Guide to EU Policies

Guide to EU Policies

Gabriel Glöckler
Lie Junius
Gioia Scappucci
Simon Usherwood
Julian Vassallo

BLACKSTONE
PRESS LIMITED

First published in Great Britain 1998 by Blackstone Press Limited, Aldine Place, London W12 8AA. Telephone 0181-740 2277

© The individual authors for their respective chapters, 1998

ISBN: 1 85431 861 6

British Library Cataloguing in Publication Data
A CIP catalogue record for this book is available from the British Library

Typeset by Montage Studios Limited, Horsmonden, Kent
Printed by Ashford Colour Press, Gosport, Hampshire

PREFACE

Jacques Delors

FORMER PRESIDENT OF THE EUROPEAN COMMISSION,
PRESIDENT OF THE RESEARCH AND POLICY UNIT
'NOTRE EUROPE'

This book draws on many years practical experience of teaching the intricacies of European Union policy-making to the postgraduate students at the College of Europe, Bruges. As President of the College of Europe, I welcome the publication of a book which will pass on the fruits of this experience to a wider public. This *Guide to EU Policies* is designed to promote understanding of how the European Union functions and to stimulate debate about its future development. It gives the reader a clear and concise picture of each of the policy areas in which the EU acts.

The growth and consolidation in the scope and depth of the EU's impact on all areas of policy-making, decision-taking and implementation has resulted in a highly complex system, all too often misunderstood beyond the narrow sphere of decision-makers and civil servants. European integration has added a new dimension to our political system and had profound effects on the lives of citizens. Without an honest open debate, based on the facts and not on the fiction of integration, the EU will never become a truly democratic and effective actor. Democracy demands transparency, simplicity, legibility. There remains much to be done, but this book represents a positive in the right direction.

European integration is not simply a question of political will — above all it is a matter of political clarification. We have to ask: 'Why do we want to live together?' In other words: 'Where are we going and why?' These questions are especially important at a time when the European Union is about to embark on a new and exciting stage in its development with the launch of a single currency and enlargement to the countries of Central and Eastern Europe. Assuring democracy in a reunited Europe depends on the commitment of its citizens to the credible common adventure that is European Integration.

The collaborative effort of the five authors brings together a refreshing range of views and approaches. The College of Europe — soon celebrating the 50th anniversary of its foundation — is a microcosm of the diversity which characterises Europe. The College unites young Europeans in an environment which encourages debate and discussion. It is in this environment that the authors have learnt that being critical can be constructive, that recognising shortcomings is as important as praising success. By the same token , we must judge the performance of the European Union on its failures as well as its achievements. By understanding the complex nature of the EU and its policies, the reader can judge for himself the ongoing struggle to put citizens' concerns at the heart of policy-making and the guarantee of peace and prosperity across our continent.

Paris, July 1998

CONTENTS

PART   I

INTRODUCTION

1 INTRODUCTION

As its name implies, this *Guide to EU Policies* is intended to provide the reader with an introduction to the various policy fields of the European Union (EU). It covers the full breadth of the EU's competences, from the original sectors of integration to the most recent. In so doing, it not only outlines the background but also the basic details of each policy field and looks to future developments. As such, it is a practical guide through the EU maze both for university and postgraduate students and for practitioners of EU business who wish to develop further their knowledge of the system.

This book is based upon work conducted by the Department of European Political and Administrative Studies at the College of Europe, Bruges, Belgium, in the framework of various courses taught there. With its masters' courses in politics, economics, law and human resources development, the College provides an ideal environment for those who wish to gain a meaningful insight into the European Union. From this academic background we have tried to develop our work for a wider audience.

The authors bring together a wide variety of backgrounds and experiences, both academic and professional. The chapters reflect this variety, hopefully to the reader's benefit. While we have limited our personal views to a minimum, it should always be kept in mind that objective fact is often used as a political tool and that one person's benefit is sometimes another person's cost.

I. SCOPE OF THE BOOK

In this book, we have attempted to cover all of the European Union's policy fields. This includes Common Foreign and Security Policy and Cooperation on

Justice and Home Affairs, which fall outside the European Community (EC), but inside the EU. Within the EC, only a very few areas have been completely excluded, while some others have been incorporated into larger sectors (research and development into industry; employment into social). So it should be possible to find most policy initiatives of the EU, one way or another.

In addition to the policy chapters, we have included several others. After a brief history of European integration since 1945, chapter 3 on the institutions of the EU provides a brief overview of how the system functions as a whole. This is intended to help those who have not studied the Union before. Within this chapter, the reader will also find the institutional reforms and innovations proposed in the Amsterdam Treaty and some future perspectives. This leads to chapter 4 on flexible integration and chapter 5 on the judicial remedies available under EC law.

Chapter 23 looks at the key challenge for the Union in the medium term, namely enlargement to the countries of Central and Eastern Europe, Cyprus and beyond. Here we look at the development of this enlargement since the fall of the Berlin Wall, how the Union has approached the question and the prospective structure of negotiations. This chapter provides an opportunity to link together various strands of policy development which have been considered within single policies.

Of course, the European Union is in constant development. The Treaty of Amsterdam (ToA) should come into force during 1998, although this is dependent upon successful referenda in various Member States. Since the text of the ToA is already agreed, it is clear what (legal) changes are intended. However, as is so often the case, other internal and external events will have an effect on institutions and policies which cannot be predicted. We have done our best to present the situation as it stands in early 1998, but for anyone with an interest in following developments, we would recommend a quality broadsheet or weekly, or a more specialist paper, such as *European Voice* or *Agence Europe*.

II. STRUCTURE OF THE CHAPTERS

We have attempted to create a common structure for our discussions of each policy field. The intention is to help the reader see patterns across policies and to structure analysis. Occasionally there are extra sections, or some of the sections have been omitted, normally because they are irrelevant or because the information cannot usefully be restructured.

In each policy chapter the first section concerns the *rationale* behind it. Before any kind of consideration of a policy can be made, it is of course necessary to understand why it exists in the first place. The reasons are often economic and political, but sometimes also social and moral. The validity of such reasonings is left to the reader.

Given that all policies derive their existence from the various treaties which have been concluded since those of Paris and Rome during the 1950s, it is logical that *legal basis, principles and objectives* should follow the rationale. The legal basis of a policy will sharply affect its development over time, both in terms of opportunities available to actors and of effectiveness of actions. The legal basis and decision-making modalities are based on the situation as they stand in the Maastricht Treaty on European Union, since the Amsterdam Treaty has yet to come into force at the time of writing. By principles, we understand those guidelines which have been fundamental to policy development, sometimes explicitly, sometimes implicitly. Objectives are somewhat more explicit, although it may well appear at times that different actors have different agendas (e.g., the Internal Market, EMU).

Under the *policy instrument* heading we set out the legal, economic and political mechanisms which the EU has at its disposal to effect its policies. These range from the basic (such as declarations) to the highly complex (such as joint actions in CFSP). For each of these instruments there is also a consideration of the process needed to enact it, since this can also vary quite substantially.

No policy is static, and so it is important to be aware of the *historical development*. Such a perspective often demonstrates how some seemingly more obvious courses of action have become unstuck and how the Union has arrived at its current priorities and processes. It also highlights the changing influence of the actors (notably the European Parliament) and the gradual enlargement of the scope of most policy fields.

Recent developments covers changes to policy which have occurred in the past few years and which may not necessarily have had time to take full effect. Under this heading, the reader will also find policy and structural innovations made in the 1997 Treaty of Amsterdam, as well as new treaty article numberings.

In *future developments* we take a more forward-looking approach to what is likely to happen. Obviously, this is clearer for some areas (EMU, enlargement) than for others, as the EU does not have a comprehensive future strategy for all policy fields, but normally some trends are apparent.

We have provided a *further reading* section for each chapter. This contains works which we think are most useful for taking the reader further into the topic. In several cases we have used ideas from these works in the text, in which case we have marked the author's name in brackets at the appropriate point. We have also tried to provide Internet websites for each chapter, given the increasingly rich body of material which is available.

Given the strong links across individual policies, we have provided cross-references to other chapters of the book.

III. GLOSSARY

If ever an organisation could be accused of impenetrable language, it is the European Union. We have attempted to refrain from complicated jargon and terminology, but sometimes it is unavoidable. To make life a little bit easier, here is a list of abbreviations and terms used in the book.

Treaties and articles

ECSC	European Coal and Steel Community, set up by the Paris Treaty of 1951. The treaty will expire in 2002.
EEC	European Economic Community, set up by the Treaty of Rome, March 1957.
TEC	Treaty establishing the European Community, also refers to the so-called first pillar of the EU, the European Community (EC).
EURATOM	Treaty setting up the European Atomic Energy Community, signed at Rome, March 1957, with the EEC Treaty.
SEA	Single European Act, signed at Luxembourg, December 1985.
TEU	Treaty on European Union, signed at Maastricht, December 1991, setting up the European Union (EU), containing the European Communities (EC), a Common Foreign and Security Policy (CFSP) and Cooperation in Justice and Home Affairs (JHA).
ToA	Treaty of Amsterdam, signed June 1997.
TEC Art.	TEC treaty article, after any TEU revision.
TEU Art.	TEU treaty article (other than TEC articles).
ToA/TEC Art.	TEC treaty article, as revised by the ToA. The ToA has instituted a process of simplification, hence changes in article numbers. A comprehensive list is given at the end of each chapter.
ToA/TEU Art.	TEU treaty article, as revised by the ToA.

Legislation

Reg.	Regulation.

Dir.	Directive.
Case	ECJ case. Case numbers have a year and a number (e.g., 73/107).
Opinion	Opinion delivered by the ECJ.
OJ	Official Journal of the European Communities.
Green Paper	Discussion paper to stimulate debate before the formal legislative process begins. Produced by the Commission.
White Paper	A first formal proposal for legislation, after the results of the Green Paper discussion have been evaluated, by the Commission.

Institutions

CFI	Court of First Instance.
CoA	Court of Auditors.
Commission	Commission of the European Communities.
CoR	Committee of the Regions.
COREPER	Committee of Permanent Representatives, prepares the Council's work.
COSAC	Committee of Specialised European Affairs Bodies.
Council	Council of Ministers of the European Union.
DG	Within the Commission, work is divided into 23 Directorates-General, each under the political control of a Commissioner.
ECB	European Central Bank.
ECHO	European Community Humanitarian Office.
ECJ	European Court of Justice.
ECOFIN	The economics finance ministers' composition of the Council.
ECOSOC	Economic and Social Committee.
EIB	European Investment Bank.
EMI	European Monetary Institute. Set up 1994 to manage stage 2 of EMU; replaced by the ECB.
EP	European Parliament.
MEP	Members of the European Parliament (currently numbering 626).
ESCB	European System of Central Banks.
European Council	The meetings of heads of state or government and the President of the Commission. An EU, not an EC, body.
GAC	The General Affairs Council is the foreign ministers' composition of the Council.

Policies

CAP	Common Agricultural Policy.
CCP	Common Commercial Policy.
CEP	Common Energy Policy.
CFP	Common Fisheries Policy.
CFSP	Common Foreign and Security Policy.
EMU	Economic and Monetary Union.
EPC	European Political Cooperation.
IS	Information Society.
JHA	Cooperation in Justice and Home Affairs.

Working Structures

Comitology	System of committee-based cooperation between Commission and Member States in the implementation of legislation.
COREU	Telex network between Member States for CFSP.
ECU	The European Currency Unit is the basket currency composed of Member States' currencies within the EMS.
EMS	European Monetary System.
ERM	The Exchange Rate Mechanism of the EMS. EMU envisages a new ERM (ERM II) between members of the single currency ('Ins') and other Member States ('Pre-ins/Outs').
IGC	Inter-Governmental Conference of Member States. Negotiates revision of the EU treaties.
MFP	Multi-annual Framework Programme.
NUTS	Statistical Nomenclature for Territorial Units, used to determine distribution of structural funds.
Troika	The Member States of the previous, current and next EU presidency, which cooperate to provide some continuity in external relations.

Funds

EAGGF	European Agricultural Guidance and Guarantee Fund.
EDF	European Development Fund, for Development Cooperation.
ERDF	European Regional Development Fund.
ESF	European Social Fund.
FIFG	Financial Instrument for Fisheries Guidance.
PHARE	Poland and Hungary: Aid for the Restructuring of Economies (extended to other Central and Eastern European countries).

Procedures

Passerelle	Procedure whereby certain competences can be moved between particular legislative procedures.
QMV	Qualified Majority Voting in the Council. Current majorities required to pass are 62 out of 87 votes.

Extra-EU bodies

ACP	African, Caribbean and Pacific states, party to the Lomé Convention.
ASEAN	Association of South East Asian Nations.
Bretton Woods	The 1944 agreement made at Bretton Woods, USA, on post-war international cooperation, providing for the setting up of the IMF, the World Bank and GATT.
CEECs	Central and Eastern European Countries.
CEN, CENELEC	European Committee for Standards, European Committee for Electrical Standards.
CIS	Commonwealth of Independent States, covering all former USSR Republics except the Baltic States.
COMECON	Council of Mutual Economic Assistance, international economic organisation of the Soviet bloc (1949–91).
Council of Europe	Intergovernmental organisation covering almost all European states, sitting at Strasbourg, with its associated European Court of Human Rights (ECHR), enforcing the European Convention on Human Rights.
CSCE, OSCE	Conference on Security and Cooperation in Europe, superseded by the Organisation on Security and Cooperation in Europe in 1992.
EBRD	European Bank for Reconstruction and Development.
EEA	European Economic Area comprising the EU and Norway, Iceland and Liechtenstein.
EFTA	European Free Trade Area, set up 1959. Members are Norway, Iceland, Switzerland, Liechtenstein.
G7, G7 + 1	Group of Seven industrialised states (USA, Canada, Japan, France, Germany, UK, Italy), now normally joined by Russia.
GATT	General Agreement on Tariffs and Trade, superseded in 1995 by the World Trade Organisation.
IMF	International Monetary Fund.

Mercosur	Southern Cone Common Market (Argentina, Brazil, Paraguay and Uruguay), set up in 1991; accession of Chile, Bolivia, Peru, Colombia in preparation.
NAFTA	North American Free Trade Area (USA, Canada, Mexico), set up 1995.
NATO	North Atlantic Treaty Organisation.
OECD	Organisation for Economic Cooperation and Development, covering most highly industrialised states. Includes the International Energy Authority (IEA).
OPEC	Organisation of Oil Producing Countries.
UN	United Nations.
WEU	Western European Union.
WTO	World Trade Organisation, set up in 1995 to supersede GATT. The WTO includes the General Agreement on Trade-Related Aspects of Services (GATS) and Trade-Related Aspects of Intellectual Property Rights (TRIPs).

Jargon

ACQUIS	The ACQUIS Communautaire of the EU is the whole of the primary and secondary instruments which makes it up and to which Member States are bound.
MS	Member States of the EU.
IM	Internal Market.
R&D	research and development.
SMEs	small and medium-sized enterprises.
☑	positive outcome.
☒	negative outcome.

IV. ACKNOWLEDGEMENTS

During the preparation of this book, the authors have being helped by countless people, who have given their time and effort in a very selfless manner. Firstly, we would like to thank the College of Europe, and in particular the Rector, Otto von der Gablentz, and the Director of Communications, Pierre-Olivier Bergeron, for providing us with a most agreeable environment in which to prepare and develop our work. The contributions from Rodolphe Muñoz and Nicola Notaro form an essential part of this book and we were very pleased when they agreed to participate in this project. Many thanks are also due to all the staff, past and present, and professors of the Departments of Political and

Administrative Studies, Law and Economics, without whom our work would have been infinitely more difficult: in this respect, special mention must be made of David Cullen, Sylvain Giraud, Hendrik Van De Velde, Professor David O'Keeffe, Professor Jörg Monar, Professor Eric De Souza, Emmanuel Le Bacon, Mercedes Garcia Perez and Frédérique Berrod. We also should thank those others who have given us their comments: Káthrin Schweren at BEUC, Brussels; Damian Stathonikos at GPC Market Access, Brussels; Christophe Hillion from the College of Europe's Natolin campus. Any mistakes which remain should, of course, be attributed to the authors.

2 HISTORICAL OVERVIEW OF THE EU

Simon Usherwood

I. INTRODUCTION

In one sense, European integration is nothing new. Ever since the Romans established the first continental empire 2000 years ago, many have tried and failed to bring Europe together. None of them succeeded in any lasting way. The reasons are not hard to find: a lack of appropriate technology to manage and control distant lands; internal power struggles within the ruling power which weakened its ability to prevent disintegration of its possessions. However, the most important factor was the necessity of the use of force to establish and maintain these empires. For obvious reasons, each and every attempt to build a European hegemonic system ultimately failed because of its use of force. And it is from here that we might take the history of post-1945 European integration: an effort to use peaceful means to build genuine integration.

One should be careful not to take the analogy between the post-war experience and cases such as the Romans, Napoleon or Nazi Germany too far. Each has its specificities and particularities: indeed, the phrase 'European integration' is rather euphemistic in these other cases, given that domination, not integration, was the primary aim. In any case, the point which should be underlined is the fundamentally different approach which has been taken by those involved. Cooperation, dialogue and consensus have been the hallmarks of the new European system, instead of competition or the pursuance of narrow national interests.

This is not to say that the post-war system sprang up spontaneously. From the Enlightenment onwards, intellectuals have often argued for the logic of a united Europe, making the then new nation states a stepping stone to a European state. The First World War provided a vivid demonstration of the dangers of rampant nationalism and gave a stimulus to the development of both intellectual and organisational bodies to promote cooperation. Intellectually, the Pan-European Union of Count Coudenhove-Kalergi was perhaps the best known, with its high-profile support from various European statesmen. Organisationally, there were both sub-regional (Benelux, Scandinavia) and international (League of Nations) efforts, the former proving rather more successful than the latter. The increasing economic problems of the late 1920s and 1930s put paid to the idea of cooperation and renewed the push towards national policies and economies, which was eventually to feed into fascism and the Second World War.

II. THE EARLY YEARS

In a much stronger way than the First World War, the 1939–45 conflict saw the development of a relatively coherent and powerful group of intellectuals and politicians who wished to make such wars a thing of the past. They proposed that through an integration of the former enemies, the negative forces of nationalism would be constrained and contained and peace would ensue. Their strength lay in the convergence during the war of the various strands of the resistance (Communist, Socialist and Christian Democrat) against fascism: consider Altiero Spinelli's *Manifesto di Ventotene* of 1941, which led to the creation of a pan-European federalist movement. This convergence carried through past 1945 into an international climate of trust across the continent, not least between the new leaders of the countries of Europe. This trust was in turn also fuelled by the external threat of the Soviet Union and the perceived need to cooperate so as not to be completely crushed by the two superpowers.

More localised cooperation — such as in the Belgium–Netherlands–Luxembourg (Benelux) trio or in the Nordic states — was planned very quickly after the end of hostilities, but it was not until 1947 and US Secretary of State George Marshall's offer of reconstruction aid that pan-West European cooperation really began. The US's motives were not totally altruistic, as they realised that unless the European economy was rebuilt, the European dollar shortage would continue and the Europeans would not be able to buy US goods. Thus, kick-starting the Europeans would help the US too. Just as importantly, the offer came at a time when relations with the Soviet Union were deteriorating sharply (Churchill had already talked of the 'Iron Curtain' in 1946), and the US was keen to use increased cooperation between the Europeans to strengthen its own position. That this was not idle speculation was highlighted by the Soviets preventing the East European states under their control from participating in the European Reconstruction Plan (ERP), as 'Marshall Aid' was formally known. After initially confused actions, the European participants were able to get together under the umbrella of the intergovernmental Organisation for European Economic Cooperation (OEEC), which became the Organisation for Economic Cooperation and Development (OECD) in 1960.

In light of the future developments of European cooperation, it is worth briefly looking at some of the various national strategic positions. For Germany, there was a need to reintegrate itself into the European and global system, to purge itself of its Nazi past and to give itself the markets which its industry needed. As a result, Germany was a prime mover in the integrative process and, because of its limited sovereignty under the Allied occupation, was more willing to give up power to supranational bodies. The French had key interests in avoiding another war with Germany, in economic modernisation and a desire to preserve France's international role. However, it was only after the failed Indochina and Suez expeditions that this latter interest was perceived to be best achieved via 'Europe' and, even then, Europe was still seen as a means to amplify French interests. Conversely, the United Kingdom still regarded (and regards) itself as a major international player, trying to balance itself between the 'three circles' of the Common-wealth, the transatlantic relationship and Europe (in that order). This meant they were loath to engage in anything more binding than intergovernmental structures, and certainly not the tight forms that the federalists were suggesting at the time.

The consequence of these three key players' attitudes was that the UK acted as a brake to integration (the Council of Europe, set up in 1949, was more to British tastes than anyone else's), which caused a certain level of frustration in large states and concern in small ones. The concern came from a fear that a Franco-German pair would dominate any organisation in which the small countries like the Benelux were involved, unless the UK acted as a balance. As such, exclusion of the UK was seen as a last resort, but the British did nothing to help their cause, being contemptuous of the viability of integration.

The Schuman declaration of 9 May 1950, calling for the creation of a European Coal and Steel Community (ECSC) to help end the possibility of war between France and Germany, marked the first real step towards the current system. The plan of the French Foreign Minister, Robert Schuman, under the guidance of the head of the French Planning Commission, Jean Monnet (later to become the first President of the ECSC's High Authority), represented a classic piece of functionalist logic, tying together the means of producing armaments in order to reduce the autarkic tendencies of the 1930s, and also setting in motion a process of 'spillover'. Once coal and steel were integrated, went the argument, then states would realise that other areas would need integration too, a virtuous circle leading to a federal system. This *finalité politique* was implicit in Schuman's call and was enough to kill any British interest in the scheme. However, Germany, Italy and the Benelux countries were all supportive and set to rapidly forming the ECSC with the Paris Treaty of April 1951.

The ECSC structure revolved around a Council of Ministers and the High Authority, a strongly supranational body with responsibility for enforcing the Treaty. A weak Assembly composed of national parliamentarians was also attached. Through the over-representation of small Member States and a clear commitment to respect the rules of the Treaty, all involved could feel that there was no structural discrimination, an important point still with relevance today. The early success of the ECSC project, in both economic and political terms, proved to be a strong fillip to pushing on with further integration among the Six, as witnessed by the Pleven plan of October 1950.

The French premier, René Pleven, was attempting to deal with one of the key challenges of the new German situation, namely rearmament. The German Democratic Republic had been building up forces since its creation in 1949, and none of the wartime allies was able to devote substantial forces to West Germany. This was heightened with the start of the Korean war, which both took away US forces and raised fears of a Soviet attack while attentions were focused elsewhere. Consequently there was pressure from the US to rearm Germany, but this clashed head on with the French fear of a resurgent Germany. Pleven proposed that by creating a European Defence Community (EDC) it would be possible to reconcile the two views. But the plan contained discriminatory elements against Germany and was lopsided as a result. The Benelux were very unhappy about going into an EDC without the balancing presence of the UK and there was a general feeling that the political and military logic underlying the whole plan was very weak. This said, a treaty was agreed upon, and even ratified by the Germans, only to hit a wall in the form of the French parliament. For two years from 1952 it was impossible to get the treaty through, and by then the international situation had changed. Stalin had died in 1953, the Korean conflict was over and the French had become highly disillusioned with the US after the disastrous defence of Dien Bien Phu in Vietnam in 1954. The treaty consequently fell and it was left to the relatively weak structure of the Brussels Treaty to extend to cover Germany and Italy, so becoming the Western European Union (see chapter 20). Ultimately, it was to be the US, through the 1949 North Atlantic Treaty Organisation, which was to become the guarantor of security in Western Europe.

III. THE EEC

Considering the setback which the EDC represented, it is perhaps surprising that the integration project was back on track as quickly as it was. Certainly, the sectoral approach of the functionalists had been damaged, but this merely seemed to stimulate other efforts. One of these was the long-standing horizontal integration of the Benelux. They proposed that dividing the economy and political system into sectors was artificial, and that what was needed was a customs union (see chapter 6). Of course, the traditionally low tariffs of the Benelux in comparison to the other Member States was another factor in the calculation, one which the French in particular were somewhat dubious about. Nevertheless, in May 1955 the Benelux made a joint proposal for a customs union and integration of the nuclear industry, a project which Monnet had also been developing.

At a summit in Messina in June 1955, the heads of government of the Six appointed Dutch Prime Minister Paul Henri Spaak to head an expert committee to discuss the proposal. May 1956 saw the adoption of the subsequent Spaak report and in March 1957, the Treaties of Rome were signed: one forming the European Economic Community (EEC) and the other the European Atomic Energy Community (Euratom). The Six had once again set the pace of integration.

The EEC Treaty, which came into force on 1 May 1957 after a very quick ratification, established a customs union, with gradual reductions in internal tariff levels over 12 years and the creation of a Common External Tariff. The barriers to movement for workers, goods, services and capital were to be eliminated and a number of common policies were to be set up, notably the Common Agricultural Policy (CAP). This combination of negative (i.e., removal of barriers) and positive (i.e., creation of common policies) integration was to be an ongoing trademark of the 'Community method'. In terms of structures, the EEC represented a step back from the ECSC, with a less powerful Commission, another weak Assembly, a consultative Economic and Social Committee (ECOSOC) and a Court of Justice ranged alongside the Council of Ministers, the main legislator (see chapter 3).

The speed and success of the EEC's creation also had effects outside the Six. Even before the Suez crisis crushed its global ambitions, the UK had been substantially marginalised in European integration. Its calls during the EEC negotiations for a wide and loose free trade area based on the members of the OECD were brushed aside by most, at least by the Six. However, other countries had strong economic links with the UK and six of them (Denmark, Norway, Sweden, Portugal, Switzerland and Austria) were prepared to take up the offer. In January 1960, the Stockholm Convention was signed, creating the European Free Trade Area (EFTA), which aimed to be nothing more than its name implied.

The consequence of all of this was to divide West Europe economically. The increased bargaining weight of the EEC Member States and the breaking of the British European 'circle' led to political problems and even the fear that the Soviet Union might become tempted to exploit the split to its advantage. The EFTA Seven were in a very weak position, as their options were severely limited. EFTA could not be deepened, as some wanted, because of British and Danish resistance, and the EEC did not really want to enlarge to include the EFTAns. The reasons for this attitude were clear; the strong UK–US relationship bred fears of 'drowning in the Atlantic' (this was particularly a problem for the French), while worries were also expressed about a slowing down of the impetus to integration if the British and the Scandinavians were inside the EEC. Whatever the reasons, the EEC was the core, and EFTA the periphery, of the West European economy and some resolution would have to be found.

IV. DEEPER, WIDER, SLOWER

The first years of the EEC's existence were relatively carefree. The coincidence of the strong economic growth of the time helped the integration process and a strengthening of the EEC's position as a permanent institution. Internal tariff reductions were speeded up and the 1965 Merger Treaty joined together the parallel bodies of the ECSC, Euratom and the EEC into one, more efficient whole. The Court of Justice was establishing the doctrine of direct effect, which gives EC citizens a right of action against their governments on the basis of certain treaty provisions (*Van Gend en Loos* 26/62), and the primacy of European law over national law (*Costa* v *ENEL* 6/64; see chapter 5).

But already the problems were mounting, first indirectly and then directly. The failure of the French-proposed Fouchet plans in the early 1960s (see chapter 20) marked the end of any major effort to integrate foreign policy for the next 30 years. The division between the EEC and EFTA continued to create tensions, not least when the British, the Danes and others applied for membership of the former in 1961, only to be vetoed by the French (or more specifically French President Charles de Gaulle) in 1963. A second attempt by the UK four years later was similarly blocked, to much disgruntlement.

But this was an external manifestation of a deeper malaise within the Community. As mentioned above, the French were enthusiastic Europeans, but largely because it suited their national interests of containing Germany and amplifying their position internationally. In the early 1960s their bluff was called, as the CAP was put into place and the financial package of the Commission was discussed. These elements would have substantially increased the supranationality of the EEC and this was difficult for the French to take, especially with de Gaulle at the helm and his vision of a *'Europe des patries'* ('Europe of nations' is an approximate translation). From June 1965, the French operated an 'empty chair' policy, refusing to participate in Council meetings, and so blocking the passage of most legislation. It took seven months until a solution could be found. In the so-called Luxembourg Compromise, Member States were allowed to prevent voting on any legislation where 'very important national interests' were at stake. The French victory allowed them to come back into the fold, but it was to dampen the EEC's progress for the next 25 years, as a slower and less efficient (in terms of integration) path of intergovernmentalism was followed.

That de Gaulle had been a key factor in the Community's slowdown was demonstrated by his resignation in 1969. His successor, Georges Pompidou, was quick to breathe life back into the system, calling for a summit to resolve the bundle of obstacles in the EEC's way. In December 1969 at the Hague, a package deal was agreed, with the opening of enlargement talks to EFTA members to be balanced by the strengthening of the EEC through the creation of own budgetary resources, an enlargement of the scope of policies, the beginnings of informal European Political Cooperation (EPC; see chapter 20) and the adoption of the Werner plan for Economic and Monetary Union by 1980 (see chapter 19). Within four years, the Community was enlarged to include the UK, Ireland and Denmark (Norway having rejected membership in a referendum) and nine Member States were participating in the first European Council meeting in Paris in 1974.

But even with the removal of the impasse, new problems were created. The Werner plan was rather vague and rapidly broke down with the collapse of the post-war Bretton Woods system in 1971–2 and the subsequent turmoil in the currency markets. Added to this was the sharp economic slowdown in the wake of the first oil crisis of 1973–4, when OPEC was able to play off the Member States against each other to good effect (see chapter 8). This in turn had a psychological impact on the new members, who came to associate membership with economic hardship: for the Six, quite the opposite had been true, and the difference was telling. Even if the UK had made the calculation that it was better to be in than out, this did not stop them making life difficult. The bias towards CAP spending in the budget meant that the British paid in much more than they got out. The initial solution was the creation of a regional policy (see chapter 13), but when a Labour government came to power in 1975, they still insisted on 'renegotiating' the terms of accession (to no obvious effect) and having a referendum on membership (which was comfortably won). All of this left relations somewhat strained, even before Margaret Thatcher's election in 1979.

The late 1970s and early 1980s were to be characterised by what was termed 'Eurosclerosis', a gradual seizing up of the institutional machinery through overloading and increased bureaucracy. The economic downturn coupled with political difficulties externally (Afghanistan and Poland) and internally (Thatcher and her quest for a budgetary rebate) to produce a generally poor perception of the Community. Even the launch of the European Monetary System in 1979 was a substantial step down from the Werner plan and the 'snake' which replaced it (see chapter 19). Efforts to promote institutional reform, such as the Tindemanns Report of 1976, were disregarded, as Member States cut back their ambitions. Greece's entry into the EEC in 1981 was largely unremarked upon, apart from concerns for the stability of its political system after the dictatorship and for the effect on Mediterranean agricultural products.

V. THE EIGHTIES' RELAUNCH

The 1980s were to highlight the ups and down of the integration process. From the depths of the early 1980s to the radically different Europe of 1989–90, the turnaround was clear and decisive.

Even in the seeming inaction of the early 1980s, there were efforts to kick-start the Community into action. From the Genscher-Colombo proposal of 1981, through the Solemn Declaration of the Stuttgart European Council in 1983, to the draft Treaty on European Union of Spinelli presented to the EP in 1984, there were those who tried to set a pace. Their immediate success was limited, but their value lay more in keeping alive the idea of closer integration. This came into its own with time, as other factors swung in their favour. First, the French, now under President Mitterrand, were forced back into the European fold as their socialist policies collapsed in front of the neo-liberal stance of most of the rest of the industrialised world. Mitterrand's finance minister, Jacques Delors, played a key role in this return to Europe and the refocusing on relations with Germany and the EEC. This effect was also felt to a lesser extent in the UK, as Thatcher watered down her government's extreme neo-liberal policies. More importantly for the UK, there was a resolution of the budget rebate at the Fontainebleau European Council in 1984, which allowed .them to concentrate on more positive aspects of membership.

Fontainebleau was also important because it set the ball rolling towards institutional reform, with the Dooge Committee created to look into the matter. The impending accession of Spain and Portugal was helping to concentrate minds, and with Delors installed as Commission president in 1985, there was a feeling that this time reform would come. Extra support for this came from unexpected quarters; as part of the privatisation and deregulation of the British economy, Thatcher wanted to create a true single market within the EEC. Market operators had similar ideas and also started to push for the freeing up of movement across borders.

All of this gave an impetus to the Commission, which produced a White Paper in 1985 on the completion of the Internal Market (IM) by 1992. The paper, prepared by Commissioner Lord Cockfield, contained 300 legislative measures to remove the current barriers to the free circulation of goods, workers, services and capital. After agreement in Milan later that year to consider also the Dooge Committee's report, negotiations began in the Inter-Governmental Conference (IGC), and in 1986 the Single European Act (SEA) was signed in Luxembourg.

The SEA both formalised existing informal policies and created some innovations. A new decision-making procedure of cooperation was introduced, giving the EP more say, if not an actual right of veto, as well as the limited use of EP assent (see chapter 3). Beyond this, the most important provision was Art. 100a, which was designed to break through the perceived previous legislative impasse to completing the IM, by use of qualified majority voting (QMV). The SEA was quickly ratified and in force by 1987.

Movement could be seen on all fronts. The budgetary crisis of the mid 1980s was a spur to the conclusion of an Interinstitutional Accord between the Commission, EP and Council in 1988, which introduced a more practical system of managing the budget. This comprised multi-annual projections (known as Delors I (for 1988–92) and II (1993–9)) and limits on the spending increases for CAP. 1988 also saw the creation of the Committee of Central Bankers, under the chairmanship of Delors, to look into new plans for EMU. The UK, which had been most vocal against monetary integration, had acquiesced in the Committee, as it considered the central bankers too proud to agree on giving up their own powers. This was to be a grave miscalculation and set in motion another round of treaty reform.

VI. MAASTRICHT AND ITS CONSEQUENCES

The Delors Committee produced its report on EMU in April 1989, and the Strasbourg European Council was able to agree upon an IGC to prepare treaty revisions in December of the same year. But even as this was happening, outside events were radically changing the very context upon which the Community had been built.

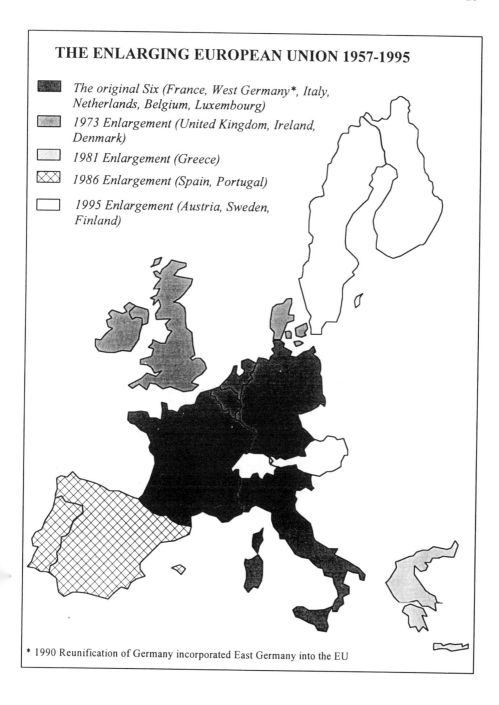

THE ENLARGING EUROPEAN UNION 1957-1995

The original Six (France, West Germany*, Italy, Netherlands, Belgium, Luxembourg)

1973 Enlargement (United Kingdom, Ireland, Denmark)

1981 Enlargement (Greece)

1986 Enlargement (Spain, Portugal)

1995 Enlargement (Austria, Sweden, Finland)

* 1990 Reunification of Germany incorporated East Germany into the EU

1989 saw the effects of Soviet perestroika and glasnost spinning out of control, as General Secretary Mikhail Gorbachev attempted to rescue the Soviet economy by engaging in détente and cooperation with the West. The countries of Central and Eastern Europe used their new-found freedom to liberalise their systems, leading to a summer of increasing migrations across the ever more porous Iron Curtain and deepening crises of legitimacy for the regimes of those states. On 9 November 1989 the Berlin Wall was opened, rapidly leading to plans for the unification of the two German states in October 1990. This represented the most dramatic change to Eastern Europe at the time, but the collapse and roll-back of Communist power first to the edge of the Soviet Union, and then beyond, was no less impressive.

However, the moves towards German unification also had internal repercussions for the Community. The old French fear of a resurgent Germany, exploiting its traditional hinterland of *Mitteleuropa*, once again came to the fore, and the British were not much less sceptical about the thought of a more powerful Germany. Indeed, the Germans themselves recognised that unification could result in their being cut loose from the Community, so losing much of their international standing. This was especially true for Chancellor Helmut Kohl, who had a very close relationship with French President Mitterrand, and who wished to demonstrate that Germany was committed to further integration. Thus, at the Dublin European Council, in June 1990, a second IGC was agreed upon, to consider questions of political union.

From the official opening of the IGCs in December 1990 to their conclusion at the European Council meeting in Maastricht one year later, there was a relatively positive air about the proceedings. Many involved in the negotiations saw the opportunity to make a qualitative leap in the level of integration. The Treaty on European Union (TEU) signed at Maastricht, created a new structure, the European Union (EU). The EU comprised three pillars. The first was the EEC, now renamed the European Community, further developed with a new co-decision procedure (TEC Art.189b; see chapter 3) for the EP; a consultative Committee of the Regions; a new selection procedure for the Commission; new competences, including provisions on citizenship of the Union; and a full programme for EMU. Alongside this strong supranational pillar were created two weaker, intergovernmental pillars. The second pillar, Common Foreign and Security Policy (CFSP), formalised EPC and created potentially strong instruments for common action. The third, cooperation in Justice and Home Affairs (JHA), reorganised the intergovernmental cooperation which had taken place before, but to no great effect (see chapter 21). On the top of the pillars was placed a set of common provisions, giving the European Council a guiding role and improved coherence between the various elements.

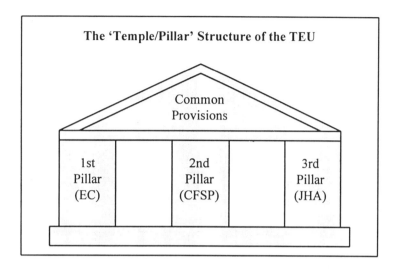

The 'Temple/Pillar' Structure of the TEU

Common Provisions

| 1st Pillar (EC) | 2nd Pillar (CFSP) | 3rd Pillar (JHA) |

If the Maastricht project was ambitious, then it showed. Even with the introduction of the subsidiarity principle, which limited the EC's actions to those which Member States could not perform better themselves, the increased profile of the Community in the wake of the '1992' programme for the Single Market meant that public interest had been awoken, along with many fears. This was true not only in traditionally sceptical countries, such as the UK and Denmark, but also in more positive members, France and Germany. The seemingly sudden appearance of the Community in all walks of life caused people to question how it had happened and, more importantly, what basis it had in terms of legitimacy. The 'democratic deficit' had already been a popular topic before Maastricht, and the TEU opened as many questions as it resolved. All of this was demonstrated vividly when the Danes narrowly voted against ratification in June 1992, followed by the tiny majority in favour in France in September. At the Edinburgh European Council in December, special arrangements and 'clarifications' were made for the Danes, allowing them to vote narrowly in favour in May 1993. Finally in November 1993, the TEU came into force, almost two years after its signature, and after a particularly tricky passage through the UK Parliament and a reference to the German Constitutional Court.

The near farce of ratification had both put a big dent in the credibility of the programme and given a boost to sceptic elements across the Union. But the underlying political commitment, from the key Franco-German pairing and from others, remained. This commitment was to be tested once again after

Maastricht, when the European Monetary System came under increasing pressure from currency speculators. The entry of the British pound, after much procrastination, in 1990 came at a time when the European Rate Mechanism was becoming increasingly rigid, as the tight Bundesbank policy clashed with other countries' economic needs, and speculators sensed a chance to break the central banks' resolve to protect parities. First in 1992 and then again in 1993, the EMS was blown apart, if not actually destroyed, and many observers thought that EMU would have to be scrapped. However, a strong political resolve rode out this storm and put EMU firmly back on track by 1996.

Another consequence of the end of the Cold War was the questioning in some other European countries of their neutrality and non-alignment policy. The economic and political benefits of membership of the EU were weighed against these policies and were convincing for most, a fact highlighted by the negotiations between the EC and EFTA on the European Economic Area (see chapter 10) in the early 1990s. Here, the EFTAns soon realised that the relationship was highly asymmetrical and that they would be obliged to take up most of the Community's *acquis* without having a say in its formulation. Consequently, applications for membership were lodged by Austria, Sweden, Finland and Norway, and in 1995 the first three of these states joined the EU, Norway having again rejected membership in a referendum. Although a largely painless enlargement, in comparison to the Southern extensions in the 1980s, the new members brought their own particularities to the EU and were to leave their mark on the next treaty revision, which the TEU had provided for.

VII. AMSTERDAM AND THE FUTURE

The follow-up IGC to the TEU was always going to face difficulties. Its timing had been based on the false assumption that by 1996 the TEU would have been in force for almost five years and so would have provided much information on that treaty's shortcomings. The ratification instead effectively took two years out of that period. Similarly, the IGC was intended more as a fine-tuning exercise than a major overhaul. This caused problems, as the momentum of the 1980s was lost to increasing systemic problems and generalised scepticism. The ERM crisis of 1992–3 produced calls for a major rethink of EMU, but political exigencies of cross-linked deals done at Maastricht meant that it was never really likely that such an important project would be renegotiated. The Germans had been sold on EMU by the close modelling of the ECB on the Bundesbank (see chapter 19) and the Southern Members by the provision of greatly increased structural aid (see chapter 13).

As such, the IGC was seen by most as 'Maastricht II', rather than 'Amsterdam I'. The impending enlargement to the East (where countries had been placing applications for membership since the early 1990s) theoretically put extra pressure on those involved to make more radical proposals for institutional reform, a key theme of the IGC, but this was countered by the political inertia of Member States. In June 1995, a Reflection Group was set up under the Spanish Foreign Minister Carlos Westendorp to consider the key points of discussion and its subsequent report was the basis of the decision at the Madrid European Council in December of that year to open the IGC in March 1996. Already it was clear that the priorities would be increased institutional efficiency, procedural questions, preparation for enlargement, transparency and improved links with the citizen. These last two points were very much at the insistence of the Nordic Member States and found a sympathetic echo across the EU in the wake of the TEU ratification.

The IGC was officially finished at Amsterdam in June 1997. It was only a partial coincidence that this date was three months after the British general election, as it had been clear that the Conservatives, in power since 1979, were probably going to lose to Labour. The importance in this lay in the increasing hard line that the British had been taking, under domestic pressure, and which other governments hoped would disappear with a new administration. This was in fact the case, and as part of Labour's new European policy the Social Charter, which had been excluded from full incorporation into the TEU, was fully communitarised (see chapter 17). Nevertheless, it was clear that it was not only the British who had reservations about the EU, and the Treaty of Amsterdam (ToA) was not the great leap forward that some had hoped for.

The ToA's prime achievements lay in the refinement of the TEU. The co-decision procedure was simplified, to give the EP full veto powers, and extended to more policy fields. CFSP was restructured and developed more fully than time had allowed in the TEU, and JHA was partially incorporated into the EC. A new chapter on employment was added, to address the growing concerns about rising unemployment in the Union. A procedure for closer cooperation between Member States was created, partly to allow the semi-incorporation of the Schengen Convention on free movement and partly to improve flexibility in light of the enlargement to the Central and Eastern European Countries (CEECs; see chapters 4 and 22). As part of a simplification process all treaty articles were renumbered sequentially (new article numbers are given at the end of each chapter of this book) and obsolete provisions deleted. But the most striking feature of the ToA is its omissions: despite the recognised need to reform the institutional structures in the face of enlargement, no agreement could be found, other than to limit the number of seats in the EP to 700. An attached protocol declared that a full institutional restructuring would have to take place when the number of Member States reached 20, with a possibility of resolving the Council vote weighting and number of Commissioners question before then. No IGC is provided for in the ToA apart from this protocol.

If Amsterdam was a damp squib, then the Commission was not going to let the occasion pass, and one month after the European Council, it announced its 'Agenda 2000' programme. This combined the Commission's opinions on the various applications to join the EU with a set of proposals for reform of Union policies (especially CAP and structural funds) and budgetary requirements (in anticipation of the end of the Delors II package in 1999). On the basis of criteria laid down at Copenhagen (1993), the Commission was in favour of opening negotiations with Poland, Hungary, the Czech Republic, Estonia, Slovenia — as well as the previously agreed Cyprus — a proposition which the Luxembourg European Council of December 1997 confirmed. For those countries not invited there would be continued links and a new European Conference, a somewhat vague idea which first took place in March 1998, but which Turkey rejected out of hand (see chapter 23).

And so the European Union finds itself in 1998 on the brink of a new phase in its existence. In the next few years it will become clear whether the EU can turn itself from a small, relatively stable group of rich West European states into a pan-European organisation, without losing its core identity and coherence. Even if the project to create a sense of being 'European' amongst its citizens has not worked to any great extent, at least the Union has been able to attempt it: in the future the larger number and diversity of states will make progress based on unanimity and consensus harder and harder, and the pressures to introduce stronger federal elements to the system will grow. The Union is far from perfect, but its attractions outweigh its faults, as the long line of applicants testifies, and it is unlikely that it might fall apart completely. Of course, a badly handled enlargement and a failed EMU in 1999 could conceivably stop integration in its tracks, but such a prospect is less than likely, given the political and economic capital which has been invested. Whatever happens, the European Union of 2010 will not be like the European Union of now.

VIII. FURTHER READING

Historical treatments of the integration process are many and varied. However, one should always be aware of the personal proclivities of any particular author. For this reason, it is suggested that several accounts of the same events should be read, in order to get a fuller and more balanced picture. For various time periods and for various perspectives; the following are useful starting points:

GERBET, Pierre: *La Construction de l'Europe*, Paris, Imprimerie Nationale, 1994.

MIDDLEMAS, Keith: *Orchestrating Europe: The Informal Politics of European Union 1973–1995*, London, Fontana, 1995 (especially pp. 1–206).

MILWARD, Alan: *The European Rescue of the Nation-State*, London, Routledge, 1992.

URWIN, Derek: *The Community of Europe, A History of European Integration since 1945*, 2nd ed., London, Longman, 1995.

PART II

THE EUROPEAN UNION: INSTITUTIONS AND PROCEDURES

3 INSTITUTIONAL FRAMEWORK

Gioia Scappucci

The purpose of this chapter is to introduce the reader to the powers and functioning of the key actors of the European Union's policy cycle, covering the preparation, taking, implementation and controlling of decisions. It will also provide the reader with the basic tools to understand the EU's decision-making process. Throughout the chapter the institutional changes included in the Treaty of Amsterdam (ToA) will be highlighted.

A. CHARACTERISTICS AND PRINCIPLES

1 Single Institutional Framework

The Union shall be served by a single institutional framework which shall ensure the consistency and the continuity of the activities carried out in order to attain its objectives while respecting and building upon the 'acquis communautaire' (TEU Art. C para. 1)

The Community pillar and the two intergovernmental pillars (Common Foreign and Security Policy and Cooperation in the Fields of Justice and Home Affairs) share the same institutions, although they play different roles in each of them. The importance of the role depends on the varying interests which are found in each pillar.

2 The Principle of Institutional Balance and Representation of Interests

The institutional framework of the EU does not reflect the principle of separation of powers: with the exception of the judicial power (entrusted to the European Court of Justice), the other powers (executive and legislative) are shared by the so-called 'institutional triangle', namely the European Parliament (EP), the Council of Ministers and the Commission. Each institution *represents a specific interest*: the peoples of the states brought together in the Community; the Member States and the general interest of the Community, respectively.

According to TEU Art. E, each institution has to exercise the powers conferred to it 'under the conditions and for the purposes provided for' by the provisions of the Treaty. Moreover, TEC Art. 4 para. 1 establishes that 'each institution shall act within the limits of the powers conferred upon it by this Treaty', reflecting the particular balance of the interests which each institution represents. If the prerogatives of an institution are endangered by other institutions acting beyond the limits of the powers conferred on them, each institution may bring an action before the ECJ to protect the *principle of institutional balance* (see chapter 5). However, this does not mean that the institutions have equal powers, but rather that the balance provided for in the treaty is respected.

3 Autonomy and Loyal Cooperation

Each institution has the power to adopt its rules of procedure. It must exercise its powers while respecting those of the other institutions. This results in a duty of *loyal cooperation* between the institutions. This principle was affirmed by the ECJ's case law on the duty of cooperation between the Member States and the institutions (TEC Art. 5).

4 Transparency

Decisions in the 'ever closer union among the peoples of Europe . . . *are taken as openly as possible*' (ToA/TEU Art. 1). When the ToA enters into force, rules on transparency which previously were contained in inter-institutional agreements and rules of procedure will become part of the EU's primary law. Their implementation will therefore be checked by the ECJ.

A general '*right of access to European Parliament, Council and Commission documents*' is established (ToA/TEC Art. 255). This right of access is, however, subject to general principles and limits to be defined by the Council within two years of the coming into force of the ToA. On the basis of these general principles and limits, the three institutions will elaborate specific provisions in their own rules of procedure regarding access to documents.

B. THE INSTITUTIONS

This section of the chapter will describe the main characteristics of the institutions listed in TEC Art. 4 para. 1, namely the Commission, the Council of Ministers, the European Parliament, the Court of Justice and the Court of Auditors. It will try to analyse the powers of these institutions, in so far as they play an influential role in the policy cycle.

Other actors such as the Economic and Social Committee, the Committee of Regions, the European Investment Bank, the institutional set-up concerning EMU, as well as interest groups, social partners and specialised committees will not be analysed in this chapter. The influence of these actors is described in the chapters on policy areas where they play a specific role.

I. THE COMMISSION

The Commission is the institution which represents the *general interest of the Community* (TEC Arts 155 and 157.2).

I.1 Main Characteristics and Functioning

I.1.1 Composition
The Commission is composed of *20 independent members* chosen on the grounds of their general competence. The number of members may be altered by a unanimous decision of the Council of Ministers. The members must be nationals of the Member States. The Commission must include at least one national from each Member State and no more than two per Member State. In practice the five 'big' Member States (France, Germany, Italy, UK, Spain) have two Commissioners (TEC Art. 157.1).

I.1.2 Organisational Structure
The College of Commissioners is helped by the *Commission's services*. The Commission is divided into 24 *Directorates-General* (DGs) dealing with the areas of Community activity (see table). Each Commissioner has one or several DGs under his/her supervision. Each DG is divided in 'Divisions', which are in turn divided in 'Units'. Each Commissioner is also assisted by a personal team of advisers, the so-called '*Cabinet*'. These 'vertical services' benefit from the support of common 'horizontal services' such as the Legal Service, the Secretariat General, the Office of Publications and the Translation Service.

The Directorates-General and Commissioners of the Commission		
DG	*Area of responsibility*	*Commissioner*
—	Horizontal services, including the Secretariat-General and the Interpreting Service. Also joint responsibility for CFSP (with VAN DEN BROEK) and monetary matters (with DE SILGUY)	President Jacques SANTER (Luxembourg)
DG I	External Relations: Commercial Policy and Relations with North America, the Far East, Australia and New Zealand	Vice-President Leon BRITTAN (UK)
DG IA	External Relations: Europe and the New Independent States, Common Foreign and Security Policy and External Missions	Hans VAN DEN BROEK (Netherlands)
DG IB	External Relations: Southern Mediterranean, Middle and Near East, Latin America, South and South-East Asia and North-South Cooperation	Vice-President Manuel MARIN (Spain)
DG II	Economic and Financial Affairs	Yves-Thibault DE SILGUY (France)
DG III	Industry	Martin BANGEMANN (Germany)
DG IV	Competition	Karel VAN MIERT (Belgium)
DG V	Employment, Industrial Relations and Social Affairs	Pádraig FLYNN (Ireland)
DG VI	Agriculture	Franz FISCHLER (Austria)
DG VII	Transport	Neil KINNOCK (UK)
DG VIII	Development	João de DEUS PINHEIRO (Portugal) for Lomé and relations with ACP states and South Africa. MARIN for development in other regions.
DG IX	Personnel and Administration	Erkki LIIKANEN (Finland)
DG X	Information, Communication, Culture, Audiovisual	Marcelino OREJA (Spain)
DG XI	Environment, Nuclear Safety and Civil Protection	Ritt BJERREGAARD (Denmark)
DG XII	Science, Research and Development	Edith CRESSON (France)
DG XIII	Telecommunications, Information Market and Exploitation of Research	BANGEMANN
DG XIV	Fisheries	Emma BONINO (Italy)

DG	Area of responsibility	Commissioner
DG XV	Internal Market and Financial Services	Mario MONTI (Italy)
DG XVI	Regional Policies and Cohesion	Monika WULF-MATHIES (Germany). Cohesion Fund shared with KINNOCK and BJERREGAARD.
DG XVII	Energy	Christos PAPOUTSIS (Greece)
DG XIX	Budgets	LIIKANEN
DG XXI	Customs and Indirect Taxation	MONTI
DG XXII	Education, Training and Youth	CRESSON
DG XXIII	Enterprise Policy, Distributive Trades, Tourism and Cooperatives	PAPOUTSIS
DG XXIV	Consumer Policy and Consumer Health Protection	BONINO
—	Immigration, home affairs and justice; financial control and fraud prevention	Anita GRADIN (Sweden)

I.1.3 Nomination (TEC Art. 158)

The Commissioners are appointed for five years. Their mandate is renewable. Since the entry into force of the TEU, the process of nomination takes place in the following way:

(a)   After having consulted the EP, the governments of the Member States (in practice the European Council) nominate, by common accord, the person they intend to appoint President of the Commission.

(b)   In consultation with the nominee for President, the governments of the Member States nominate the other persons they intend to appoint as Members of the Commission.

(c)   At this stage, in practice, the governments of the Member States also agree on the portfolios to assign to each person they intend to appoint.

(d)   The nominees are submitted to individual hearings before the EP parliamentary committee corresponding to the foreseen portfolio of the nominees. This procedure was used for the nomination of the Santer Commission (1995), and is not foreseen by the treaty.

(e)   The nominee for President and the other persons nominated to be Members of the Commission are submitted to a vote of approval by the EP.

(f)   The President and the other Members of the Commission are appointed by the governments of the Member States.

I.1.4 Voting Modalities and Working Structures

The Commission's Rules of Procedure establish the general principle of *collegiate decision-making*. According to this fundamental principle, the Commissioners are bound as a college by the decisions they take, and bear the responsibility of these collectively: there is no individual decision-taking, consequently there is no individual responsibility.

The Commission meets once a week. The meetings are convened by its President. Proposals to take decisions are put forward by a member of the Commission. Decisions are taken by simple majority (TEC Art. 163).

I.1.5 Motion of Censure (TEC Art. 144)

The Commission has to *resign collectively* if a motion of censure on its activities is approved by the EP. The EP has never managed to pass one. If it does, the Commission must continue to deal with current business until it is replaced.

I.2 Role in the Policy Cycle

I.2.1 Policy Initiator

Except for rare cases (EMU and the uniform election procedure for the EP), the Commission is the policy initiator *par excellence* in the Community pillar as it enjoys a *monopoly of legislative initiative*. It decides when it is best to launch an initiative in a specific policy area. Its proposals set the framework for the decisions to be adopted by the Council and, where provided, by the EP. The procedural requirement of unanimity voting in the Council to adopt an act constituting an amendment to the Commission's proposal strengthens the Commission's initiatives (TEC Art. 189a.1).

Before putting forward a proposal, the Commission collects information and advice from the other institutions and other key actors such as lobbies, national expert groups and social partners. It does so through various means such as Green and White Papers. Its ideas on the development of the policies are generally contained in Action Programmes.

In the second and third pillars of the TEU, where the interests of the Member States are strong, the Commission shares the right of initiative with the Council. In some areas of common interest in Justice and Home Affairs, the Commission has no right of initiative at all.

I.2.2 Guardian of the Treaty (TEC Art. 155, 1st indent)

The Commission also plays a decisive role in the control phase of the policy cycle (see chapters 5 and 11). It has to make sure that the Treaty's provisions are applied by the Member States (TEC Arts. 169, 170, 92 and 93), the institutions (TEC Arts. 173 and 175) and economic agents (TEC Arts. 85–7 and 90).

I.2.3 Pool of Expertise (TEC Art. 155, 2nd indent)
The Commission *formulates recommendations or delivers opinions* on matters dealt with in the Treaty. The Commission may do so when it considers it necessary, but the Treaty expressly provides the Commission with *consultative powers* in matters of a 'constitutional nature' such as the revision of the Treaties (TEU Art. N) and applications to join the EU (TEU Art. O).

I.2.4 Decision-making (TEC Art. 155, 3rd indent)
The Commission has its own power of decision and participates in the shaping of measures taken by the Council and the EP in the manner provided for in the Treaty (e.g., Art. 90 para. 3: the Commission can address Directives and Decisions to the Member States to ensure the application of the provisions concerning the behaviour of public undertakings).

I.2.5 Management (TEC Arts 155, 4th indent and 145, 3rd indent)
The Commission is commonly described as the executive body of the Community, since it normally manages EC policies. Nonetheless, the Treaty of Rome did not clearly reserve such a power to it: in fact, it conferred management powers on the Council. Originally, the Council could delegate its management powers to the Commission for the implementation of rules it had laid down. As the amount of secondary legislation increased, the Council systematically delegated management powers to the Commission. The Council coupled the delegation of powers with the creation of ad hoc committees to supervise the Commission's adoption of implementing measures. The Single European Act codified (TEC Art. 145, 3rd indent) the existing practice, making the attribution of implementing powers to the Commission the rule and their exercise by the Council an exception. It also recognised the Council's right to submit the attribution of implementation powers to certain requirements. The Council did so in the so-called *Comitology* decision (1987), which foresees *three types of committees* (advisory, management and regulatory) to supervise the Commission while adopting implementing measures. Under certain conditions the management and regulatory-type committees can block the Commission's measures in favour of measures adopted by the Council.

I.2.6 Representation Powers
Within the Member States, the Community as a legal person is represented by the Commission (TEC Art. 211; *internal representation*). It also enjoys

important *external representation* powers as it maintains relations with all international organisations. It does this with all UN organs and UN specialised agencies (TEC Art. 229). Moreover, in areas where the Community has competence in the first pillar, the Commission *negotiates international agreements* with third countries or international organisations on the basis of negotiation directives adopted by the Council (TEC Art. 228).

I.3 Reforming the Commission

The ToA strengthened the *role of the President of the Commission*, establishing that: 'The Commission shall work under the political guidance of its President' (ToA/TEU Art. 219). This leading role is further explained in a Declaration 'on the organisation and functioning of the Commission', which is annexed to the ToA and which foresees that 'the President of the Commission should enjoy broad discretion in the allocation of tasks within the College, as well as in any reshuffling of those tasks during a Commission's term of office'.

The role of the EP in the appointing of the Commission was also substantially enhanced by the ToA, thus reducing the current 'democratic deficit'. The *EP will have to give its assent to the nomination of the Commission President* (it will continue to give its approval to the team of Commissioners). The nominee for President will also be given the right of assent on the choice of the members of the College.

The issue of ensuring an optimal division between conventional portfolios and specific tasks within the Commission, as well as a corresponding restructuring of the Commission's subdivisions, was scheduled for the year 2000. The sole clear target set by the IGC in this respect was that there should be *a vice-president responsible for all external relations* (currently, foreign policy and external commercial relations are split up between six Commissioners).

II. THE COUNCIL OF MINISTERS

The Council of Ministers is the institution which represents the *governments* of the Member States (TEC Art. 146).

II.1 Main Characteristics and Functioning

II.1.1 Composition (TEC Art. 146)
The Council consists of a representative of each Member State at the ministerial level, who is authorised to commit the government of that Member

State. The office of President is held in turn by each Member State for a term of six months. Council Decision 95/2 fixed the following order for the Presidency.

Year	Presidency held by	Year	Presidency held by
1996	Italy Ireland	2000	Portugal France
1997	Netherlands Luxembourg	2001	Sweden Belgium
1998	UK Austria	2002	Spain Denmark
1999	Germany Finland	2003	Greece

In the second half of 2003, assuming there has been no enlargement, Italy will begin the cycle again.

II.1.2 Working Structures
There is *one Council* of Ministers but, according to the matter discussed, it meets in *different formations*. The original formation, the General Affairs Council (foreign affairs ministers), deals with a great variety of issues and has assumed a function of coordination of the other specific formation Councils: ECOFIN (finance ministers: EMU), Agriculture Council (agriculture ministers: CAP); JHA Council (ministers of justice or of internal affairs: JHA) etc.

The Council organises its work on *three levels*:

(a)   Council level — ministers;

(b)   Committee of Permanent Representatives of the Member States, so-called 'COREPER' (TEC Art. 151.1) — either permanent representatives (COREPER II, which covers foreign affairs and ECOFIN) or deputy permanent representatives (COREPER I, which covers IM and connected policies);

(c)   Working groups — national experts.

At each level the Presidency plays both an administrative (managing of meetings) and a political (consensus building) role. All levels benefit from the technical assistance of the General Secretariat (TEC Art. 151.2).

A Commission proposal in the Council of Ministers starts at the expert level and works its way up (it can go up and down several times!). The working group level is responsible for the analysis of the technical implications of a proposal. The national experts, together with experts from the Commission, discuss the proposal word by word. If agreement is found on certain points, these are transmitted to COREPER as 'I points' (no further discussion necessary) on the agenda, whereas unsolved issues are marked as 'II points'. COREPER prepares the Council's work. It also tries to solve certain issues at its level. The matters where consensus has been reached appear as 'A points' on the Council's agenda and do not require further debate. The Council has to solve all open problems ('B points', generally the most sensitive issues).

II.1.3 Voting Modalities

(a)   *Simple majority*: if no particular voting modality is provided for the adoption of an act, the Council votes on it by simple majority. This is very rarely the case.

(b)   *Unanimity*: this is the normal voting modality for the adoption of acts which touch directly upon sensitive interests of the Member States and for 'constitutional' matters. Abstentions are not calculated as votes against the adoption of an act.

(c)   *Qualified majority*: the votes are weighted as foreseen in TEC Art. 148.2. The weighting of votes is based on demographic and economic considerations. The total number of votes is 87 and the threshold for qualified majority voting (QMV) is 62. In 1993, the European Council preparing the enlargement of the EC to Austria, Sweden, Finland and Norway discussed the need to modify the weighting mechanisms in order not to disrupt the initial equilibrium reflected in the weighting of votes. It did not succeed in altering the weighting. In 1994 the deadlock was solved through a compromise on the threshold for a 'blocking minority' (between 23 and 26 votes — Ioannina compromise, 1994). The issue of the weighting of votes in the Council was postponed to the 1996 IGC for a definitive solution.

Country	Votes
Belgium	5
Denmark	3
Germany	10
Greece	5
Spain	8
France	10
Ireland	3
Italy	10
Luxembourg	2
Netherlands	5
Austria	4
Portugal	5
Finland	3
Sweden	4
United Kingdom	10

The rule and the practice
In practice the Council tries to avoid voting. It prefers working on a consensual basis. The occasions when the Presidency actually calls for a vote are rare. Nonetheless, the threat of calling a vote helps to build up compromises and reach solutions. After the 'empty chair crisis' (1965–66, see chapter 2) when the Council effectively adopted all its decisions by unanimity (Luxembourg compromise), the Commission's role in the policy cycle was weakened as the Council could always depart from its proposal. The extension of QMV with the SEA demonstrated the Member States' willingness to limit the practice of unanimity voting, even though this has not produced the massive improvements in the speed and volume of legislation which were promised at the time.

II.2 Role in the Policy Cycle

II.2.1 Decision Preparation
The Council may request the Commission to submit to it any appropriate proposal (TEC Art. 152). Legally, the Commission is not obliged to satisfy the request. Nonetheless, the Commission generally acts on such requests, since they reflect the Member States' concerns for action in specific policy areas.

II.2.2 Decision-making (TEC Art. 145, 2nd indent)

'To ensure that the objectives of this Treaty are attained, the Council shall ... have power to take decisions': the Council is the *primary decision-taker* in the EU policy cycle even though the EP has acquired increasing powers with each IGC. The Council's fundamental role in decision-making reflects the interest of the Member States to influence strongly what is being decided at the Community level, since the acts adopted will bind them at the national level.

II.2.3 Decision Implementation (TEC Art. 145, 3rd indent)

Acts adopted at the EC level which are not directly applicable in the Member States must be transposed into national law. The day-to-day implementation of Community acts is carried out by national administrations. Under certain conditions, it is necessary that implementation measures be adopted at the Community level. These are adopted by the Commission but, as explained above, the Council may take back the powers conferred.

II.2.4 Coordination of Economic Policies (TEC Art. 145, 1st indent)

The Council has the responsibility of coordinating the general economic policies of the Member States (see chapters 6 and 9).

II.2.5 External Representation (TEU Art. J.5.1)

The Presidency of the Council represents the Union in matters concerning Common Foreign and Security Policy (see chapter 20).

II.3 Reforming the Council

II.3.1 New Voting Modalities

The *extension of QMV* was identified by the 1996 IGC as one of the most important reforms needed to increase the efficiency of the Council's decision-making. The ToA did not go as far as one might have expected. Nonetheless, QMV was indeed extended, within certain limits, to the second and third pillar. In the second pillar, new procedures ('constructive abstention' and the so-called 'Amsterdam compromise') should also facilitate the taking of decisions. In the third pillar, new cases of 'extra-qualified' majority voting are provided for (see chapters 20 and 21).

The ToA created new cases where the Council acts by QMV without the EP being involved: employment policy guidelines and recommendations; implementation of social partner agreements, etc.

Unanimity was chosen for a series of new competences such as the implementation of the Schengen *acquis* or the determination of a breach of the Union's principles. Since these new cases may be categorised as quasi-constitutional matters, unanimity may be considered appropriate. However, some exceptions to this categorisation exist; for example, the adoption of measures against discrimination or the provision on international agreements, as well as some existing competences such as industrial policy (Nentwich & Falkner, 1997).

II.3.2 Weighting of Votes

The temporary solution contained in the 'Ioannina compromise' and the prospect of an enlarged Union demanded that a lasting solution be found for a new mechanism of weighting of votes in the Council. No consensus on how the mechanism should be readapted was possible. In fact, the 'Protocol on the institutions with the prospect of enlargement', annexed to the ToA, merely reaffirms that the system of weighted votes in the Council will not be abandoned and that it needs to be strengthened. However, there is no suggestion of a way of doing that.

II.3.3 New 'Transparency' Requirements

In line with the need to respect the newly introduced principle of transparency (see above, A.4), ToA/TEC Art. 207.3 requires the Council to define the cases in which it is to be regarded as acting in its legislative capacity because it will be obliged to allow 'greater access to documents' when it acts as a legislator. This increased transparency needs to be balanced with the need to preserve 'the effectiveness of its decision-making process'. This condition might complicate the implementation of the new transparency requirements. The ToA therefore stresses that anyhow, when acting as a legislator, results of votes, explanations of votes and statements in the minutes have to be made public regardless of the possible negative impact on the effectiveness of the Council's decision-making process.

III. THE EUROPEAN COUNCIL

Meetings of the Heads of State or of Government of the Member States and the Commission President are referred to as European Councils.

The European Council originates from the Member States' perceived need to extend their cooperation to fields outside the scope of the EC Treaty and to do so without the straitjacket of the decision-making procedures of the Council of Ministers. It was formalised by the SEA and further clarified by the TEU, which defined it as a body of the Union. Even though it is *not an 'institution'* in the sense of TEC Art. 4, it is a key actor in the intergovernmental pillars of the TEU and plays an important role also in the Community pillar. Given its peculiarity, it is worth briefly describing its functioning and powers.

III.1 Main Characteristics and Functioning

III.1.1 Composition

> The European Council shall bring together the Heads of State or
> Government of the Member States and the President of the Commission.
> They shall be assisted by the Ministers of Foreign Affairs of the Member
> States and by a Member of the Commission (TEU Art. D para. 2)

The involvement of the President of the Commission in this intergovernmental
body highlights the necessity to coordinate harmoniously the interests of the
Member States with the general interest of the Community.

III.1.2 Meetings (Summits)

In practice, the European Council meets at least once during each Presidency,
usually in December and June. Extraordinary meetings to discuss specific
issues can take place at other times (see chapter 17). The meetings are very
informal and discussion is not constrained by procedures (the so-called 'fireside
chats'). The European Council does not produce any legally binding acts. At
the end of each summit, the Presidency draws the conclusions of the meeting.
These contain highly influential guidelines for future action to be undertaken
by the EU's institutions.

III.2 Role in the Policy Cycle: Policy Initiator

> The European Council shall provide the Union with the necessary impetus
> for its development and shall define the general political guidelines thereof.
> (TEU Art. D para. 1)

The position of the European Council in the policy cycle lies essentially in the
'decision preparation' phase. In practice it affects policy in three different ways:

    (a)   it puts forward concrete suggestions concerning actions to be taken or
instruments to be created in the different policy fields (e.g., the adoption of the
Social Charter in Strasbourg in 1989);

    (b)   it acts as a problem solver trying to find solutions to deadlocks in the
Council of Ministers on particular issues (e.g., the reform of CAP in the early
1980s);

    (c)   it defines the general guidelines for the evolution of the EU integration
(e.g., constitutional and institutional reforms, enlargement, EMU, etc.).

IV. THE EUROPEAN PARLIAMENT

The European Parliament is the institution which represents the *peoples* of the states brought together in the Community (TEC Art. 137).

IV.1 Main Characteristics and Functioning

IV.1.1 Election Procedure
The Treaty of Rome provided for an 'Assembly' composed of persons designated by the national parliaments, which would draw up proposals for elections to take place by direct universal suffrage in accordance with a uniform procedure in all the Member States. In 1975 a proposal was submitted to the Council and in 1976 it adopted an Act concerning the election of the representatives of the Assembly by direct universal suffrage. The first *direct universal elections* took place in 1979. By then, the Assembly had changed name and was being referred to as the European Parliament.

The *uniformisation of the election procedure* has still to be realised: the elections take place in all the Member States at the same time and the term of office of the European Members of Parliament (MEPs) is the same (five years), but the procedure to elect them remains different between Member States, causing considerable problems of proportionality in representation.

At present there are 626 MEPs and the number of seats for each Member State is established by TEC Art. 138.2. Since the entry into force of the TEU, it is possible for every citizen of the Union — residing in a Member State of which he or she is not a national — to vote and stand for elections for the EP in the Member State where he/she resides (TEC Art. 8b). The next election will be held in 1999.

Country	Number of MEPs
Belgium	25
Denmark	16
Germany	99
Greece	25
Spain	64
France	87
Ireland	15
Italy	87
Luxembourg	6
Netherlands	31
Austria	21
Portugal	25
Finland	16
Sweden	22
United Kingdom	87

IV.1.2 Working Structures

The EP's seat is in Strasbourg, where one-week plenary sessions are held once a month. The EP also holds plenary sessions in Brussels. The Secretariat of the EP is located in Luxembourg.

During the plenary sessions, MEPs may speak on their own behalf, as committee rapporteurs or as representatives of a political group. They never speak on behalf of a certain Member State. As in any Parliament, the MEPs' work is organised in specific structures.

Leadership structures

These are the coordinating organs of the EP. They are elected by the MEPs at the beginning of their mandate. Among them are:

(a) *President*: opens and closes the Parliament's sittings; chairs the meetings of the Conference of Presidents and the Bureau; represents the EP.

(b) *14 Vice-Presidents*: they preside over plenary sessions; represent the EP externally when the President cannot.

(c) *Five Quaestors* (College of Quaestors): they are responsible for administrative and financial matters directly concerning the MEPs (office equipment, etc.).

(d)   *Conference of Presidents* (President of EP and chairs of political groups): drafts the agenda and deals with the other institutions; proposes membership of committees; adjudicates disputes on competencies of committees.

(e)   *Bureau* (President and Vice-Presidents): internal financial organisational and administrative tasks; responsible for staff policy (sending members on missions, etc.).

Political groups
They reflect the various political and ideological orientations and cleavages of the Member States' political systems. There are nine major political affiliations: the Party of European Socialists (PSE); the European Peoples Party (EPP); the Liberal, Democratic and Reformist (ELDR), the European United Left/Nordic Green Left; Forza Europa; European Democratic Alliance (EDA); the Greens; European Radical Alliance; Europe of Nations Group. None of these affiliations has led to corresponding 'transnational European parties'. All groups are transnational in composition. The two biggest groups are the PSE and the EPP, which effectively control the EP.

Committees
The detailed work of the EP is prepared in committees. The MEPs are divided up among 20 'standing committees', each specialised in a particular field (Foreign Affairs; Agriculture and Rural Development; Social Affairs and Employment; Development and Cooperation; Legal Affairs and Citizen's Rights; Institutional Affairs, etc.). Ad hoc committees on particular issues may also be set up.

IV.1.3 Voting Modalities
(a)   *Absolute majority of the votes cast (AMUC)*: the majority (50% + 1) of the MEPs present in the room.

(b)   *Absolute majority of the constituent members (AMCM)*: this is the majority of all MEPs (since MEPs are 626, the AMCM is 314). Absent MEPs effectively vote against.

(c)   *Strengthened majorities*: these are the most difficult to obtain. There are two types:

(i)   AMCM + 2/3 AMUC (e.g., for motion of censure of the Commission; to reject the Community budget);

(ii)   AMCM + 3/5 AMUC (e.g., to increase the fixed maximum rate of expenditure).

IV.2 Role in the Policy Cycle

IV.2.1 Decision Preparation

The EP may adopt resolutions calling on the Commission and the Council to develop or modify existing policies or to introduce new ones. As such it can have a political driving force role. Moreover, like the Council, the EP may request the Commission to submit any proposal (TEC Art. 138b).

IV.2.2 Decision Taking: from No Role at all to Co-legislator

The role of the EP varies (see C) according to the procedure to be used in the decision-making process: it may range from no role at all (when not even consultation is provided for) to an extremely influential role (the power to block the adoption of an act). This broad spectrum of influence is the result of a struggle which may be summarised in four major phases:

(a)   First the EP gained the final say on the non-compulsory expenditure of the Community (1970 and 1975 budgetary reforms).

(b)   Then it exploited the ECJ's jurisprudence on the importance of consultation by asking the Commission to integrate its opinion in a revised proposal so that the Council could decide differently only by unanimity. In 1986 the SEA codified this practice by creating two new procedures (cooperation and assent).

(c)   The TEU recognised the EP's right to reject an act (co-decision).

(d)   The ToA effectively transformed the EP into a true co-legislator by reforming and extending co-decision.

IV.2.3 Control

The control that the EP exercises in the EU policy cycle is essentially political:

(a)   The *motion of censure* expresses the possibility for the institution representing the interests of the peoples of the Member States to dismiss the Commission if it does not act in the interest of the Community.

(b)   Even when it has no role in the decision-making procedure, the EP is *always informed* by the other institutions. This right to be informed gives it the possibility to react by stressing its interests on each issue.

(c)   The EP may set up *temporary committees of inquiry* (TEC Art. 138c) to investigate alleged contraventions or maladministration in the implementation of Community law, unless these are already the subject of judicial proceedings. These Committees submit reports with their findings to the EP.

(d)   Since the entry into force of the TEU an *Ombudsman* is appointed by the EP (TEC Art. 138c) to receive complaints concerning maladministration by the Community's institutions from citizens or any legal person in the Member States. The Ombudsman submits an annual report to the EP containing its findings.

IV.3 Reforming the EP in View of Enlargement

IV.3.1 Representation in the EP
The ToA limits the number of MEPs to 700 (ToA/TEC Art. 189 para. 2). In the event of amendments to the Treaty's allocation of seats per Member State, the 700 ceiling has to be combined with the need to secure 'appropriate representation of the peoples of the States' (ToA/TEC Art. 190.2). How to guarantee such appropriate representation has not been agreed upon.

IV.3.2 National Parliaments' Involvement in the Process of European Integration

The 'Protocol on the role of national parliaments in the European Union' annexed to the ToA does not refer to a greater involvement of national parliaments in the sense of formal participation in the decision-making process, but rather through increased exchanges of views. To this end, specific provisions are contained in the Protocol *to assure an improved transfer of information.* The Protocol stipulates that Green and White papers and communications should be sent directly to the national parliaments whilst legislative proposals will continue to be forwarded to them via national governments. Theoretically, national parliaments will be able to scrutinise the activities of their governments at the European level, and influence them, since it is established that the Commission proposals should be made available to them in good time. Moreover a period of six weeks should elapse between a proposal being made available in all languages to the EP and the Council by the Commission and the date when it is first placed on a Council agenda for decision. This does not apply in cases of urgency.

COSAC (Conférence des Organes des Parlements Spécialisés dans les Affaires Européennes) will have the right to make any contribution it deems appropriate for the attention of the EU institutions, either on its own initiative or when a specific legislative proposal is forwarded to it. It will also be able to comment on proposals and initiatives related to the establishment of the area of freedom, security and justice (see chapter 22), the application of the principle of subsidiarity and questions regarding fundamental rights. COSAC's contributions are to be forwarded to the institutions but will neither bind the latter nor prejudge the position of the national parliaments.

V. THE EUROPEAN COURT OF JUSTICE

The ECJ ensures that in the interpretation and application of the TEC the law is observed (TEC Art. 164). It represents *the rule of law*.

V.1 Main Characteristics and Functioning

V.1.1 Composition
The ECJ consists of 15 Judges (TEC Art. 165). These are assisted by eight Advocates-General (TEC Art. 166). Judges and Advocates-General are persons whose 'independence is beyond doubt' and who possess the qualifications required for appointment to the highest judicial offices in their respective countries (TEC Art. 167).

V.1.2 Nomination
The judges are appointed by common accord of the governments of the Member States for a term of six years. A system of partial replacement is provided for. The President of the ECJ is elected by its members for a term of three years and may be re-elected (TEC Art. 167).

V.1.3 Working Structures
The ECJ sits in plenary sessions in Luxembourg. In order to undertake preparatory inquiries or to adjudicate on particular categories of cases, it may form chambers consisting of three, five or seven judges (TEC Art. 165). The Advocates-General assist the judges. Their duty is to make reasoned submissions in open court on cases brought before the ECJ. The judgment of the ECJ may differ from the Advocate-General's conclusions.

Since the entry into force of the SEA, a *Court of First Instance* (CFI) has been attached to the ECJ. It is composed of one judge from each Member State appointed as the judges for the ECJ. According to TEC Art. 168a, the CFI has jurisdiction to hear and determine, at first instance, 'subject to a right of appeal to the Court of Justice on points of law only', certain classes of action or proceedings. These were determined by the Council on the basis of a request of the ECJ and after having consulted the EP and the Commission (TEC Art. 168a.2). They are:

(a)   disputes between the Community and its staff;

(b)   all actions brought by natural or legal persons other than anti-dumping cases;

(c)   actions brought against the Commission under the ECSC Treaty.

V.2 Role in the Policy Cycle

V.2.1 Policy Initiator

Given its nature, the ECJ obviously has no formal role in the decision-preparation phase of the policy cycle. Nonetheless one should highlight the important influence its case law may have in the determination of the scope of the competences of the Community. Through the interpretation of Community law the ECJ may therefore play a policy-initiator role (see chapter 17).

V.2.2 Control

The ECJ plays a fundamental role in terms of control (see chapter 5): it has to ensure that the law is observed in the interpretation and application of the TEC (TEC Art. 164). By adjudicating disputes among the Member States and the institutions on the interpretation, application or failure of application of Community acts, it assures the uniform enforcement of the rules agreed upon in the policy cycle.

TEU Art. L excludes from the ECJ's jurisdiction the TEU common provisions, the Second and Third Pillar (with one exception; see chapter 21).

V.3 Amsterdam: Broadening of ECJ Jurisdiction

ToA/TEU Art. 46 extends the powers of the ECJ to:
    (a)   police and judicial cooperation in criminal matters (see chapter 22);
    (b)   the activities of the institutions affecting respect for fundamental rights (ToA/TEU Art. 6.2);
    (c)   the provisions on closer cooperation (see chapter 4).

VI. THE COURT OF AUDITORS

The Court of Auditors (CoA) represents the desire to guarantee a *transparent control* and audit of the Community budget.

It was established in 1977 under the Financial Provisions Treaty of 1975 to carry out the audit (TEC Art. 188a). A need to increase control had been felt since the 1975 budgetary reforms had guaranteed the EP the sole responsibility of discharging the Commission of its responsibility concerning the accounts of the Community.

VI.1 Main Characteristics and Functioning

VI.1.1 Composition
The CoA consists of 15 members whose 'independence must be beyond doubt' (TEC Art. 188b). Its members are chosen from persons who belong or have belonged in their respective countries to external audit bodies or who are especially qualified for the office (TEC Art. 188b.2).

VI.1.2 Nomination
The members of the CoA are appointed for a term of six years by the Council, acting unanimously after consulting the EP. The members of the Court appoint their President for a term of three years which is renewable (TEC Art. 188b).

VI.2 Role in the Policy Cycle: Financial Watchdog

The role of the CoA in the policy cycle is limited to the control stage. It examines the legality and regularity of the accounts of all revenue and expenditure of the Community. It also does this for the accounts of all bodies set up by the Community, unless the constituent instrument of any such body expressly precludes it from doing so. It provides the EP and the Council with a statement of assurance as to the reliability of the accounts and the legality and the regularity of the transactions. After the close of every financial year it draws up an annual report which it forwards to the other institutions and which is published in the Official Journal (TEC Art. 188c).

The CoA assesses both the financial soundness of the operations carried out and whether the means used to do so were the most efficient and economic. Its role is therefore that of ensuring openness and transparency. This role influences the other institutions' behaviour and puts constraints on them, since its reports highlight wasted resources in specific policy areas and the need to redirect resources to other policy areas.

VI.3 Amsterdam: A Strengthened Role for the Court of Auditors

The new provisions concerning the role of the CoA should increase transparency. The CoA will have control over the premises of any entity which manages expenditure on behalf of the Community. It *must report any instance of irregularity* when examining the legality and regularity of revenue and expenditure and when trying to ensure sound financial management. The statement of assurance as to the reliability of the accounts and the legality and regularity of the underlying transactions, which the CoA must submit to the EP and the Council, *must be published* in the Official Journal of the European Communities.

C. THE DECISION-MAKING PROCEDURES

The *institutional balance* explained above is mirrored in the choice of the procedure to be followed to take decisions. According to the interests at stake in the various policy areas where the EU has competence to act, there might be a preference for a procedure which gives more power to the Council or the EP, which gives greater or less influence to the Commission, or which gives the ECJ jurisdiction or not. Nonetheless one should stress that there is *no clear-cut procedural division of labour between the institutions in the EU policy cycle* as, according to the rules applied in the policy area in question, decisions are taken in different ways. This complexity makes it very difficult to identify who is the decision-maker of the system. It is practically impossible to identify the person responsible for efficient or inefficient policies. The purpose of this section of the chapter is to highlight the influence of the Commission, the Council and the EP in the decision-making system of the EU by sketching the main stages of the different decision-making procedures.

Originally, the Commission submitted proposals to the Council; the EP would give its opinion where 'consultation' was provided for in the Treaty; and the Council would adopt the final act. As explained above, the EP has progressively increased its power and influence in the decision-making procedures. The evolution of the role of the institution representing the interests of the peoples of the Member States reflects the historical development of the integration process. Thanks to the ECJ's case law, the institutional balance has adapted to these evolving roles. These have been enshrined in the Treaty each time it was revised. Through the extension and reform of co-decision, the ToA marks a further increase in the legislative role of the EP. Nonetheless, the ToA also extends the use of other procedures. Consultation is provided for in new provisions concerning authorisation for closer cooperation, measures against discrimination, most decisions on asylum and immigration etc. The ToA also introduces new cases of non-involvement of the EP: decisions on closer cooperation, the suspension of rights deriving from the Treaty for a Member State in breach of fundamental principles of the Union, the implementation of social partner agreements in social policy etc.

I. CONSULTATION

I.1 Working of the Procedure

This was the original procedure and it still exists in some areas such as CCP. Like all procedures, it starts with a proposal from the Commission which is transmitted to the Council which has to decide on it. Before doing so the Council has to ask for the EP's opinion.

I.2 Influence of the Institutions

The EP's opinion is not legally binding but, according to the ECJ's jurisprudence, it is an *essential procedural requirement*, the non-observance of which results in an annulment of the act in question. The opinion represents an essential element of the institutional balance designed by the authors of the TEC. It represents their desire to ensure the *respect of the democratic principle* of participation of the institution representing the peoples of the Member States in the legislative process of the Community (*Roquette* case, commonly known as 'Isoglucose', C-70/88).

II. ASSENT

II.1 Working of the Procedure

For acts to be adopted with this procedure an agreement of both the Council and the EP is needed. The EP gives its assent in the following cases:

Article	Field	EP majority required
TEC Art. 8a.2	Facilitating the rights of citizenship	AMVC
TEC Art. 105.6	ECB tasks	AMVC
TEC Art. 106.5	Amendments of the ESCB statute	AMVC
TEC Art. 130d.1	Tasks, priority objectives and organisation of structural funds	AMVC
TEC Art. 138.3	Uniform electoral procedure for the EP	AMCM
TEC Art. 228.3	Association agreements	AMCM

II.2. Influence of the Institutions

The EP has the power to say 'yes' or 'no' to an act, nothing more. It cannot, in principle, propose any amendment. In practice, it uses its possibility of saying 'no' as a threat to subordinate its assent to the taking up of its suggestions.

III. COOPERATION (TEC Art. 189c)

III.1 Working of the Procedure

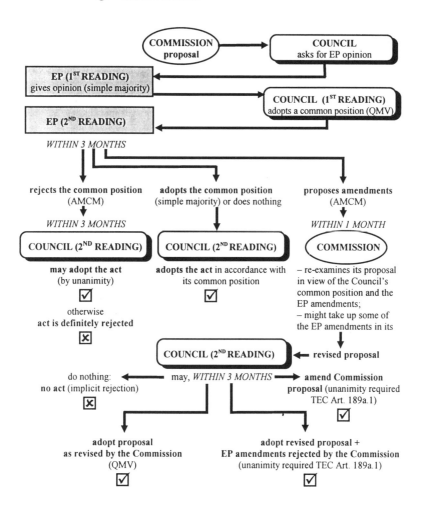

III.2 Influence of the Institutions

The EP's opinion on the Commission's proposal has to be taken into consideration by the Council when elaborating its common position. In the second reading the EP has the possibility of amending the common position. This obviously grants it an important role in the elaboration of Community legislation. Here the EP has the power to reject an act. However, the rejection is not definitive, since the Council may, by unanimity, adopt the act anyhow. The Council remains the institution that takes the final decision.

The Commission also plays a notable role in this procedure as it intervenes with a new proposal before the Council's second reading. This means that if the Council wants to depart from the revised proposal it has to do so by unanimity (TEC Art. 189a.1). If the Commission has incorporated EP amendments in its revised proposal, their chances of being accepted by the Council are strengthened because this would have to exclude them by unanimity.

IV. CO-DECISION (TEC Art. 189b)

IV.1 Working of the Procedure

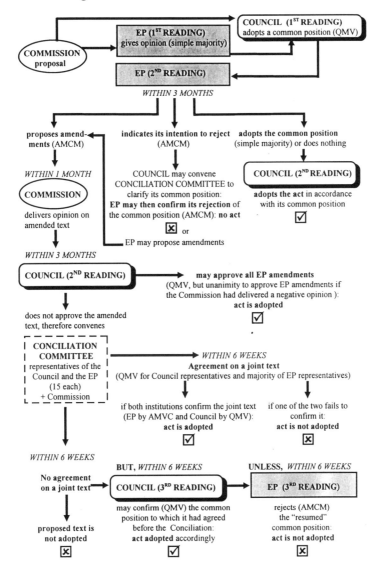

IV.2 Influence of the Institutions

The EP further increases its power as a co-legislator: indeed it gains the power to reject an act definitively. The Council cannot, as in the cooperation procedure, save the act by adopting it unanimously even if the EP does not approve it. The voting modalities needed for the EP to decide differently from the Council reflect a certain caution in the attribution to the EP of an increased role: they generally are very difficult to reach and whenever the EP does not act, its silence is interpreted as an approval of the Council's positions whereas the same does not happen for the Council (its silence is deemed as disapproval of EP suggestions).

The Council still plays an extremely influential role. Its common position is actually the text which, after the initial proposal of the Commission, will be adopted as an act. Indeed, from the second reading onwards the Council and the EP discuss the contents of the common position. The Council may alter it as it wishes (no unanimity is required as it is not the Commission's proposal).

The Commission's role is weakened as the game is essentially played between the EP and the Council. The Commission does not submit a revised proposal after the EP's second reading: it merely delivers an opinion on the amended common position. If the opinion on the EP's amendments is negative, the Commission's view is strengthened by the procedural requirement of unanimity for the Council to adopt the amendment. In the Conciliation Committee the Commission plays a mediator role: the EP and the Council are not obliged to take into consideration the Commission's suggestions.

IV.3 Amsterdam: Reforming and Extending Co-decision

With the ToA co-decision replacing cooperation in all provisions unchanged from the TEU (except for EMU), it is the most frequently used procedure. This means that the EP is co-legislator in an increased number of areas (changes for specific policy areas can be found in the relevant chapters).

The ToA also simplifies the procedure. According to ToA/TEC Art. 251 co-decision shall work as follows:

CO-DECISION PROCEDURE (TEC/ToA Art. 251)

COMMISSION
proposal

EP (1ST READING)
gives opinion (simple majority)

COUNCIL (1ST READING)

if agreement to EP's opinion,
act adopted accordingly

☑ or

EP (2ND READING)

adopts a common position
(QMV)

WITHIN 3 MONTHS

proposes amendments
(AMCM)

rejects the common position
(AMCM)
no act
☒

adopts the common position
(simple majority) or does
nothing: act deemed adopted
☑

WITHIN 1 MONTH

COMMISSION
delivers opinion on
amended text

*WITHIN
3 MONTHS*

COUNCIL (2ND READING)

may approve all EP amendments
(QMV, but unanimity to approve EP amendments if
the Commission had delivered a negative opinion):
act is adopted
☑

does not approve the amended text,
therefore convenes
WITHIN 6 WEEKS

WITHIN 6 WEEKS
Agreement on a joint text
(QMV for Council representatives and
majority of EP representatives)

CONCILIATION COMMITTEE
representatives of the Council
and the EP (15 each) + Commission

WITHIN 6 WEEKS

if both institutions confirm the
joint text (EP by AMVC and
Council by QMV):
act is adopted
☑

if one of the
institutions fails to
confirm the joint text:
act is not adopted
☒

WITHIN 6 WEEKS
**No agreement
on a joint text**
↓
proposed text is not adopted
☒

Comparing TEC Art. 189b and ToA/TEC Art. 251 the most significant changes are:

1st reading
If the Council agrees to the EP's amendments it may adopt the act at this early stage.

2nd reading
— *The EP can reject* the common position *right away*: it no longer has to notify the Council of its intention to reject it (consequently no conciliation can take place at this stage).
— If the EP *does not act* within three months, the act is deemed to be adopted in the version of the Council's common position.
— If the EP *approves* the Council's common position, the act is deemed to be adopted without being referred back to the Council.

— If the Council agrees to the EP's amendments, the act is also deemed to be adopted without any further formal decision.

— If the Council does not agree to the EP's amendments, it *must convene* the conciliation committee *within six weeks.*

3rd reading
If the Conciliation Committee does not succeed, the Council may *no longer approve again* its original common position, consequently there is no act.

The ToA also attempts to limit the duration of the procedure. While the 1st reading remains without time limits, the period between the EP's 2nd reading and the outcome of the whole procedure should *not exceed 9 months.*

The simplification of co-decision results in a *re-balancing of powers to the EP*: its veto on the adoption of an act is transformed into a requirement for its approval to adopt an act. This leaves just one last formal inequality: during the second reading the EP's silence will continue to result in the adoption of the act in the version of the Council's common position; whereas the Council's failure to reach a decision on the EP's amendments in the second reading does not entail an adoption of the act in the EP's version (Nentwich and Falkner).

D. INSTITUTIONS UNPREPARED FOR ENLARGEMENT

The institutional reforms of the ToA are incomplete, since the reforms necessary to prepare the institutions for enlargement were postponed. Open questions remain, regarding:

   (a)   the number of Commissioners;
   (b)   the weighting of votes and a new threshold for a blocking minority in the Council;
   (c)   the system of representation in the EP.

Reference is made to these questions in the 'Protocol on the institutions with the prospect of enlargement' annexed to the ToA. It establishes that at the date of entry into force of the first enlargement (no precise number of states referred to), the Commission shall comprise *only one Commissioner per Member State*, but the issue of the *re-weighting of the votes in the Council* has to be settled at the same date. This apparent agreement on the reduction of size of the Commission is in fact a postponement of the decision. Anyway, the Protocol recognises that, because the institutional reforms necessary to prepare the EU to face the next enlargement were not met, *as soon as the number of EU Member States exceeds 20, there must be a new Integovernmental Conference to deal with all of the institutional questions.*

E. FURTHER READING

CORBETT, Richard, JACOBS, Francis and SHACKLETON, Michael: *The European Parliament*, London, Cartermill, 1995.

EDWARDS, Geoffrey and SPENCE, D. (eds): *The European Commission*, London. Cartermill, 1994.

HARTLEY, T. C.: *The Foundations of European Community Law*, Oxford, Clarendon Press, 1994.

NENTWICH, M. and FALKNER, Gerda: *The Treaty of Amsterdam: Towards a New Institutional Balance*, European Integration Online Papers, August 1997, available at website: http://olymp.wu-wien.ac.at/eiop/texte/1997-015.htm.

NUGENT, Neill (ed.): *At the Heart of the Union: Studies of the European Commission*, London, Macmillan, 1997.

REVUE FRANÇAISE DE SCIENCE POLITIQUE: *La Commission européenne: cultures, politiques, paradigmes*, Vol. 46, No. 3, June 1996.

RIDEAU, Joël: *Droit institutionnel de l'Union et des Communautés européennes*, L.G.D.J., 1995.

SIMON, Denys: *Le système juridique communautaire*, Paris, PUF, 1997.

WALLACE, Helen and HAYYES-RENSHAW, Fiona: *The Council of Ministers*, London, Macmillan, 1997.

WESSELS, Wolfgang: 'Institutions of the EU system: models of explanation' in ROMETSCH, Dietrich and WESSELS, Wolfgang (eds): *The European Union and Member States: Towards Institutional Fusion*, Manchester, Manchester University Press, 1996, pp. 20–36.

WESTLAKE, Martin: *The Parliament and the Commission: Partners and Rivals in the European Policy-Making Process*, London, Butterworths, 1994.

Websites

European Commission	http://europa.eu.int/comm/index.htm
Council of Ministers	http://ue.eu.int/en/summ.htm
European Parliament	http://www.europarl.eu.int/sg/tree/en/default.htm
European Court of Justice	http://europa.eu.int/cj/index.htm
Court of Auditors	http://www.eca.eu.int/

Institutions not covered in the chapter:

Committee of the Regions	http://www.cor.eu.int/
Economic and Social Committee	http://www.esc.eu.int/en/default.htm
European Investment Bank	http://eib.eu.int/
European Ombudsman	http://www.euro-ombudsman.eu.int/media/en/default.htm
European Central Bank	http://www.ecb.int

CO-DECISION PROCEDURE (TEC/ToA Art. 251)

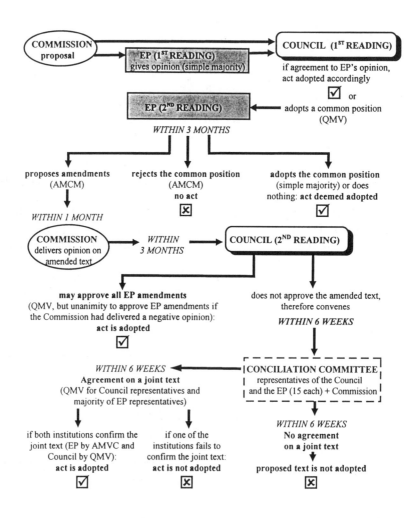

4 FLEXIBILITY AND CLOSER COOPERATION

Gabriel Glöckler

The Treaty of Amsterdam includes, for the first time, a chapter on 'closer cooperation' as a means to a more flexible, differentiated mode of integration. By *flexible integration* we understand the 'general mode of integration strategies which try to reconcile heterogeneity within the EU. The aim of flexibility is to allow different groupings of Member States to pursue an array of public polices with different procedural and institutional arrangements' (Stubb).

I. RATIONALE

What is the rationale behind the inclusion of a flexibility clause into the treaty? Following Wallace and De La Serre, the following factors led to the clause being included:

(a) *Enlargement* — a larger, more diverse Union needs more flexible mechanisms, so as to maintain the integration dynamic in a Europe of 25 + Member States (see debate on 'deepening v widening' and 'differentiation v fragmentation').

(b) *Coping with dissidence and intransigence* — to avoid blockage by one Member State (e.g., UK, Denmark) of generally desired further integration; in order not to let slowest ship in the convoy determine the speed of all others.

(c)   *'Avant-garde' and lever to further integration* — a smaller circle of
Member States with common projects, strengthened commitments and
solidarity can practise a quasi-federal model.
   (d)   *Preventing a Europe à la carte outside EC institutional framework*:
      (i)   attempt to avoid repetition of cooperation exercises outside the
treaty framework (e.g., Schengen — see chapter 21).
      (ii)   prevent the constitution of a directorate, e.g., Bosnia Contact Group
(comprising only Germany, France and the UK from the EU side).
   (e)   *Dealing with the unpredictable* — given the EU's pan-European
perspective, a Treaty clause on flexible integration — agreed upon by (only) 15
Member States and enshrined in the treaty — may turn out to be a crucial
safeguard to the integration process in a Europe of 25 + Member States.

II. PAST EXPERIENCES

Transition periods
History shows that the introduction and application of EC rules occurred
according to different rhythms and capabilities;
   Recent enlargements provide numerous examples of long transitional
periods for the full application of *acquis*, e.g., Spain enjoyed a temporary
derogation from the Common Fisheries Policy regime for 10 years. But the EC
always insisted on the uniformity and indivisibility of *acquis*; the acceptance
of common aims and objectives was essential. EMS, EMU are examples *par
excellence*: a multi-speed model was institutionalised, Member States 'willing
and able' to deepen monetary integration form a sub-group, with set criteria
and regulated relations between 'ins' and 'pre-ins' (see chapter 19).

Opt-out formulae (also 'opt-in', 'opt-up' etc.)
These formulae have become necessary when the integration process has
reached critical depth for certain Member States (UK, Denmark). The opt-out
of smaller Member States (such as Denmark) is no real problem, because it has
a negligible impact in political or economic terms. The UK is a critical case:
   (a)   in economic terms, the UK's opt-out of the Social Agreement could
have been perceived as a clear competitive advantage for a weighty economic
actor on the otherwise level playing field of the IM (see Chapter 17);
   (b)   in political terms: former Prime Minister John Major advocated a
proliferation of opt-outs as a model of European integration — leading to an 'à
la carte' Europe of permanent disjuncture and weakening of solidarity between
an inner circle and Member States that 'opted out'.

Parallel cooperation
Cooperation agreements tailored to the needs and ambitions of the respective participants, be it within the EU or parallel to it, have existed since the very beginning of the integration process, e.g., TEC Art. 233 explicitly recognises Benelux cooperation.

Further examples include the Schengen Group; the Nordic Council; the WEU; as well as special bilateral relationships (e.g., the Franco-German couple, UK-Ireland relations).

Protocols and declarations
To account for national particularities or specific arrangements (e.g., Portugal's monetary relationship with Azores, or France's with the CFP franc zone), numerous protocols and declarations were annexed to the treaties — a subtle and proliferating form of flexibility.

III. CONCEPTUAL CLASSIFICATION

Obviously, the EU has attempted to steer a pragmatic course and to differentiate the integration process. The numerous experiences, however, do not fit a clear overarching concept; a plethora of labels and proposals confuses the issue. A useful classification has been provided by Stubb (1996):

Variables	TIME	SPACE	MATTER
Concept	Multi-Speed	Variable Geometry	À la carte
Definition	Mode of differentiated integration according to which the pursuit of common objectives is driven by a core group of Member States which are both willing and able to go further, assuming that the others follow later.	Mode of differentiated integration which admits unattainable differences within the main by allowing permanent or irreversible separation between a core group and less developed integrative units.	Mode of differentiated integration whereby respective Member States are able to pick and choose in which policy area they would like to participate while maintaining a minimum number of common objectives.
Examples	Transitional periods for new entrants, EMU.	Outside the Treaties Schengen, WEU, EMS.	UK opt-out of Social Protocol.
semantic variations, jargon	*'plusieurs vitesses',* 'Abgestufte Integration'	*'Concentric circles',* 'Noyau dur', 'Kerneuropa'	*'Opt-in', 'Opt-up',* etc., 'Ad libitum integration'.

IV. THE TREATY CLAUSE

The ToA provides for a new Title VII (ToA/TEU Arts. 43–5): 'Provisions on closer cooperation':

(a)   A general clause on closer cooperation stipulating the following principles. The closer cooperation:

   (i)   aims at pursuing the objectives of the treaty;
   (ii)   preserves the single institutional framework;
   (iii)   is a 'last-resort' measure;
   (iv)   is favoured by a majority of Member States;
   (v)   does not affect the *'acquis communautaire'*;
   (vi)   respects the rights of non-participants;
   (vii) is open to all other Member States.

(b)   specific clauses applicable to first pillar (ToA/TEC Art. 11) and third pillar (ToA/TEU Art. 40).

Trigger mechanism to establish a closer cooperation:

(a)   QMV, but no vote in case one Member State opposes enhanced cooperation 'for important and stated reasons of national policy', leading to reference to European Council where consensus is required.

(b)   Specific clause for TEC: request from concerned Member States induces initiative from the Commission, consultation of EP.

(c)   For third pillar: only opinion from the Commission, information of EP.

(d)   when developing an *'acquis'* specific to the sub-group: all Member States take part in deliberations, but only ministers from participating Member States vote; but EP, Commission and ECJ remain indivisible institutions.

(e)   Financing of operations under closer cooperation (other than administrative costs) borne by participating Member States.

(f)   If latecomer wants to opt into a new application of closer cooperation, it has to apply the full *acquis* developed in the sub-group. For first pillar closer cooperations, the Commission judges if applicant Member States is capable of joining closer cooperation, in third pillar applications, 'ins' decide.

V. POTENTIAL APPLICATIONS OF CLOSER COOPERATION

First pillar
Ex ante exclusion of Community polices; but potential development of EMU policies (fiscal, economic or social) in the subgroup of 11 Euro-ins.

Second pillar — application in CFSP very questionable:
— *constructive abstention* is the main instrument to overcome veto (see chapter 10);

— only for cooperation between certain Member States (e.g., Belgium and France in Africa) in order to provide EU endorsement, closer cooperation in foreign policy has to be open to all to avoid the feared directorate of the more powerful Member States (e.g., Bosnia Contact Group);
— common defence questionable given UK and neutrals' objections to defence role of EU.

Third pillar
Inclusion of Schengen into TEU requires some form of flexibility, especially for UK and Ireland (see chapter 22).

Generally, there appears to be little use for closer cooperation for the coming enlargement, since the applicant countries are likely to ask for flexibility on IM measures (harmonisation, competition rules, etc.), which are *a priori* excluded. The Commission's Agenda 2000 stresses internal reform (CAP, structural funds, institutions) *precisely because* sector-by-sector differentiation (e.g., excluding new entrants from expensive CAP) is to be avoided.

VI. EVALUATION

Closer cooperation is unlikely to be able to deal with dissidence and intransigence, because the 'outs' must not be affected — which is (almost) impossible in the highly interdependent EU. Closer cooperation cannot work in case of real and deep-seated problems (e.g., EU foreign policy in Balkans against Greece or developing EU defence against UK objections is inconceivable under current clause).

In sum, closer cooperation is conceived as a measure of last resort, i.e., when all other 'normal' procedures do not work. Yet closer cooperation is no escape route from decisional impasse; it will only work under *conditions of full cooperation* between the 'ins' and 'outs', e.g., under a scenario of 'benign neglect' of one Member State for the closer cooperation of the others (Wessels).

Generally, the inclusion of the clause in the Treaty is a proof of the accepted legitimacy of a smaller group of Member States to proceed faster with deeper integration. But the actual application of closer cooperation is restrained by high hurdles, conditions which avoid — successfully — a marginalisation of non-participants. It has a potential application in the third pillar, namely to integrate the Schengen '*acquis*' into the Treaty.

But there are also considerable dangers:

(a)   potential erosion of existing system (sense of belonging to one and the same Community and solidarity within);

(b)   possible weakening of the Commission's role of initiative;

(c)   fragmentation of EC legal order (the various 'inner' circles would develop their own *acquis*);

(d)   encouragement of opt-outs;

(e)   no prevention of 'Europe à la carte' because the clause only applies to policy fields *within* the treaty, thus new policy areas cannot be developed;

(f)   resurrection of the Luxembourg Compromise (see Chapter 2);

(g)   more complex procedures, less understanding among citizens.

Briefly the new chapter on flexibility in its current form is not a solution to the EU's problems, nor does it provide a quick-fix alternative to comprehensive institutional reform.

VII. FURTHER READING

EHLERMANN, Claus: *Differentiation, Flexibility, Closer Cooperation: The New Provisions of the Amsterdam Treaty*, Florence, European University Institute, 1997.

MOUVEMENT EUROPÉEN, FRANCE: *L'Europe à quelques-uns? Les Coopérations renforcées*, Paris, Mouvement Européen, 1996.

STUBB, Alexander: 'A categorisation of differentiated integration', *Journal of Common Market Studies*, vol. 33 (1996), pp. 283–295.

WALLACE, Helen and DE LA SERRE, Françoise: *Flexibility and Enhanced Cooperation in the European Union: Placebo rather than Panacea?* Research and Policy Paper (No. 2), Paris, Groupement d études et de recherche 'Notre Europe', 1997.

WESSELS, Wolfgang: Discussion during a round table conference on 'The results of Amsterdam' at the College of Europe, 19–20 September 1997.

5 JUDICIAL REMEDIES

Rodolphe Muñoz

I. INTRODUCTION

The purpose of this chapter is to equip the reader with the tools to understand how the European Court of Justice (ECJ) controls the implementation of the policies analysed in this book. The different roles played by the Member States, the institutions, legal and natural persons will be analysed highlighting, for each procedure examined, its purpose, main characteristic and functioning.

According to TEC Art. 219 the ECJ has *exclusive jurisdiction* concerning the interpretation or application of the Treaty and all Community acts. A Court of First Instance, attached to it since 1989, deals with cases brought by individuals (TEC Art. 168a). TEU Art. L excludes the second and third pillars and TEU Title I common provisions from the jurisdiction of the ECJ.

The *ToA will extend the ECJ's jurisdiction* to the third pillar under certain conditions (see chapter 22) to the provisions on closer cooperation (see chapter 4) and those on the respect of fundamental rights with regard to the action of the institutions in so far as the ECJ has jurisdiction under the Treaties (ToA/TEU Art. 6.2).

The ECJ ensures that in the interpretation and application of the Treaty the law is observed (TEC Art. 164) which is the application of the notion of *rule of law*. This implies that 'a *complete system of legal remedies* and procedures' (*Les Verts* 294/83) is designed by the Treaty to permit the protection of all interests at stake (Member States, institutions, EC legal order and individuals). The legal remedies *provided by the Treaty* are:

— actions for enforcement (TEC Arts. 169–171);
— action for annulment of an EC act (TEC Arts. 173, 174 and 176);
— action for failure to act (TEC Arts. 175 and 176);
— preliminary ruling on interpretation and validity (TEC Art. 177);
— extra-contractual liability of the EC institutions (TEC Arts. 178 and 215);
— litigation between the Community and its servants (TEC Art. 179);
— specific litigation (TEC Arts. 180 to 183);
— exception of illegality (TEC Art. 184);
— interim measures (TEC Art. 186).

It is not only for the ECJ to protect EC rights, it is also the *task of any national judge*, by application of the principle of direct effect (*Van Gend and Loos* 26/62) and the primacy of EC law (*Costa* 6/64).

These two means have been first designed to protect the uniformity of application of EC law (the so-called *first generation* of the effects of primacy and direct effect) and have been developed by the ECJ to afford an effective protection of EC rights (the so-called *second generation rights*) through the right to a judicial process (*Johnston* 222/84), the right to interim measures (*Factortame I* C-213/89 and *Zuckerfabrik* 143/88 and C-92/89). This movement also permits the development of a secondary protection of individuals in case a Member State infringes Community law by reimbursement of undue paid taxes (*San Giorgio* 199/82) and the possibility of an action for State liability (*Francovich* C-6 and 9/90; *Brasserie du Pêcheur* C-46 and 48/93).

This new range of Community rights is essentially protected by national judges following the principle of institutional and procedural autonomy. The linkage between the two legal orders is anyway assured by an efficient means of cooperation (TEC Art. 177).

In this chapter the national remedies will not be considered as such but the cooperation mechanism (TEC Art. 177) will be analysed. The chapter will focus on the main remedies available at the Community level (TEC Arts. 169, 173, 175 and 177).

II. ACTIONS FOR ENFORCEMENT (TEC Arts. 169–171)

Three actions against Member States which have failed to fulfil an obligation exist under the EC Treaty:

(a)   Article 169: action against a Member State brought by the Commission;

(b)   Article 170: action against a Member State brought by another Member State;

(c)   Article 171: action for enforcement on the basis of arts 169 and 170.

The *purpose* of these articles is to *control the implementation of and respect for Community law by the Member States*. They reflect the specificity of the EC legal order. Member States have to comply with Community rules otherwise the Commission or another Member State is entitled to bring an action before the ECJ to condemn the infringement. The general rule of international law, *exceptio inadempleti contractus*, does not apply. The EC is a legal framework where non-application of EC rules has to be controlled by an independent body: the ECJ (see chapter 3).

II.1 TEC Art. 169

If the Commission considers that a Member State has failed to fulfil an obligation under this Treaty, it shall deliver a reasoned opinion on the matter after giving the State concerned the opportunity to submit its observations.

If the State concerned does not comply with the opinion within the period laid down by the Commission, the latter may bring the matter before the Court of Justice.

II.1.1 Purpose
TEC Art. 169 has a *double role*:
(a)   It enables the Commission to *protect the interests of the EC* (see chapter 3).
(b)   It allows for the *interpretation* of Community law: through this mechanism the ECJ can solve problems of interpretation arising between the Commission and the Member States.

II.1.2 Characteristics

Basic conditions to be fulfilled in order to lodge a *complaint*:
(a)   It has to be in written form.
(b)   It has to specify which part of Community law has been violated.
(c)   It has to ask expressly that the Commission acts.
The *initiation* of such an action is in the *hands of the Commission*. The Commission has the right to decide not to bring an action under TEC Art. 169 even if there is a violation. This discretion has to be understood as a 'political' control: for any reason the Commission may decide not to sue a Member State, because the Commission acts in the interest of the Treaty as a whole. Therefore it could be in the interest of the Treaty not to bring an action for a minor violation or for any political reason. Another reflection of the Commission's role of guardian of the Treaty is the fact that prejudice is not necessary to enable it to use TEC Art. 169 which means that it acts without any necessary interest to act.

Consequently, it is not posible to bring an action for failure to act under TEC Art. 175 (see IV) if the Commission does not bring an action before the ECJ under TEC Art. 169 (*Lütticke* 48/65). The Commission has the right to stop the procedure at any time.

The action is mainly aimed at *avoiding a judicial procedure*. It allows the Member State and the Commission to discuss the matter before going to the ECJ. Indeed most cases under TEC Art. 169 do not arrive before the ECJ, since the Member State manage to explain themselves and find solutions to implement Community rules or they find a compromise with the Commission.

The objective of a TEC Art. 169 procedure is to avoid any infringement of obligations arising under:

(a)   the Treaties;

(b)   Community secondary legislation;

(c)   agreements between the Community and third countries.

II.1.3 Procedure

The procedure may start in one of four different ways:

(a)   a *complaint* by an individual to the General Secretariat of the Commission;

(b)   an *inquiry* of the Commission in a specific sector on its own initiative;

(c)   a *petition* sent to the Commission;

(d)   a *check* by the services of the Commission which can result from a parliamentary question or events leading the Commission to think that a Member State is not complying with Community law.

The procedure is divided into *two main stages: administrative and judicial.* The administrative stage:

(a)   Informal discussions between the Commission and the Member State. During this preliminary stage only an *exchange of letters* between the Commission and the Member State takes place. This exchange of letters is important since it can often lead to the end of the procedure.

(b)   If the infringement continues, a *letter of formal notice* is sent from the Commission to the Member State. This letter is not mentioned in TEC Art. 169, but it is necessary for the Commission to let the Member State know exactly what infringement has occurred.

(c)   If the Member State does not comply, the *Commission sends it a reasoned opinion* listing the infringements and informs the Member State that it will submit the matter to the ECJ. The Commission usually gives the Member State a deadline to comply with its Community obligations. According to the ECJ, this deadline has to be 'reasonable' in order to give the Member State the possibility to comply with Community law, otherwise the ECJ could declare the procedure inadmissible (*Commission v Belgium* 85/85).

The judicial stage: reference of the case to the ECJ. The ECJ might decide to follow up the procedure even if the Member State has complied with its Community obligations after the time limit. This is linked to the aim of TEC Art. 169 which is to condemn any attempt by Member States to infringe Community law.

The ECJ declares in its judgment whether EC law has been respected or not. If not, the Member State has the responsibility to comply with these conclusions.

II.2 TEC Art. 170

A Member State which considers that another Member States has failed to fulfil an obligation under this Treaty may bring the matter before the Court of Justice.

II.2.1 Characteristics
Only Member States can initiate this procedure. It is very rare that a Member State is willing to sue another Member State because it risks starting a vicious circle, since it is always possible to find some area where a Member States does not comply with Community law. There have been two cases to date and only one of these procedures was pursued to a final judgment (*France* v *United Kingdom* 141/78).

The *Commission is still present in the procedure* and plays an important role even if it is not the only head of jurisdiction.

II.2.2 Procedure
The procedure is divided into *two main stages: administrative and judicial.*

The administrative stage:
(a)   The Member State brings the matter before the Commission.
(b)   The defendant submits its observations.
(c)   The Commission delivers a reasoned opinion.

If the Commission has not delivered an opinion within three months from the date on which the matter was brought before it, the absence of such an opinion does not stop the matter being brought before the ECJ by the Member State directly.

II.3 TEC Art. 171

1.   If the Court of Justice finds that a Member State has failed to fulfil an obligation under this Treaty, the State shall be required to take the necessary measures to comply with the judgment of the Court of Justice.

2.   If the Commission considers that the Member State concerned has not taken such measures it shall, after giving that State the opportunity to submit its observations, issue a reasoned opinion specifying the points on which the Member State concerned has not complied with the judgment of the Court of Justice.

If the Member State concerned fails to take the necessary measures to comply with the Court's judgment within the time limit laid down by the Commission, the latter may bring the case before the Court of Justice. In so doing it shall specify the amount of the lump sum or penalty payment to be paid by the Member State concerned which it considers appropriate in the circumstances.

If the Court of Justice finds that the Member State concerned has not complied with its judgment it may impose a lump sum or penalty payment on it.

This procedure shall be without prejudice to Article 170.

II.3.1 Characteristics

Since the entry into force of the Maastricht Treaty, TEC Art. 171 gives the Commission more power to *force Member States to implement decisions of the ECJ*. This was an attempt to try to decrease the number of cases where decisions of the Court were not implemented.

II.3.2 Procedure

The ECJ's initial judgment in infringement proceedings is declaratory. If the Commission considers that the Member State has not taken measures to comply with the judgment of the ECJ after giving the Member State the opportunity to submit its observations, *the Commission issues a reasoned opinion* specifying the points on which the Member State concerned has not complied with the judgment. *The Commission can decide to bring the case before the ECJ and indicate the fine it wants to impose on the Member State.*

With the 1996 communication of the Commission (OJ C 242/96) a list of fines based on the GDP of each Member State has been issued.

III. ACTION FOR ANNULMENT (TEC Art. 173)

The Court of Justice shall review the legality of acts adopted jointly by the European Parliament and the Council, of acts of the Council, of the Commission and of the ECB, other than recommendations and opinions, and of acts of the European Parliament intended to produce legal effects vis-à-vis third parties.

It shall for this purpose have jurisdiction in actions brought by a Member State, the Council or the Commission on grounds of lack of competence, infringement of an essential procedural requirement, infringement of this Treaty or of any rule of law relating to its application, or misuse of powers.

The Court shall have jurisdiction under the same conditions in actions brought by the European Parliament and by the ECB for the purpose of protecting their prerogatives.

Any natural or legal person may, under the same conditions, institute proceedings against a decision addressed to that person or against a decision which, although in the form of a regulation or a decision addressed to another person, is of direct and individual concern to the former.

The proceedings provided for by this Article shall be instituted within two months of the publication of the measure, or of its notification to the plaintiff, or, in the absence thereof, of the day on which it came to the knowledge of the latter, as the case may be.

III.1 Purpose

The respect of the rule of law. Since the Community is based on the rule of law, the legality of Community acts is subject to judicial review.

III.2 Characteristics

III.2.1 Limits to the Use of TEC Art. 173
The use of this article has been reduced through *procedural and time limit requirements* in order to protect the legal certainty of Community law.

Strict criteria have been established by the ECJ for such proceedings to be admissible in relation both to the acts open to review as well as to the type of potential applicants.

III.2.2 After the TEU, an Important Change
The EP and the European Central Bank (ECB) have been added as 'semi-privileged'(see III.3.4) applicants and authors of acts which are reviewable.

III.3 Type of Acts under Review

The first paragraph of TEC Art. 173 deals with the institutions whose acts are open to judicial review and the types of acts which are subject to judicial review.

III.3.1 Institutions whose Acts are Open to Judicial Review

—Commission.
—Council.
—ECB.
—EP. Only acts producing legal effects vis-à-vis the third parties concerned can be challenged. Consequently, acts which are purely internal measures of the EP cannot be reviewed (see *Les Verts* 294/83).

III.3.2 Type of Acts Subject to Judicial Review
All the acts of the EC institutions with the exception of recommendations and opinions. 'Acts' here means regulations, directives and decisions as laid out in the TEC Art. 189. However, according to the ECJ 'any measure' (*ERTA* 12/70) may be subject to review: an action for annulment must therefore be available in the case of all measures adopted by the institution, whatever their nature or form, which are intended to have legal effect.

The essential criterion used by the ECJ is therefore the legal effect of the act, i.e., its ability to affect the legal position of subjects of Community law. The limit of this approach has been underlined in *IBM* v *Commission* (60/81), where the ECJ stated that it was not possible to bring a TEC Art. 173 action against a preparatory measure necessary to issue a final decision.

III.4 Definition of Applicants

The second and third paragraphs of TEC Art. 173 define the different categories of applicants for judicial review.

III.4.1 The Privileged Applicants
The 'privileged' applicants are:
—Commission.
—Council.
—Member States.
These three applicants can challenge EC acts 'on grounds of lack of competence, infringement of an essential procedural requirement, infringement of this Treaty or of any rule of law relating to its application, or misuse of powers'.

They have an *automatic and absolute right to bring proceedings* under TEC Art. 173. This reflects their crucial role in the decision-making process of the EC. They are presumed to have an interest in contesting the legality of all types of Community acts (see chapter 3).

III.4.2 The Semi-privileged Applicants
The 'semi-privileged' applicants are:
— EP.
— ECB.
They have the right to bring an action for annulment only in order to defend their own prerogatives (*Chernobyl*, 70/88). This right was introduced to guarantee full respect for the principle of institutional balance (see chapter 3).

III.4.3 The Non-Privileged Applicants
The 'limited' applicants are natural and legal persons. They have limited possibilities to bring an action for annulment of EC acts in order to avoid a multiplication of such actions and so enhance the legal certainty of the EC legal order.

Only three situations allow a natural or legal person to bring an action under TEC Art. 173:

(a)   If the act is a decision which is addressed to the applicant then the latter is able to challenge the decision.

(b)   If the decision is addressed to another person (including a Member State), the applicant has to prove that he is individually and directly concerned by the decision even if it is not addressed to him (see below).

(c)   In principle, it is not possible for a natural or legal person to challenge a regulation. A regulation (TEC Art. 189) is a normative act of general application. Nevertheless, in *Confédération nationale des producteurs de fruits* v *Council* (16 and 17/62), the ECJ held that the Court cannot restrict itself to considering the official title of the measure but must first take account of its object and content. As such, it appears possible that a natural or legal person may bring a TEC Art. 173 action against a regulation *if it directly and individually concerns the applicant*. This means that the decision affects the applicants by reason of certain attributes which are peculiar to them or by reason of circumstances in which they are differentiated from all other persons and by virtue of these factors distinguishes them individually just as in the case of the person addressed (*Plaumann* v *Commission* 25/62).

In the case *Gibraltar* v *Council* (C-298/89), the ECJ has also implicitly accepted that an individual can challenge a Directive.

III.4 Time Limit

According to the last paragraph of TEC Art. 173, proceedings must be brought before the ECJ *within two months* of the publication of the act.

Once the time limit is over it is impossible to seek annulment of an EC act. The only other possibility is to rely on the so-called 'incident procedures' (TEC

Arts. 177 and 184) whereby the ECJ will consider whether the act is valid for a specific case. The ECJ held in *TWD* (C-188/92) that it is impossible for an applicant authorised to bring an action under TEC Art. 173, but who did not do so within the time limit, to use the TEC Art. 177 validity procedure instead.

This limit is aimed at *protecting legal certainty* and *securing the legal order* of the EC.

III.5 Judicial Consequences of a TEC Art. 173 Action: TEC Art. 174

If the action is well founded, the ECJ will declare the *act* concerned to be *void*. In the case of a regulation, the ECJ may state which of the effects of the act it has declared void shall be considered as definitive.

IV. ACTION FOR FAILURE TO ACT (TEC Art. 175)

Should the European Parliament, the Council or the Commission, in infringement of this Treaty, fail to act, the Member States and the other institutions of the Community may bring an action before the Court of Justice to have the infringement established.

The action shall be admissible only if the institution concerned has first been called upon to act. If, within two months of being so called upon, the institution concerned has not defined its position, the action may be brought within a further period of two months.

Any natural or legal person may, under the conditions laid down in the preceding paragraphs, complain to the Court of Justice that an institution of the Community has failed to address to that person any act other than a recommendation or an opinion.

The Court of Justice shall have jurisdiction, under the same conditions, in actions or proceedings brought by the ECB in the areas falling within the latter's field of competence and in actions or proceedings brought against the latter.

IV.1 Purpose

The aim of TEC Art. 175 is to *force the institutions to define their position or to take action in accordance with the Treaty*. Therefore this article does not oblige the institution to take a positive action but merely to define its position. Consequently, once the institution has done so the ECJ stops the procedure and dismisses the case.

IV.2 Characteristics

TEC Art. 175 is linked to TEC Art. 173: the first requests the defendant to define its position, while the second is aimed at requesting the annulment of the act once it has been adopted by an institution.

It is often difficult to define when the institution has taken a 'position' which delimits the scope of TEC Art. 175.

IV.3 Institutions which can be Sued for Failure to Act

Before Maastricht:
— Commission.
— Council.
— EP.

After Maastricht also :
— ECB.
— EMI until the end of the transitional period (see chapter 19).

IV.4 Different Categories of Applicants

IV.4.1 The Privileged Applicants
These are 'the Member States and the other institutions' (TEC Art. 175 para. 1). 'Institutions' included are those listed in TEC Art. 4 (the EP, the Council, the Commission, the ECJ and the CoA). The ECJ should be able to bring a TEC Art. 175 action as an institution but never has.

These are considered privileged applicants because they can bring an action *at any time* to challenge the failure to make *any type of Community act* having legal effects *without having to demonstrate an interest to act*.

IV.4.2 The Semi-privileged Applicant
The ECB is considered as a semi-privileged applicant because it can only bring an action 'in the areas falling within [its] field of competence' (TEC Art. 175 para. 4).

IV.4.3 The Non-privileged Applicants
An application may be made by 'any natural or legal person' (TEC Art. 175 para. 3), which is a large enough expression to encompass all sorts of possibilities.

They are considered as ordinary applicants because they can only bring an action for failure to act under certain conditions:

(a)   The institution has failed to address to that person any act other than a recommendation or an opinion.

(b)   The act has to be subject to judicial review (*Chevalley* 15/70) i.e., the act has to have legal effects or to be a necessary procedural step for issuing an act having legal effect. It is not possible to bring an action for failure to adopt a legislative act (*Lord Bethel* 246/81).

Since the *ENU* Case (C-107/91), *locus standi* is now given if the act requested should have been formally addressed to the applicant or if it should have been de facto addressed to him. This is the same definition as the one given by the Court in relation to TEC Art. 173: the act would have concerned the applicant directly and individually.

IV.5 Procedure

TEC Art. 175 para. 2 describes the procedure that has to be followed in the case of a failure to act. It is a compulsory procedure: any irregularity in its implementation would lead the ECJ to declare the action inadmissible.

Time limit to start an action
According to the ECJ's case law, the question of determining the period within which it is possible to bring an action under TEC Art. 175 has to be resolved by applying the 'reasonable time limit' theory, i.e., for the sake of protecting legal certainty, the applicant has to act as soon as possible.

It is necessary to ask the relevant institution to act
In the case of an act which is the result of a succession of acts taken by different institutions and when the final act is missing only because a procedural act has not been adopted by another institution, the request shall be addressed to the latter institution.

It has to be clearly stated that the institution has to act and what action it has to take
The ECJ insists that the request to act has to be as clear as possible, otherwise it will consider the request inadmissible (*EP* v *Council* 13/83).

The institution has two months to reply
This applies *only if the institution has an obligation to act*. This entails, for example, that an action for failure to act in order to oblige the Commission to bring a TEC Art. 169 action is inadmissible since the Commission has discretionary powers in bringing the case before the ECJ (see II).

During this time, the institution can take an action which may not suit the applicant, in which case the applicant will have to stop the TEC Art. 175 procedure and bring a TEC Art. 173 action.

The applicant has two months to bring an action before the ECJ
During these two months or during the proceedings, should the institution adopt the requested measures, the ECJ will stop the proceedings and dismiss the case.

IV.6 Judicial Consequences of TEC Art. 175 Action

The effect of a judgment for failure to act is to *force the institution to take action* to comply with the judgment (TEC Art. 176). Nevertheless, the *Treaty does not provide a time limit* during which the institution has to adopt the act. The ECJ held in *EP v Council* (13/83) that the institution should act in a reasonable time limit. Therefore, the effect of such a judgment will not automatically lead to the institution's action as it remains a discretionary power in so far as the deadline to act is concerned.

V. PRELIMINARY RULING FOR INTERPRETATION AND VALIDITY (TEC Art. 177)

The Court of Justice shall have jurisdiction to give preliminary rulings concerning:

(a) the interpretation of this Treaty;

(b) the validity and interpretation of acts of the institutions of the Community and of the ECB;

(c) the interpretation of the statutes of bodies established by an act of the Council, where those statutes so provide.

Where such a question is raised before any court or tribunal of a Member State, that court or tribunal may, if it considers that a decision on the question is necessary to enable it to give judgment, request the Court of Justice to give a ruling thereon.

Where any such question is raised in a case pending before a court or tribunal of a Member State against whose decisions there is no judicial remedy under national law, that court or tribunal shall bring the matter before the Court of Justice.

V.1 Purpose

It is necessary to provide a mechanism which permits uniformity of interpretation and implementation of EC law.

There is no judicial hierarchy between Community law and national law. The necessity of creating linkages has been solved through judicial cooperation between these two legal orders, organised by TEC Art. 177.

V.2 Main Characteristics

There are two types of preliminary references:

(a)   Preliminary reference concerning *interpretation*. This allows national courts or tribunals to ask the ECJ for its interpretation on specific points of EC law.

(b)   Preliminary reference concerning *validity*. This gives national courts or tribunals the chance to ask the ECJ to decide upon the invalidity of Community legislation. This is possible even once the time limit imposed by TEC Art. 173 has expired under the strict conditions imposed by the ECJ in *TWD* (see III).

It is an *autonomous consultative procedure*. The preliminary reference can be made at any point of the national procedure. During preliminary reference the trial before the national court or tribunal is suspended.

It is an *objective procedure*. It is a cooperation between judges, therefore there are no parties during the proceeding before the ECJ.

There are *three steps* in a TEC Art. 177 action.

(a)   *Before the national judge*. The national judge decides to refer a question to the ECJ (subject to complying with certain conditions, see below).

(b)   *Before the European judge*. The ECJ rules on the admissibility of the question and then deals with the interpretation or the validity of the Community rule in question.

(c)   *Before the national judge*. The national judge receives the answers to his questions and applies them to the case.

V.3 Acts which may be the Subject of a Preliminary Ruling

This first part of TEC Art. 177 establishes *which acts can be referred* to the ECJ.

V.3.1 In Case of Interpretation

'This Treaty' (TEC Art. 177 para. 1.a)
In fact the scope of interpretation is wider since it comprises all Treaties amending or supplementing the EC Treaty.

The power of interpretation of the Treaties has been limited by the TEU which excludes the possibility of interpreting the common provisions (TEU Arts. A–F) and those of the second and third pillar. The ToA expands the ECJ's scope of jurisdiction to the third pillar under certain circumstances (see chapter 22) as well as to the common provisions, including those on the protection of fundamental rights (ToA/TEU Art. 6) and to the provisions on closer cooperation (see chapter 4).

'Acts of the institutions of the Community and of the ECB' (TEC Article 177 para. 1.b)
This covers all forms of Community acts. It includes both *binding acts* (regulations, directives, decisions) and *non-binding acts* (recommendations and opinions), as laid out in TEC Art. 189.

However, the Court has not limited its power of interpretation and considers also as part of its competence the interpretation of *international agreements concluded by the Community* under the powers given by the Treaty, including association agreements and the acts adopted by the legislative bodies set up by them. In the 1970s there was a question as to whether the ECJ was competent to give a preliminary ruling on the GATT. The answer should have been negative because the EC was not formally a party to the GATT. Basing its reasoning on the specificity of the obligations resulting from the GATT for the Community, the ECJ considered the Community as part of the agreement and therefore recognised its own competence to interpret the provisions of this agreement (*International Fruit Co.* 21–4/72).

On the other hand, the ECJ *cannot give preliminary rulings on international agreements concluded solely by Member States, nor is it competent to give preliminary rulings on questions of national law.*

'The statutes of bodies established by an act of the Council, where those statutes so provide' (TEC Article 177 para. 1.c)
The ECJ's scope of action does not cover statutes which do not clearly state that they allow for ECJ interpretation.

V.3.2 Validity
A decision on validity can be given only for *acts of the institutions* of the Community and of the ECB, including *international agreements legally binding for the EC* (Opinion 1/75). The purpose of this limitation is to *avoid uncertainty* in the framework of European law. ECJ case law cannot be referred to for an appreciation on validity (*Wünsche* 69/85).

V.4 Applicants

TEC Art. 177 para. 2 covers who may bring an action before the ECJ and how.

V.4.1 Who may bring an action
According to the Treaty only 'a court or tribunal of a Member State' is allowed
to bring an action but this notion has been defined in detail by the ECJ.

The phrase 'court or tribunal' does not refer to a national definition. The ECJ
has stressed the importance of giving a *Community definition* of this concept.
This definition results from the ECJ's case law and refers to *all the courts or
tribunals of the Member States recognised as such by national systems.*

The ECJ has also broadly interpreted the term 'Member State'. Using TEC
Art. 127, it has added the tribunals of French Overseas Departments and those
European territories for whose external relations a Member State is responsible,
e.g., Gibraltar and the Isle of Man.

V.4.2 How is an action referred to the ECJ?
The power of national courts or tribunals to refer to the ECJ is linked with the
phrase 'a decision . . . to enable it to give judgment' (TEC Art. 177 para. 2).

It appears that national courts or tribunals have *total discretion in referring
a question* to the ECJ *at any time of the procedure*. It is not possible for national
procedural law to prevent national courts or tribunals from asking for a
preliminary reference (*Rheinmühlen* 166/73 and *Peterbroeck* C-312/93). The
national court or tribunal can refer a question if one of the parties asks for it. It
can also raise it on its own motion.

However, this discretion is and has been limited by EC procedural law and
the interpretation of the ECJ:

(a)   In relation to *validity* the *ECJ has obliged all national jurisdictions*, in
case of doubt on the validity of an EC act, to refer a preliminary ruling in order
to preserve the uniformity of Community law (*Foto Frost* 314/85).

(b)   In relation to *interpretation*, the ECJ cannot make a ruling on the
question when procedural law forbids national courts or tribunals from
referring to the ECJ if the case has been taken off the record by the withdrawal
of one of the parties. It is also impossible for the ECJ to hear a reference for a
preliminary ruling *when the procedure before the national court or tribunal
making the reference has already been concluded.*

Through its case law the ECJ has limited the power of national courts or
tribunals to refer a question on interpretation of EC law. The ECJ declares the
question inadmissible:

(a)   In case of artificial or hypothetical questions. The case has to be a real
one and not the consequence of an artificial agreement by the parties in order
to obtain an answer to a specific question (*Foglia Novello* 104/79).

(b)   In case of a consultative opinion on future legislation. The ECJ refuses to use TEC Art. 177 as a way of analysing present or future national legislation. The ECJ does not have to play an advisory role (*Mattheus* 93/78).

(c)   In case of general questions with no direct link with the case. The ECJ answers only questions necessary to solve existing problems of interpretation (*Lorenzo Dias* C-343/90).

(d)   In case of lack of information on national law which apply to the case. The ECJ asks national jurisdictions to provide all necessary information on facts and law to answer the question (*Telemarsicabruzzo* C-320 to 322/90).

Nevertheless, the ECJ has softened its policy through different means as it reformulates, completes or even transforms the questions of national jurisdictions in order to be able to answer them.

V.4.3 Obligation to refer a question to the ECJ

There is an *obligation for national jurisdictions to bring an action if they are the last instance*. Other courts simply have the faculty to ask for a preliminary ruling (TEC Art. 177 para. 3).

Exceptions to this obligation are possible concerning the interpretation of Community law:

(a)   It is possible for these courts or tribunals not to refer to the ECJ if the question has already been the subject of a preliminary ruling in a similar case or whenever it is not necessary for the outcome of the case.

(b)   The last instrument is to use the doctrine of *acte clair*, which states that if Community law is clear enough, then the national judge may apply it. This theory is applicable only under very limited conditions to avoid any distortion in the uniformity of application of European law (*CILFIT* 283/82).

V.5 Validity: Parallelism and Links between TEC Arts 173 and 177 Actions

On the merits of the case, the ECJ uses the same methods for both TEC Arts. 177 and 173 actions (see III).

Given that there is no time limit in TEC Art. 177, the ECJ can decide to limit its judgment *ex nunc* to protect legal certainty (*Defrenne* 43/75) otherwise decisions always take effect *ex tunc*.

VI. FURTHER READING

ARNULL, Anthony: 'Private applicants and the action for annulment under Art. 173 of the EC Treaty', *Common Market Law Review*, vol. 32, 1995, pp. 7–49.

CONSTANTINESCO, Vlad; KOVAR, Robert and SIMON, Denys (under the direction of): *Traité sur l Union Européenne commentaire article par article*, Paris, Economica, 1995.

HARTLEY, Trevor C.: *The Foundations of European Community Law*, 3rd ed., Oxford, Clarendon Press, 1994.

MATTERA, Alfonso: 'La procédure en manquement et la protection des citoyens et des opérateurs lésés', *RMUE*, 3/1995, pp. 122–64.

O'KEEFFE, David and BAVASSO, Antonio: *Judicial Protection of Fundamental Rights and the European Citizen*, Symposium of the European Lawyers' Union, Brussels, 1997.

O'KEEFFE, David: 'Is the spirit of Article 177 under attack?', in *Scritti in onore di G. Mancini*, Milano, Giuffrè, 1998, pp. 695–729.

POMMIES, Bernard: 'Cour de Justice: recours en carence', in *Juris Classeur*, Fasc. 340, 3, 1991.

SIMON, Denys: *Le système juridique communautaire*, Paris, PUF, 1997.

Website

| European Court of Justice | http://europa.eu.int/cj/index.htm |

PART III

THE POLICIES OF THE EUROPEAN COMMUNITY

6 THE INTERNAL MARKET

Gabriel Glöckler

I. RATIONALE

Originally, i.e., in the 1957 Rome Treaty (TEC), there were two main rationales for establishing an Internal Market (IM): to avoid the national protectionism of the inter-war period and to ensure peace and a generous welfare state through economic expansion, by creating a large common market for European producers to rival the US market (i.e., to face up to the *défi américain*). Indeed, European integration as a whole was seen as a purely economic project by some Member States such as Denmark and the UK. The perceived economic advantages of the 'Common Market', and the cost of being left out, strongly motivated those countries' entry in 1973.

Changing circumstances altered the rationale and justification of the IM project. By the mid-1980s, Member States' economic policies converged around the neo-liberal paradigm of economic policy, and the completion of the IM was seen as means to ensure competitiveness and face up to global competition (i.e., *défi japonnais*). In the 1990s, the European agenda focused on liberalisation, deregulation and re-regulation at European level, advocating competition in the IM to counter protected national markets and monopolies (e.g., in utilities, telecoms, etc.).

The IM is a step in the process of full economic integration.

Theory of Economic Integration (after Balassa, 1975)

1. Free Trade Area. Tariffs and quotas are eliminated on trade between participating countries but are maintained with third countries (e.g., NAFTA); may allow the free movement of all goods within the territory of the participating states, or only of specific categories of goods.

2. Customs Union. Countries remove barriers to trade and adopt a Common External Tariff vis-à-vis third countries. Requires a common customs policy.

3. Common Market/Internal Market. A customs union in which all goods enjoy the freedom of movement and where the free movement of workers/people, capital and services are guaranteed. The realisation of the four freedoms requires harmonisation of further policy areas. Accompanying polices, e.g., social and regional polices, competition policy, need to be pursued in common.

4. Internal Market preparing for Economic and Monetary Union. IM plus relative monetary stability by establishing an exchange rate system (such as the EMS). Exchange rate stability requires some kind of coordination of macroeconomic policies.

5. Monetary Union. IM with a single currency. A common monetary policy is instituted and institutionalised in a common central bank. Closer coordination of fiscal polices and macroeconomic conditions may prove necessary, yet without establishing a comprehensive common economic policy.

6. Full Economic Union. A genuine IM with a single currency, a common macroeconomic policy and a larger number of other common policies which together make a 'political union'. No obvious or hidden barriers obstruct the free movement of goods, services, people and capital; the common market should operate exactly as if it were one single national market.

The IM is not an objective in itself, but rather one of the principal instruments (together with EMU and the implementation of common policies) for achieving a whole series of objectives, such as balanced and sustainable growth respecting the environment, high levels of employment and social protection, better standards of living and economic and social cohesion (TEC Art.2).

II. LEGAL BASIS, PRINCIPLES, OBJECTIVES

II.1 Legal Basis

TEC Art. 2 sets out the objectives of the EC (see I) and TEC Arts. 3 and 3a define the means of achieving these objectives (the Community's policies, e.g., commercial, competition, agricultural, transport policies, etc.).

TEC Art. 7a defines the IM as an *area without internal frontiers in which the free movement of goods, persons, services and capital is ensured.* The basic rules which ensure that these conditions can be achieved are stipulated in the TEC:

— Art. 6 prohibits any discrimination on grounds of nationality between Member States and their nationals.

— Art. 8a establishes the right of citizens to move and reside freely within the EC.

— Arts. 9–12 require the abolition of customs duties between the Member States.

— Arts. 30–6 prohibit quantitative restrictions on trade in goods and establish the conditions for exceptions (derogations).

— Arts. 48–51 establish the principles which ensure the free movement of workers; TEC Arts. 52–7 ensure freedom of movement and freedom of establishment for self-employed people and Art. 58 for companies.

— Arts. 59-66 provide for the freedom to offer services.

— Art. 73b provides for the abolition of restrictions on the free movement of capital.

— Arts. 85 and 86 prohibit anti-competitive behaviour by undertakings which could otherwise negate the effects of the internal market. Art. 90 ensures that the competition rules apply to public undertakings.

— Art. 92 establishes strict conditions for state aids.

— Art. 95 concerns the obligation of Member States not to discriminate in fiscal matters.

TEC Art. 100a sets out the legislative procedure: QMV in the Council, co-decision procedure for the EP for the approximation of laws whose objective is the establishment or functioning of the IM. Its five paragraphs stipulate in detail which conditions apply to harmonisation measures and regulate the derogation regime.

Derogations

The TEC provides for derogations to the removal of intra-EC barriers, most notably Art. 36, which allows Member States to prohibit or restrict imports, exports and goods in transit on grounds of public morality, public policy and public security; protection of health and life of humans, animals and plants; safeguarding of national heritage; etc. The ECJ interprets these provisions very stringently, thus restricting abuse by the Member States.

The Treaty articles have been fleshed out by a whole raft of secondary legislation, mostly in the form of directives to lay down broad aims or essential conditions, while leaving room for traditional and preferred national approaches in the transposition. Nevertheless, many directives are very specific and technical, requiring extensive expert input.

II.2 Objectives

The Four Freedoms form the heart of the IM: the free movement of goods, services, capital and people across intra-EC borders must not be hindered by national laws and practices (see IV). In addition, a true IM only functions if the Member States pursue a set of policies in common, such as a competition policy, commercial policy etc. as listed in TEC Art. 3.

III. KEY ACTORS

European Commission

Key player; policy initiator, used IM programme to relaunch European integration process. Before proposing legislation, the Commission makes use of an extensive network of experts and advisers, and takes into account the views of interest groups.

Council

Main legislator; since the Single European Act, IM measures are adopted by QMV.

European Parliament

Gradual extension of scope of its involvement from consultation (Treaty of Rome) to cooperation (SEA) to co-decision (TEU).

European Court of Justice
Ultimate interpretation of treaty provisions on IM, adjudicates disputes over
IM regulation, enforces common rules through judgments (see IV.3).

European standardisation agencies
Gained profile in the wake of Commission's 'New Approach' as voluntary
standard-setting bodies, e.g., European Committee for Standards (CEN) and
European Committee for Electrical Standards (CENELEC). Currently nearly
300 technical committees are devising some 10,000 standards.

Pressure and interest groups
Influence and provide specific technical expertise to the Commission. Given
the far-reaching economic impact of IM legislation for specific sectors, a
plethora of interest groups, many of them with powerful backing and financial
capacity, have penetrated the EC policy process.

IV. POLICY INSTRUMENTS

IV.1 Achieving the IM

IV.1.1 General Legislative Procedure
Originally, the approximation of laws followed TEC Art. 100, requiring
unanimity in the Council — which soon led to an institutional impasse. The
Commission in its proposals pursued a policy of 'total harmonisation' (through
excessively detailed EC rules, e.g., exact size of apples, etc.) to push integration
towards a truly common market. This produced political backlash in Member
States and the emergence of non-tariff barriers as protectionist measures
('Eurosclerosis').

In relaunching the process of economic integration with the '1992
programme' (see V) Member States set an ambitious timetable for the
completion of the IM (31 December 1992). The constitutional remedy for an
increasingly lengthy harmonisation process came with the SEA (1986), which
introduced TEC Art. 100a allowing for *qualified majority voting* on IM matters
(as well as EP involvement via cooperation procedure). Since Maastricht,
co-decision increased the EP's power. Fiscal harmonisation, free movement of
persons and employees' rights are exempted from the TEC Art. 100a
procedure.

The introduction of QMV was balanced by the existence of an escape clause,
TEC Art. 100a.4, allowing Member States to apply more stringent national
rules than EC harmonised laws, e.g., relating to protection of the natural or

working environment. These national measures are to be communicated to the Commission. The ECJ has to be convinced of the justifiability of the derogation; until now, there has been only one application of TEC Art. 100a.4.

IV.1.2 Achieving the Free Movement of Goods

1968 saw the first step towards establishing the free movement of goods, the customs union which abolished customs duties and most quantitative restrictions between Member States. Yet *non-tariff barriers* (NTBs), e.g., physical, technical or fiscal barriers, were still obstructing the functioning of a true IM.

Removing physical barriers

Administrative formalities at border crossings (tax formalities, health controls, etc.) present physical barriers to the free movement of goods within the IM. In order to remove them, the EC:

(a)   introduced a standard EC-wide document and harmonised rules for plant and animal health controls according to TEC Art. 100a;

(b)   simplified administrative formalities (resulting in cost reduction for Member States and businesses);

(c)   cut down the number of documents necessary for transport of goods across EC borders from 30 to one Single Administrative Document, which now also has been abolished.

Removing technical barriers

National standards, specifications and technical regulations are technical barriers. Originally intended to ensure public safety of products, yet used maliciously to defend domestic producers, such barriers fragment the IM (e.g., a producer anywhere in the EC could only introduce and market a product in the European market when simultaneously satisfying the local rules in all Member States).

Removing these barriers required new methods and policy innovations:

> *Principle of Mutual Recognition*
> (1979 ECJ ruling *Cassis de Dijon* — see IV.3)
> - Any good circulating legally in one Member State must also be free to circulate in any other part of the Community, except where a Member States can demonstrate that the rules of the Member State of origin do not afford equivalent protection of the essential public good (TEC Art. 36 derogations).
> - Harmonisation of many regulations and standards became unnecessary. Fears of 'harmonisation by the lowest common denominator' have not been substantiated (e.g., environmental standards).
>
> *New Approach*
> (Commission proposal 1985)
> - Replaced the strategy of 'total harmonisation' (where lengthy bargaining produced excessively detailed EC rules).
> - Establishes limited number of essential safety requirements and those necessary to protect the public interest for technical harmonisation.
> - More detailed rules are left to European standards agencies (e.g., CENELEC) to be agreed upon on a voluntary basis. Thus, standard-setting became a technocratic discussion rather than political bargaining.

It was the principle of mutual recognition which allowed the Commission to adopt the 'New Approach'; both were essential to remove technical barriers by the 1992 deadline.

Removing fiscal barriers

Differing rates of indirect taxes (e.g., VAT) and excise duties are fiscal barriers which distort the market.

The harmonisation of tax rates requires unanimity in the Council, hence progress is very slow and cumbersome. After long bargaining, a 1991 agreement set:

(a) the minimum standard rate of VAT throughout the IM (1 January 1993) at 15%;

(b) a list of minimum rates for excise duties (since 1 January 1993).

Even though Member States failed to agree on a harmonisation of VAT rates by 1997, as originally planned, the prospect of EMU has provided a new impetus to tackling tax harmonisation or at least to set up some form of coordination, e.g., the 1997 Commission proposal on a Code of Conduct on business taxes to avoid harmful tax competition.

IV.1.3 Achieving the Free Movement of People

TEC Art. 8a and more specifically, TEC Art. 48, enshrine the concept of free movement and right of residence of persons. Member States may refuse entry on grounds of public policy, security or health, and non-national workers are excluded from public service employment. For many years, a narrow definition of 'workers' prevailed, but was extended to students and pensioners in 1992.

EC legislation in this area is divided into:

(a)   rules which ensure harmonious development of the labour market and prevent distortions of competition (people/workers are conceived as factors of production, whose free movement must be assured);

(b)   rules establishing the conditions of access for citizens from other Member States (e.g., residence permits, right of entry, restrictions on extradition and family allowances). This also includes some form of harmonisation/coordination of social services to guarantee full social rights for EC migrant workers.

Generally, legislation concerning the free movement of persons is closely linked to the freedom to provide services, especially services requiring minimum professional qualifications. Thus, the EC has attempted to harmonise rules (e.g., uniform architects', doctors' or nurses' qualifications). Recently, it has introduced the principle of mutual recognition of diplomas (horizontal approach laying down general conditions), e.g., the 1989 General Directive on the Mutual Recognition of Diplomas which requires some degree of mutual recognition of higher education courses of at least three years.

Measures concerning free movement of people in general require unanimity in the Council with the assent of the EP except where otherwise provided for in the Treaty (in some instances co-decision procedure and QMV).

(For a more detailed treatment of the free movement of people across internal EC borders, see chapters 21 and 22.)

Freedom of establishment

Moving beyond the mere right to reside in another Member States the Treaty also enshrines the right of establishment, which includes self-employed persons as well as the right to set up and manage companies in another Member State (TEC Arts. 52–8). Since companies should be treated in the same way as natural persons for the purposes of free movement and right of establishment (TEC Art. 58) some form of harmonised governance of undertakings is required, e.g., through EC company law. Recently, some progress on an EC

Company Statute has been achieved. To date, there is still not full 'free movement' for companies in matters such as changing domicile.

IV.1.4 Achieving the Free Movement of Services

On basis of TEC Arts. 59–66 (referring to both the free movement of services and the freedom to provide services) EC legislation tackled the conditions under which certain services can be offered. This was necessary because Member States' legislation — even if it did not overtly discriminate against non-nationals — varied too much to allow free movement to be achieved by simply applying the principle of mutual recognition:

(a)   much of the legislation concerns the financial services sector, laying down minimum prudential requirements (e.g., for the authorisation of banks or insurance companies);

(b)   gradual opening up of national markets in areas traditionally dominated by national monopolies, e.g., telecommunications, parts of the transport and energy sectors, also television.

IV.1.5 Achieving the Free Movement of Capital

Originally, TEC Arts. 67–73 were rather limited in their aims, providing only for progressive abolition of restrictions on payments made between residents of the Member States — capital controls having been an instrument of macroeconomic policy for most Member States.

A new impetus for a full liberalisation of capital movements came with the monetarist, neo-liberal paradigm shift in the 1980s, which justified free movement of capital on economic grounds and pursued it as a condition for the free movement of financial services and of persons.

TEC Arts. 73b–g contain broader prohibitions on restrictions; using those, a full liberalisation of capital movements within the Community could be achieved recently.

The Maastricht blueprint for EMU also stipulated fully liberalised capital movements as a precondition for the introduction of a single currency (see chapter 19).

In order to pass measures, the Council decides on proposals from the Commission by QMV except for measures constituting a step backwards (restitution of restrictions) which require unanimity.

Derogation

TEC Arts. 73f and g provide for EC-wide or unilateral national emergency measures to restrict free movement of capital with third countries (but not with another Member State) in case of serious political reasons or grounds of urgency. These measures require QMV in the Council after consultation with the ECB; the EP is to be informed.

IV.2 Implementing the IM

Many of the nearly 300 legislative measures of the '1992 Programme' were directives which needed to be transposed into national law in order to be fully applicable to economic actors. As of 1998, 79% of measures demanded in the 1985 White Paper were transposed by all 15 Member States. Problems of transposition are either technical problems or caused by deliberate delays (new entrants Finland, Austria, but also Greece, Germany, Italy).

Country	IM directives transposed (as of 1 February 1998)
Finland	97.7%
Sweden	97.5%
UK	97.5%
Denmark	97.4%
Netherlands	97.4%
Spain	95.9%
Luxembourg	94.2%
Portugal	94.2%
Ireland	94.0%
Greece	93.8%
Italy	93.2%
France	93.0%
Germany	92.7%
Austria	92.7%
Belgium	92.0%

Source: European Commission

Moreover, certain sectors or issues were completely excluded from harmonisation (defence industry, transport and energy sectors, taxation, company law) and are only slowly brought into the remit of IM rules (see VI).

IV.3 Enforcing the Rules of the IM

Member States' acceptance and application of the EC legislation presupposes an effective enforcement system which discourages cheating and builds up trust in the uniform application of the common rules. To that end, the Treaty itself provides a set of judicial instruments and procedures (see chapter 5). Market integration requires economic adaptation in the Member States and often meets with fierce resistance of national governments and/or sectoral interests. Yet the supremacy of ECJ rulings has managed to break this opposition, ensure the functioning of the IM and move forward the process of European integration.

The respected authority of the ECJ as the ultimate adjudicator of legal disputes regarding common rules underlines the EC's nature as a 'Community of law'.

Some landmark judgments have had a great impact on Member States' relations with each other and economic actors' opportunities within the IM. These relate in particular to national measures having effects equivalent to trade barriers. The Court emphasised that barriers which had been abolished in the early years of the EEC must not be re-erected by other means, i.e., by measures having equivalent effect.

(a)   *Diamantarbeiders* (1969; C-2 and 3/69) — relates to TEC Art.12 (abolition of customs duties). ECJ prohibits new customs duties and equivalents by ruling unlawful any charge imposed on goods because they cross intra-EC borders (charges having equivalent effect to customs duties).

(b)   *Dassonville* (1974; C-8/74) — relates to TEC Art. 30 (prohibition of quantitative restrictions). Defines charges having equivalent effect to quantitative restrictions as all Member States trading rules capable of hindering, directly or indirectly, actually or potentially, intra-EC trade. Extensive interpretation, potentially allowing great ECJ interference in Member States' affairs.

(c)   *Cassis de Dijon* (1978; C-120/78) — relates to TEC Art. 30:

    (i)   established the principle of mutual recognition (see IV.1.2);

    (ii)   free movement of goods can be restricted to satisfy certain 'mandatory requirements' (e.g., public health, fairness of commercial transactions, consumer protection etc.). In practice, the judgment enlarged the scope of the derogation regime under TEC Art. 36.

(d)   *Keck and Mithouard* (1993; C-267 and 268 /91) — relates to TEC Art. 30. Court ruled that it is not an infringement of the free movement of goods, if national provisions on 'certain selling arrangements' apply to all traders equally, both of domestic and other Member States' goods. It thus limits the extensive definition put forward in *Dassonville*.

V. HISTORICAL DEVELOPMENT

The establishment of a Common Market was the central idea of the European Economic Community (EEC) which was set up by the 1957 Treaty of Rome. In the following decade economic integration progressed speedily. By 1 July 1968 the customs union was achieved, and the eradication of quotas and quantitative restrictions on the free movement of goods was under way but had not been fully achieved yet. During the 1970s the climate changed as West European economies went into decline. In that period of rising unemployment and inflation and low growth, Member States' commitment to the EC waned and national protectionism was on the rise again, as governments sought to safeguard their domestic markets and to keep foreign competition out. However, traditional protectionist tools (duties and quotas) are no longer available, so non-tariff barriers (NTBs) proliferated and were used maliciously to exclude imports. The result was a near re-fragmentation of the common market. Together with the institutional impasse of unanimity voting in the Council and the fading enthusiasm of the Member States for 'Europe', this stagnant period in European integration became known as 'Eurosclerosis'.

The re-launch of the Common Market

With the economic recovery of the late 1970s, Member States turned their attention once again to the EC — afraid that the economic advantages of the EEC would be lost with the fragmentation of the IM. In 1981, on request of the European Council, Commission President Gaston Thorn drew up a report on the state of the common market, suggesting:

(a)   the eradication of NTBs;
(b)   the simplification of border formalities;
(c)   an increase in competition in public procurement;
(d)   a further liberalisation in the trade in services.

In 1983, the Stuttgart European Council made the completion of the IM a priority aim.

By the mid 1980s, a favourable constellation of events allowed the re-launch of the IM:

(a)   President Mitterrand discontinued the French Keynesian experiment and introduced '*rigueur*' into economic policy;

(b)   a general convergence of Member States' economic policies on the monetarist, neo-liberal paradigm;

(c)   the European Summit of Fontainebleau solved the UK budgetary contribution;

(d)   Jacques Delors was chosen as the new Commission President (1985).

The 1985 Brussels European Council assigned the 1992 deadline to the completion of the IM and asked the Commission to prepare a detailed programme with a specific timetable. The '1992 Programme' (set out in Lord Cockfield's White Paper) aimed to remove all NTBs; it contained some 300 legislative proposals to be agreed and implemented before 1 January 1993. The White Paper was accepted at the 1985 Milan European Council.

Member States increasingly recognised that the creation of a true IM within the 1992 deadline required a reform of cumbersome decision-making procedures (e.g., a directive on the harmonisation of the permitted levels of noise interference by domestic lawn mowers had taken five years). The Brussels European Council also called for an intergovernmental conference (IGC) on the reform of the decision-making process. British Prime Minister Thatcher was opposed to convening an IGC but cooperated because the IM was her key goal (see chapter 2).

The *1986 Single European Act* was the first major Treaty revision and introduced, *inter alia*, the cooperation procedure which gave the EP a greater say in decision-making in certain areas and introduced QMV in the Council on most IM matters.

With the legislative programme on track, the Commission sought to gather support for the IM programme from industry and the public at large by demonstrating the IM's advantages. The *1988 Cecchini Report,* entitled *The Cost of Non-Europe*, was a major study of the effects on the European economy of completing the IM. It contained 28 special studies of various sectors and problem areas, including a macroeconomic model to back up the report's findings. The report estimated:

(a)   net increase 5% of the EC's GDP over the medium term as result of IM;

(b)   direct cost effects of the removal of barriers to trade, i.e., protective public procurement, divergent standards, regulatory diversity and other restrictions on services and manufacturing;

(c)   economies of scale through increased production, better use of existing capacity, higher investment;

(d)   efficiency gains with more competitive industrial structures and management methods;

(e)   other macroeconomic benefits (a price drop by 6%, higher employment, reduced budget deficits and improved trade balances).

The report was greeted with academic criticism on grounds of methodological inconsistencies, over-optimistic predictions and statistical inaccuracies. But even so, the Commission's aims for the report were in fact fulfilled: it managed to convince business, and provided arguments which helped to win public support for the IM.

The IM provided the Delors Commission with a policy centrepiece which fitted in with the traditional philosophy of the EC (functionalist extension of Community activities) and which was in line with the prevailing free-market paradigm of the EC's political leaders in the mid 1980s. It was also a way of competing with Japan and the US, both in terms of economies of scale and in attracting investment for employment and research and development. The SEA package deal was the result of a coincidence of Member States' national interests and provided the necessary legislative and institutional environment to complete the IM.

VI. RECENT DEVELOPMENTS

VI.1 Association of Central and Eastern Europe

Since 1991, the EU has entered into Association Agreements with 10 applicant countries in Central and Eastern Europe. These 'Europe Agreements' provide, *inter alia*, for the establishment of a free trade area for industrial goods between the EU and the CEECs by 2001 (see chapter 10). The 1994 Pre-Accession Strategy and the planned Pre-Accession Partnership (Agenda 2000) provide for far-reaching approximation of CEECs' legislation to the *acquis communautaire*.

VI.2 The European Economic Area (1994)

The EEA joins together in *one single market* the EU's 15 members with the members of EFTA, Iceland, Liechtenstein and Norway (Switzerland is also in EFTA but has not ratified the EEA Agreement). The agreement:

(a) grants the four freedoms of the IM to the three partner countries;

(b) requires them to adopt most EU policies on mergers, state aids, consumer protection, labour markets and the environment;

(c) induced comprehensive cooperation in other areas (e.g., R&D, education, social policy, environment);

(d) led to reinforced political cooperation (in 1995).

VI.3 Evaluating the Effects of the Internal Market

The effects of the IM have been considered in the 1996 Commission Communication on the Impact and Effectiveness of the Single Market.

Generally, evaluation of benefits and opportunities of IM is clouded by the varying degrees of transposition and implementation of IM directives in the Member States (see IV.2). Despite these methodological problems, the Commission analysis detects 'significant change in the European economy, though it is too early for many Single Market measures to have taken full effect'. According to the Commission's analysis, the IM brought about:

(a) a net increase of 300,000–900,000 jobs (i.e., more than would have existed without the IM);

(b) a net increase of EU GDP of 1.1–1.5% (in 1994);

(c) a net reduction of inflation rates of 1.0–1.5%;

(d)   a net increase in intra-EU manufacturing trade by 20–30%;

(e)   intensified competition; increased merger and takeover activity; acceleration of industrial restructuring, concentration of European industries; net gains in competitiveness;

(f)   economic convergence and cohesion within the EU (particularly for peripheral regions such as Ireland and Portugal);

(g)   greater attractiveness for investment;

(h)   greater intra-EU mobility of workers, students, retirees.

Yet there has been no discernible effect on growth. The impact on employment and GDP is far below that predicted in the Cecchini Report. Nevertheless, the Member States remain committed to the IM project.

VI.4 A New Agenda of Liberalisation, Deregulation and EU Re-regulation

With the '1992 programme' moving towards completion, the Commission has shifted — since the early 1990s — the focus of its initiatives to sectors which are currently still exempted from EU rules. Slowly, but surely, 'Brussels' has managed to push through — against fierce national and sectoral resistance — the liberalisation of protected industries and national monopolies:

(a)   telecoms market (1998 — see chapter 18);

(b)   postal services (to be transposed by early 1999);

(c)   gas market (currently under discussion — see chapter 8);

(d)   electricity market (early 1999 — see chapter 8);

(e)   rail and road transport, airlines (see chapter 9);

(f)   tentative cooperation in armament industries.

Liberalisation, deregulation and market-opening make national regulation and intervention redundant, yet necessitate *re-regulation at the EU level*. This phenomenon extended the influence and jurisdiction of the Commission and EU regulatory bodies (e.g., the European Patent Office) to the extent that the EU system functions as a 'regulatory state' (Majone).

VI.5 Amsterdam and the Consolidation of the Treaties

Current TEC provisions	Provisions after Amsterdam
Art. 7a (Aim of creating Internal Market)	Art. 14 — QMV to ensure balanced progress
Art. 8a (Right to free movement of EU citizens)	Art. 18 — Council unanimity and EP assent becomes co-decision (Art. 251)
Art. 9 (Customs union)	Art. 23 — unchanged
Art. 10 (Free circulation of imports)	Art. 24 — references to transition period removed.
Art. 12 (Non-introduction of new customs duties)	Art. 25 — unchanged
Art. 30 (Prohibition on quantitative restrictions on imports)	Art. 28 — unchanged
Arts. 31–3 (Transitional provisions)	Repealed
Art. 36 (Exemptions to Art. 30)	Art. 30 — unchanged
Art. 48 (Free movement of workers)	Art. 39 — unchanged
Art. 52 (Right of establishment)	Art. 43 — unchanged
Art. 59 (Free movement of services)	Art. 49 — unchanged
Art. 73b (Free movement of capital)	Art. 56 — unchanged
Art. 100 (Approximation of laws)	Art. 94 — unchanged
Art. 100a (Approximation of laws for the IM)	Art. 95 — more detailed procedure for Member States' provisions.

VII. FUTURE PROSPECTS

VII.1 Commission Action Plan for the Completion of IM (Amsterdam 1997)

In view of the mixed record of implementation of IM rules in the Member States (see IV) as well as Member States' preoccupation with EMU convergence, the Commission has pointed out the so far unfinished state of the IM. The Action Plan attempts to remedy these deficiencies by defining four strategic targets:

(a) *Making the rules more effective*: improving enforcement mechanisms of common rules and simplifying EC and national rules to reduce the burden on business, *inter alia*; through the SLIM project (Simpler Legislation for the Internal Market);

(b) *Dealing with key market distortions*: i.e., fresh attempts to overcome tax barriers (e.g., 1997 code of conduct) and anti-competitive behaviour;

(c) *Removing sectoral obstacles to market integration*: filling the gaps in the IM framework, changing national administrations' attitudes towards the IM;

(d) *Delivering a Single Market for the benefit of all citizens*: enhancing the social dimension of the IM, better information for citizens, consumer protection.

Implementation will be under a three-phase timetable: accelerated transposition in Member States immediately; rapid adoption of a number of existing proposals; attainment of maximum possible agreement on thorny issues (e.g., by way of priority treatment under an informal fast-track approach in Council and EP) before 1 January 1999.

The Commission will publish regularly a Single Market Scoreboard indicating the state of the IM and Member States' level of commitment in implementing the Action Plan. This 'peer group pressure' among the Member States is seen as a means to the completion of the IM.

VII.2 Economic and Monetary Union (Transition Phase 1999–2002)

According to the Commission's argument, the full benefits of economic integration are not yet fully exploited — which is partly due to the continued existence of 14 national currencies within the IM (see chapter 19). Exchange rate risk, transaction costs, and differing monetary and economic policy parameters in the Member States hinder the IM from working properly. EMU remedies this situation by:

(a) irrevocably fixing exchange rates and introducing a single currency, the euro;

(b) centralising monetary policy in an independent European Central Bank;

(c) closely coordinating and monitoring Member States' economic policies (e.g., through the 'Euro-11' informal economic policy forum of EMU 'ins');

(d) fully integrating the financial services and banking industries of the Member States;

(e) providing a further compelling incentive for tax harmonisation.

Potentially, the benefits are as large as the risks involved in the project:

(a) complete or partial failure of EMU could jeopardise the stage of integration reached today;

(b) friction between EMU 'ins' and 'outs' could lead to fragmentation of the IM;

(c) macroeconomic policy is insufficiently coordinated to produce the appropriate policy mix (relation between fiscal and monetary policies) at EU level.

VII.3 Enlargement

With the coming enlargement, the EU's IM will be extended by 11 national economies (with 110 million consumers) which — with the exception of Cyprus — have immature and underdeveloped market economies. In order for the IM to function, despite the inevitable lengthy transition periods in the wake of accession, the Commission has identified the 'core *acquis*' which is absolutely essential for the functioning of the IM in the new entrants.

The 1995 White Paper on the Preparation of the Associated CEECs for Integration into the IM:

(a)   sets out 'key measures' for priority approximation of laws with detailed recommendations to the CEECs;

(b)   establishes a two-stage approach to provide a guide for sequencing of CEECs' work programmes, yet without a definite timetable;

(c)   offers specialised technical advice from the EU and the Member States to the CEECs, e.g., sector-by-sector technical and specialist advice, access to up-to-date EC legislation, qualification and training of national administrators in IM matters.

VII.4 Free Trade Area with the Mediterranean Partners by 2010

The EU and its Mediterranean partners agreed in 1995 at Barcelona to establish, by the year 2010, a free trade zone characterised by *free circulation of manufactured products, and gradual liberalisation of trade in agricultural products*. Until 1997, progress has been rather limited:

(a)   free trade between the EU and Israel (since 1989, new agreement in 1995);

(b)   customs union between Turkey and EU in early 1996;

(c)   association agreements with Tunisia (1995) and Morocco (1996).

Currently, heightened tension in the Arab-Israeli conflict overshadows the multilateral negotiations and hinders serious progress towards trade liberalisation. As a result, meeting the 2010 deadline seems increasingly unlikely (see chapters 10 and 14).

VIII. FURTHER READING

BALASSA, Bela: *European Economic Integration*, Amsterdam, North-Holland, 1975.
MAJONE, Giandomenico: *Regulting Europe*, London, Routledge, 1996.
PELKMANS, Jacques: *European Integration: Methods and Economic Analysis*, Harlow, Longman, 1997.

REVUE DU MARCHÉ COMMUN ET DE L'UNION EUROPÉENNE, 409, June 1997: special section on Evaluer les effets du Marché unique, pp. 380–406.

TSOUKALIS, Loukas: *The New European Economy Revisited: The Politics and Economics of Integration*, 3rd ed., Oxford, OUP, 1997.

WALLACE, Helen and YOUNG, Alasdair: 'The Single Market: a new aproach to policy' in WALLACE, Helen and WALLACE, William (eds): *Policy-Making in the European Union*, Oxford, OUP, 1996, pp. 125–56.

Websites

DG XV (Internal Market and Financial Services)	http://europa.eu.int/comm/dg15/en/index.htm
DG XXI (Customs and Indirect Taxation	http://europa.eu.int/comm/dg21/dg21.html
Office for Harmonisation in the Internal Market (Trade Marks and Design)	http://europa.eu.int/agencies/ohim/ohim.htm
CENELEC	http://server.cenelec.be/
CEN	http://www.cenorm.be/

7 COMMON AGRICULTURAL POLICY

Lie Junius[1]

I. RATIONALE

Member States have a long tradition of state intervention in the agricultural sector, be it for technical reasons such as the sector's vulnerability to weather conditions and crop diseases, or for economic reasons, e.g., to avoid fluctuation of prices or to protect EU agricultural producers from price competition from outside. Agricultural policy also has strong political relevance: not only is the sector considered part of the national heritage, but food security is of paramount importance to the consumers. Finally, agriculture weighs heavily in national politics: agricultural lobbies and interest groups are well-organised and influential, and the 'farm vote' is an important factor in electoral politics.

CAP at EC level was established in the wake of the EEC, largely as part of a trade-off between France (likely to lose out in the IM, but prospective beneficiary from CAP) and Germany (likely to shoulder large part of CAP's financing, but prospective beneficiary from the IM). Moreover, CAP could be seen as a welfare institution at the EC level, intended to maintain employment and population levels in rural areas (Rieger, 1996).

[1] The author would like to thank Sylvian Giraud for his valuable contribution to this chapter.

II. LEGAL BASIS, PRINCIPLES, OBJECTIVES

II.1 Legal Basis

TEC Art. 3 provides that the Community's activities are to include: 'a common policy in the sphere of agriculture and fisheries'.

TEC Part Three Title II *'Agriculture'* (Arts. 38–47) includes:
(a)   Art. 39: objectives of CAP.
(b)   Art. 40: basic organisation of CAP.
(c)   Art. 41: social dimension of CAP.

II.2 Objectives

(a)   to increase agricultural productivity through modernisation;
(b)   to ensure a fair standard of living for farmers;
(c)   to stabilise markets;
(d)   to assure the availability of supplies;
(e)   to ensure reasonable prices for consumers.

II.3 Principles

(a)   *Unity of the market*: free movement of agricultural products in a single market and common prices.

(b)   *Community preference*: the needs of the market are to be provided primarily by European production. This entails protection from imports and world price fluctuations. A system of prices is a way to enforce this principle.

(c)   *Financial solidarity*: the Member States are jointly responsible for all the charges of the common policy: common budget and redistribution.

Since the 1980s:

(d)   *Co-responsibility*: farmers have to share the burden of the costs implied by CAP.

III. KEY ACTORS

III.1 Decision-making Process

The Council adopts legislative acts by qualified majority on proposal of the Commission and after consulting the European Parliament (TEC Art. 43). The decision-making process is characterised by a high level of secrecy, technocracy, a closed network, and an extensive involvement of interest groups. The environment in which CAP is elaborated could be described as a policy network (arena in which the often diverse interests of governments and pressure groups are mediated).

III.2 The Actors

Commission
DG VI is in charge of CAP, and with its highly specialised civil servants it is a powerful entity inside the Commission. Other DGs are involved to a much lesser extent in CAP. In the policy-initiation phase, DG VI moved from a cautious to a more active approach, putting forward several documents with reform proposals. In the implementation phase the Commission plays a central role. The Commissioner responsible for agriculture is Franz Fischler (Austria).

European Parliament
EP involvement is limited to consultation. Since CAP is part of the compulsory expenditure, the power to influence the agricultural budget is limited. The Parliament's strategy has long consisted of pushing for a reduction of the agricultural budget by using its wider powers (e.g., global refusal to vote on the budget or refusal to vote on the discharge).

Council
Agriculture ministers have very close links with their client lobbies. This can lead to rivalries with other Councils, for example, the Environment Council. A basic feature of the Agriculture Council is the use of package deals and issue linkage to reach solutions. The main body for preparing the Council meetings is the Special Committee on Agriculture (SCA), which is the 'COREPER for Agriculture'.

Committees
Committees of different types are involved in the elaboration and implementation of CAP. Most of the decisions are not taken at political level but by civil servants in meetings and during negotiations in a web of highly specialised committees.

The Commission consults the committees specialised in the various products in the process of elaborating its proposals. These are composed of representatives of farmers' organisations and national administrations.

The work of the Council and SCA is prepared by committees and expert groups.

The decisions on the implementation of CAP are adopted through the comitology procedure in coordination between the Commission and management committees (one for each product), composed of representatives from national administrations. The day-to-day management of the common market organisations is supervised by other management committees which control the implementation carried out by the Commission. Highly specialised experts serve in those committees.

Agricultural lobbies

Similar to many national farmers' organisations, the Committee of Agricultural Organisations in the European Union (COPA) represents a powerful, well-organised and financially strong pressure group in the EC policy process.

IV. POLICY INSTRUMENTS

IV.1 The Common Market Organisations (CMOs)

Basic principles of a CMO:
(a)   free movement of agricultural goods;
(b)   common price;
(c)   financial solidarity: CMO operations are financed directly by the EC budget.
TEC Art. 40.2 provides for three forms of CMO:
(a)   only common competition rules;
(b)   coordination of the various national market organisations;
(c)   a single European common organisation.
TEC Art. 40.3 lists the various measures that may be taken in the framework of a CMO:
(a)   regulation of prices;
(b)   aids for the production, marketing, storage and carryover of the products;
(c)   common mechanisms for stabilising imports and exports.

IV.2 The Price Support Mechanism

Internal wing

Target price: artificial price fixed by the EC: lucrative enough for farmers and reasonable enough for consumers.

Intervention price: the minimum guaranteed price below which the Community buys the agricultural product through intervention agencies and withdraws from the market all stocks presented to it (Harrison, 1995).

External wing

Threshold price: the price at which imports enter the EC market. The target price will be raised to avoid any undercutting.

Import levy: the difference between the world price of imports entering the EC and the threshold price.

Export restitution: subsidies provided to exporters amounting to the difference between the world price and the EC intervention price.

IV.3 Agro-Monetary Instruments

Currency fluctuations within the IM affect the common price system. In order to compensate the effects of currency de/revaluations, 'green rates' have been introduced, aiming at maintaining the original exchange rate in real terms.

In 1969, Monetary Compensatory Amounts were introduced, consisting of levies charged on imports into a Member State while its exports benefit from a premium.

Since 1993, the Monetary Compensatory Amounts have been abolished.

In 1995, the 'green rates' were frozen at the current rates until 1 January 1999, but Member States are free to direct national subsidies to farmers affected by intra-EC export losses.

IV.4 The Financial Instrument: The European Agricultural Guidance and Guarantee Fund (EAGGF)

The guarantee section finances the functioning of the CMOs, the price support mechanisms and the agro-monetary expenditures. This section takes up the bulk of the budget of the fund.

The guidance section finances, along with other funds (e.g., EIB), structural actions in the field of agriculture and rural development (see chapter 13).

In 1995, the EAGGF absorbed about 48% of the total EU budget.

IV.5 Structural Instruments

Direct aids aiming at social and regional development (financed by the EAGGF guidance section). The structural component of CAP developed very slowly. The 1968 Mansholt memorandum (which was too radical to be implemented) gave the first impetus. It was followed by the 1972 socio-structural directives providing for the modernisation of exploitations, early retirement schemes for farmers, and training programmes for young rural populations. A 1975 regulation dealt with the less favoured agricultural areas.

V. HISTORICAL DEVELOPMENT

V.1 Development of the CAP

At the end of the Second World War, the European farm sector was relatively backward and characterised by a high number of small farms with low productivity and unmodernised farming methods (Harrison, 1995).

The Treaty of Rome left open several options for the development of the policy but it was decided to merge the national protectionist systems into a joint European system due to the special nature of agricultural products.

The 1958 Stresa conference set up the basic functioning of the policy. It was decided that the agricultural prices were to be brought up to a common level and, as such, agricultural markets had to be managed.

1962–6: establishment of the CAP: CMOs and price-support system; the structural policy part as proposed in the Mansholt plan was not followed up by Council legislation.

The 'success/surplus crisis' period: the vicious circle of a price policy leading to production surpluses and consequently to high costs.

V.2 Reform of the CAP

V.2.1 Reasons for Reforming the CAP

(a)   Inherent distortions of the price-support mechanism: overproduction, especially by big farms and the excessive cost of the CAP (storage of surpluses, export restitutions).

(b)   International tension with trade partners:

(i)   the principle of Community preference had become increasingly incompatible with the rules of free trade;

(ii)   the impact on Third World countries: the contradiction between stated objectives of EU development policy and the refusal to allow in agricultural products from certain Third World countries became more and more obvious;

(iii)   the permanent call for free trade: the dynamics of the GATT/WTO negotiations exerted mounting pressure on the EU to reform its protectionist organisation of agriculture.

(c)   high costs for consumers;

(d)   environmental consequences of the CAP: air pollution, water pollution, loss of natural habitats and reduction of biodiversity, etc.;

(e)   budgetary difficulties for the EC budget, the slowing down of the common market project, the favouring of short-termism and piecemeal reforms.

V.2.2 The First Reforms (1980s): to Reduce Price Support and Discourage Production

Introduction of incentives to reduce overproduction: the co-responsibility principle
This principle was introduced to make the farmers aware of the surplus crisis and to give an incentive to reduce production and limit the budgetary expenditure. Two types of instruments were used:

(a)   *Stabilisers*: thresholds (maximum guaranteed quantities) beyond which farmers either:

(i)   will not benefit from the full guaranteed price but will receive a reduced price, or

(ii)   will have to pay a special tax (co-responsibility levy), or

(iii)   will not be able to sell their surpluses to the CMO intervention authorities.

(b)   *Quotas*: production quotas.

Renovation of the structural policy
Structural action — also aiming at the reduction of production — was introduced at the same time: aid to diversification, additional income aids for set-aside of land, aid for extensification, and measures for early retirement of farmers.

Budgetary discipline
These reforms were pursued in the framework of strict financial guidelines. At the Fontainebleau European Council in 1984 an agreement was reached after a long conflict with the UK over the budget. The deal provided for a limitation

on the increase of an agricultural expenditure: an increase in CAP expenditure cannot be higher than the increase in the Community's own resources. In 1988 an inter-institutional agreement was reached and the institutions passed a multi-annual program of 'financial perspectives' (Delors I). A strict ceiling to limit the increase in the CAP budget was set up: the agricultural budget could not increase by more than 74% of the growth rate of the Community's GNP.

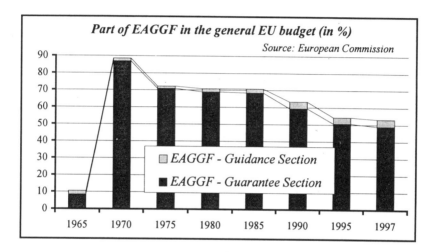

V.2.3 The 1992 MacSharry reform

Context
The limits of the previous reform: prices did not fall enough to have an impact on production and the stabilisers and quotas were insufficient to reduce expenditure in the long run. The structural measures failed to produce a real incentive to reduce production because of the low level of the premiums granted.

The coming EFTA enlargement: an increase of the expenditure was inevitable, in order to finance special schemes for less favoured areas in subarctic areas and in the Alps with resultant agro-environmental pressures.

The Uruguay Round: pressures to bring about a necessary price reduction. There was no formal linkage between the MacSharry reforms and the external negotiations in the GATT, but the latter could not have happened without the former. The GATT agreement on agriculture is intended to reduce the general levels of farm subsidy in all developed countries over a six-year period, and in particular to reduce levels of subsidised farm exports on the world market and to cut restrictions on imports of farm goods.

Main objectives and instruments
The heart of this plan is the attempt to decouple financial support from the price mechanism:

(a)   progressive reduction of prices in arable and beef sectors over a period of three years, to come closer to world market levels;

(b)   compensation for the reduction in price by direct payments to farmers;

(c)   direct aid conditioned on reducing production (by set-aside of land and extensification);

(d)   quotas and stabilisers remain in operation;

(e)   Accompanying measures: agro-environmental measures aimed at developing more environmentally friendly types of farms, afforestation and other types of land management, EU finance for early retirement scheme.

An Assessment of CAP in the 1990s

Achievements of the 1992 reform:
(a)   Farmers' incomes have increased.
(b)   Stocks have recovered a normal level.
(c)   The renewed CAP is flexible.

But major deficiencies of CAP remain, because of the limits of the 1992 reform:

(a)   Complete decoupling was not achieved: the link between direct payment and production remained.

(b)   High costs in the medium term because the price reduction is compensated by an increase of direct payments.

(c)   Still a high subsidy level.

(d)   The limited impact of the set-aside requirement.

(e)   The 1992 reform has increased the possibility of fraud.

VI. CHALLENGES and FUTURE PROSPECTS

VI.1 Can the CAP Survive Eastern Enlargement?

The agricultural sector in the CEECs is, on average, considerably larger than the EU's, both in terms of percentage of GDP and employment, the agricultural surface is two thirds as big as the EU's and the CEECs' production is equal to a significant part of the Community production. Prices and environmental standards are lower and the farming structure (size of plots) differs markedly from country to country.

In addition, the CEECs are facing some structural problems:

(a)   The agricultural sector has been in crisis since the shift towards a market economy: loss of the former USSR markets, perturbations caused by agricultural products of the Union, etc.

(b)   Other structural problems include the difficulties of organising land tenure because of the lack of a proper system of agricultural credit, lack of management and marketing experience among farmers and shortcomings of the food-processing industry.

With an unchanged CAP, enlargement would cause big problems, both with the budget and with the price levels. And clearly, with current prices in CAP some two or three times higher than the internal CEEC prices, an unreformed system would be an incentive to produce more in the CEECs.

VI.2 Possible Options for the Future

Three options can be put forward regarding the future of the CAP:

(a)   *Completion of the 1992 reform*:
    (i)   generalisation to all agricultural products;
    (ii)   full decoupling and cross-compliance with environmental and social objectives;
    (iii) the end of full compensation.

(b)   *An integrated rural policy*: a more integrated approach, taking into account structural and regional policy instruments in order to promote rural industries, activities in the field of tourism, protection of the environment and countryside, encouraging rural residence, etc.

(c)   *The renationalisation option*: a process whereby sovereignty is transferred back, at least partially, from EU institutions to Member States.

Different options to handle the impact of Eastern enlargement of CAP (Grant, 1997):

(a)   A two-tier CAP with a lower price level for the new eastern Member States:
BUT: not politically acceptable, would create problems with the IM.

(b)   Long transitional period for the new entrants:
BUT: delays difficult decisions on reform, also problems with IM.

(c)   Imposition of various quantitative controls on the new Member States.

(d)   Admit new Member States into a new, reformed CAP where compensatory aid is abolished.

VI.3 The Commission's Answer: 'Agenda 2000'

Agenda 2000 was launched in July 1997, together with an opinion on the accession of the applicant countries. This was followed up by legislative proposals in Spring 1998. The Commission proposes to build on the 1992 reforms, opting for direct aid to farmers instead of price support. The CAP's future objectives should be:

(a)   to improve the Union's competitiveness through lower prices;

(b)   to guarantee the safety and quality of food to consumers;

(c)   to ensure stable incomes and a fair standard of living for the agricultural community;

(d)   to make its production methods more environmentally friendly and respect animal welfare;

(e)   to integrate environmental goals into its instruments;

(f)   to seek to create alternative income and employment opportunities for farmers.

Cereals, beef and milk would be the main products affected by the reform. This means a reduction of 20% in the cereals intervention price in 2000 combined with an area payment, a 30% cut in the beef price between 2000 and 2002 and compensations with direct payments, and a 15% cut in the average support price for dairy products, while retaining the present quota system.

Other important elements of the reform proposal focus on the development of a *rural policy*, emphasising agro-environmental measures and the use of the countryside for recreation, and a change in the management of the CAP by simplifying the rules and applying them in a more centralised way.

The Commission has thus tried to combine the different options:

(a)   decentralised management of the CAP;

(b)   reform in line with the 1992 reform and control of the budget;

(c)   rural policy.

VI.4 Amsterdam and the Consolidation of the Treaties (1997)

Current TEC provisions	Provisions after Amsterdam
Art. 38 (Common market in agriculture)	Art. 32 — references to transition period removed
Art. 39 (Objectives)	Art. 33 — unchanged
Art. 40 (Common market organisations)	Art. 34 — references to transition period removed
Art. 41 (Supporting programmes)	Art. 35 — unchanged
Art. 42 (Competition)	Art. 36 — unchanged
Art. 43 (Set-up of CMOs)	Art. 37 — references to transition period removed
Art. 44 (Abolition of duties and quotas)	Repealed
Art. 45 (Transition arrangements)	Repealed
Art. 46 (Countervailing charges)	Art. 38 — unchanged
Art. 47 (ECOSOC involvement)	Repealed

VII. FURTHER READING

RIEGER, Elmar: 'The Common Agricultural Policy: external and internal dimensions' in WALLACE, Helen and WALLACE, William (eds): *Policy-Making in the European Union*, Oxford, OUP, 1996, pp. 97–123.

FENNELL, Rosemary: *The Common Agricultural Policy: Continuity and Change*, Oxford, Clarendon Press, 1997.

FRIES, ʹFabrice: *Les Grands Débats Européens*, Paris, Sevil, 1995, pp. 273–299.

GARDNER, Brian: *European Agriculture: Policies, Production and Trade*, London, Routledge, 1996

GRANT, Wyn: *Crisis or Opportunity? Agriculture and the EU*, Centre for European Union Studies, University of Hull, 1995.

GRANT, Wyn: *The Common Agricultural Policy*, London, Macmillan, 1997.

HARRISON, D. M.: *The Organisation of Europe*, London, Routledge, 1995, pp. 129–150.

OCKENDEN, Jonathan and FRANKLIN, Michael: *European Agriculture: Making the CAP Fit for the Future*, London, Pinter, 1995.

Websites

DG VI (Agriculture)	http://europa.eu.int/en/comm/dg06/index.htm
COPA	http://www.copa.be

8 ENERGY POLICY

Simon Usherwood

I. RATIONALE

Energy policy represents something of an exceptional case amongst the EC's policies. It was developed in a parallel body before the Community even existed, and even to this day it has not been fully integrated into the Treaty.

The end of the Second World War left the states of Europe in a profound state of shock. By integrating coal and steel sectors of the former antagonists, it was hoped that the means of producing war materials would become so interdependent that future conflict would be avoided. This was certainly the explicit motivation behind the Schuman Declaration of May 1950.

At the same time, there were also economic reasons for the proposition. Germany lacked iron ore and France lacked coal, so each had an interest in accessing the other's market for materials. The post-war boom had created an increased demand for these products (for the reconstruction of infrastructure and industry) and the economies of scale which could be utilised in a common market were highly evident.

In the later period of integration, energy policy was driven by the exigencies of the Internal Market (IM) and the need for reliable supplies. At the same time, the primary obstacle to integration, the divergence of national interests, has persisted.

II. LEGAL BASIS, OBJECTIVES

II.1 Legal Basis

Because there is no legal basis in the Treaty for energy policy per se, measures have been adopted under general provisions.

Until the Single European Act (SEA) in 1986, the Community tried to develop its energy provisions (the ECSC and Euratom Treaties notwithstanding) through TEC Art. 235, which allows for actions to fulfil the Community's objective when no specific legal basis exists. This requires unanimity in the Council, and so was a rather ponderous way to proceed.

The SEA brought with it a new set of provisions, which the Commission used to get around both the continued lack of legal basis and the requirements of TEC Art. 235. The Commission has been able to utilise the IM provisions under TEC Art. 100a, which only required QMV in the Council, and environmental provisions (TEC Arts. 130r–t).

Of course, as with any other industrial sector, the energy sector is covered by the rules on competition (TEC Arts. 85–90), although it has only been since the mid 1980s that the rules have been fully applied (see chapter 11).

The Treaty on European Union (TEU) created trans-European networks (TENs) under TEC Arts. 129b–d, including energy networks (also see chapter 9).

II.2 Objectives

Despite a lack of formal objectives, the Commission has gained the support of the Council and EP on the broad development of energy policy, as outlined in its White Paper, *An Energy Policy for the European Union* (COM(95)682 of 13 December 1995). This White Paper suggests four key objectives and challenges:

(a) *Managing external dependency to secure energy supply.* Given that external energy dependency of the EC currently stands at around 50%, and looks set to rise in the future, there is a need to ensure security of supply. This requires diversification and flexibility of supply, promotion of renewable energy sources (such as wind and solar) and more closely integrated energy markets. Closer cooperation with supplier states will be essential, especially with the issues of market access to an integrated EC market.

(b) *Integration of EC energy markets.* Energy costs are relatively high in the EC, explained largely by a lack of competition between suppliers. Therefore liberalisation is needed, although some balance between free access to networks and public service obligations is required.

(c)   *Coordination of energy and environmental objectives.* Clearly, energy use has environmental impacts and the EC should aim to make the two more compatible, through rational use of fossil fuels and improved efficiency of use.

(d)   *Development of energy technologies.* By developing new, more efficient technologies, it will be possible to achieve the other objectives more easily.

III. KEY ACTORS

The Commission
The Commission has responsibility for initiating policy. However, given the particular status of energy policy there is an internal power play to gain primacy. While DG XVII (Energy) has largely retained the dominant position, DG IV (Competition) has made big increases in its role since the mid 1980s. This jostling for position has been intensified by the DGs' different approaches: DG XVII is seen as being generally responsive to interests within the energy industry, while DG IV has a more confrontational style — in keeping with its carefully cultivated image as a tough player. At the same time, DG XI (Environment) has been more cooperative with DG XVII, supporting it particularly in those legislative proposals which attempt to reconcile energy requirements with environmental protection (although the arguments over the carbon tax form a notable exception).

In general, despite these internal problems, the Commission has taken a proactive stance, working to extend its competences (see VI) and to break stalemates between other actors.

The Council
If the Commission is proactive, then the Council tends towards reaction, delay and postponement. Even with substantial brokerage before the biannual Energy Council meetings, both by the Presidency and the Commission, the Council finds that agreement is still relatively hard to find. This can be attributed to the strong lobbying of Member States by the industry and to the persistence of national interests.

European Parliament
The EP plays a relatively small role in energy policy, although that role has increased over the years since the SEA. Its influence lies primarily in representing and promoting consumer and environmental issues, rather than in overall policy development. This also explains to some extent the EP's favouring of a Common Energy Policy (CEP) for the EU, as this would provide more opportunities to influence the other actors.

Interest groups
Interest groups, and particularly industry ones, have been rather successful in transposing their national influence to a European level. All energy producing sectors have their European federations: Europia for oil, Eurogas, Foratom for nuclear power, CEPCEO for coal and Eurelectric. All of these groups have strongly resisted the development of the internal energy market, largely out of fear of an attack on dominant or monopoly positions in their respective territories (see V). They also lobbied very hard (and finally successfully) against the carbon tax proposal, as this would have set highly problematic precedents and incurred substantial costs.

Other industrial lobby groups, on the other hand, have favoured the internal market and a freer access to energy supply, especially when their industry is an energy consumer. This has been true for sectoral interests, such as the chemicals industry, and for industry as a whole (as represented by UNICE).

IV. POLICY INSTRUMENTS AND ACTIONS

IV.1 Security of Supply and International Cooperation

Diversification of supply

Development of relations with suppliers:
— Energy Charter (see VI).
— Bilateral agreements with CEECs, CIS, Mediterranean, Gulf states, etc.
— Extension of TENs into third countries.

Diversification of resources:
— Encouragement of new and renewable energy sources (ALTERNER programme).
— Balance of potential nuclear resources with safety and non-proliferation.

Action on energy demand
Promotion through SAVE, JOULE and THERMIE energy-saving programmes.

International aid and cooperation

Technical assistance:
— Use of PHARE, TACIS and MEDA programmes to assist and co-finance efficient and effective energy sectors in CEECs, CIS and Mediterranean (see chapters 10 and 23).
— Programme with Latin America, to optimise energy resources.

—European Development Fund (EDF) available for Lomé states to develop new energy structures.

Developing EC priorities: the SYNERGY programme covers cooperation on energy with third states, as with the Euro-Mediterranean Energy Forum.

Preparation for enlargement: as part of the Essen pre-accession strategy, the EC and CEECs began a structured dialogue on harmonisation of policies, reform of legislation to conform to the *acquis* and energy sector restructuring. This will be replaced by the new accession partnerships (see chapter 23).

Cooperation with international organisations: The Commission works with the International Energy Agency (IEA) and the International Atomic Energy Agency (IAEA), which are the primary international coordinators of energy cooperation.

Crisis measures: together with the IEA, the EC has developed a system of oil stocks in case of supply disruption.

IV.2 Integrating Energy Markets

Internal energy market

Internal market in electricity: directive adopted in December 1995, in force since early 1997, providing for real competition, whilst protecting public service requirements. One third of market to be open by 2003; full implementation of the IM and of competition rules; tightening of state aid.

Internal market in gas: ongoing negotiations, as several Member States are concerned about the effect of liberalisation on long-term contracts with current suppliers.

TENs for energy: these are being developed to resolve missing connections and insufficient capacities.

Taxation of energy products: proposals are currently being tabled to harmonise the taxation of all energy products with a view to removing trade distortions.

Energy and economic and social cohesion
A good energy balance, rational use and use of renewables are all important in regional planning. As such, half of the actions in the THERMIE programme are in Objective 1 and 2 regions. Other regional programmes involved with

energy include Interreg (cross-border cooperation) and REGIS (remote regions).

IV.3 Promotion of Sustainable Development in Energy

The Commission has pushed for much in the way of environmentally compatible legislation at a European level. The concern over carbon dioxide emissions led to some moves towards substantial target setting in the early 1990s, not least in the UN Framework Convention on Climate Change. However, progress has stalled somewhat with the failure of the carbon tax legislation (see COM(95)172 final of 10 May 1995) and the reticence of other global players (notably the USA) to pursue these targets. As a consequence — despite the creation of programmes such as SAVE, JOULE, THERMIE and ALTERNER — their impact has been rather marginal.

IV.4 Research and Development

The Research Framework programme has a research and development element (JOULE) and a demonstration element (THERMIE), and it is within this framework that most activities are focused. The programme covers rational use, development of renewables and improved use of fossil fuels. There are also actions concerning nuclear power, notably the Joint European Torus (JET) project.

V. HISTORICAL DEVELOPMENT

Historically, there have been major blocks to integration in the energy sector. These have come from the very different production volumes, import requirements and consumption patterns for each Member State. When coupled to the perception of energy as an essential element of national planning (because of its knock-on effects in the economy) and the various attempts to reduce external dependency, it can be seen that national policies are both well-developed and highly resilient.

V.1 ECSC and Euratom

The creation of the ECSC in 1952, following the Schuman Declaration of May 1950, was initially hailed as a great success. With its strong supranational element (the High Authority) it was seen as the best way forward in the sectors' development. Tariffs and quotas were abolished and non-tariff barriers were reduced; assistance was given to restructuring; and both output and interstate trade were increased. But when the first serious challenge came in the winter of 1958–9, the ECSC failed completely.

The mildness of the winter reduced consumption of coal, just at the time when cheap oil from the Arabian Gulf was entering the market. The consequence was huge surplus capacity, which the High Authority wanted to contain by production limits. However, the Member States were against this and overruled the proposal.

The reasons for the weakness of the ECSC were multiple. As had been demonstrated, the High Authority was unable to push through policies all the way to completion, not least because the members of the High Authority itself pushed their respective national positions. More generally, the growth of oil and gas demonstrated the need for a common energy policy, rather than sectoral policies for coal and steel in isolation.

If the ECSC had enjoyed at least initial success, the European Atomic Energy Community (Euratom) was not so fortunate. The USA wanted to retain its role in European nuclear programmes, much to French disgust and distrust. Euratom, the French hoped, would create a European industry, within which they could develop their own *force de frappe*. However, the US promise to provide cheap uranium to Germany meant that the final agreement in 1957 was so full of loopholes (particularly on secrecy) that the organisation never really had a chance: the US became the primary supplier of materials and France developed its own industry.

V.2 The End of the Boom

The weakness of the Community was brutally exposed in 1973–4, when the Organisation of Petroleum Exporting Countries (OPEC) decided to sharply restrict their supply of oil to the West, as retaliation for the Yom Kippur War. This sent energy prices sky-high and caused a major economic downturn. The effect on energy policy was principally to reinforce national objectives, not least because OPEC were very successful in their strategy of divide and rule, making bilateral agreements with the various Member States. Indeed, it was only through US intervention that there was any international cooperation, in the form of the IEA.

In the subsequent period up until the SEA, the EC found itself limited to little more than producing guidelines for national policies in matters such as security of supply and conservation.

V.3 Single European Act

The SEA itself came out of a realisation of the need for efficient markets to boost growth and the new paradigm of deregulation and liberalisation to promote that efficiency (see chapter 6). However, neither the White Paper nor the SEA itself mentioned energy integration at all, because it was felt to be far too problematic to even attempt to tackle. That said, by 1988 the necessity of such integration was apparent, in terms of both the need to free up energy markets to complete the IM and the overdependence on external supplies. In 1989 DG XVII produced its proposals.

The resultant legislative push came in two main stages. In the first (1989–91) directives were agreed on opening access to gas and electricity supply. In the second (from 1991), draft directives were proposed to open up these areas further, through the use of Third-Party Access (TPA). TPA works in two stages: first, the supply grids for gas and electricity are opened up to other grid providers, and then to any third party.

At the same time as this legislative element, there was also a much increased use of competition rules (which had previously proved difficult, given the possibility of a TEC Art. 36 exemption under public security) and an attempt to integrate environmental concerns (both in terms of legislation and of external relations).

While Member States were generally in favour of the internal energy market, they were still very wary of losing national control to the Community, not least because the Commission was proving rather successful in carving a niche for itself. TPA, for example, implied some kind of centralised agency to coordinate it (i.e., the Commission), while extra leverage was gained through financing TENs and applying competition policy to the sector. In short, the Commission successfully managed to make itself be seen as a major energy policy-maker by lobbies and interest groups, which in turn enhanced its role vis-à-vis the Member States.

Problems still remain in completing an internal energy market. Structurally, the sector has been characterised by unstable markets and vulnerability of supply, which has led to an emphasis on security of supply, and in turn vertical integration of producers, transmitters and distributors. There is still a need to implement fully the directives already agreed, break down further the vertical integration and introduce some TPA before a true internal energy market can be said to exist.

VI. RECENT DEVELOPMENTS

Since the SEA there have been no great developments, at least in terms of legal standing. TENs got a legal base in the TEU, but otherwise the Commission failed in its attempts to gain a definitive article on energy policy inserted, either at Maastricht or at Amsterdam. Indeed, Amsterdam limited itself to little more than a renumbering of the relevant articles:

Current TEC provisions	Provisions after Amsterdam
Art. 129b (TENs objectives)	Art. 154 — unchanged
Art. 129c (TENs procedures and instruments)	Art. 155 — unchanged
Art. 129d (TENs decision-making)	Art. 156 — all measures and guidelines to be decided under co-decision

At the same time, progress on the internal energy market has continued afoot. Though there was success in the agreement on electricity in 1995, there was also ongoing frustration about gas. The balance between market liberalisation (as espoused by the UK) and the need to maintain public service obligations (as argued by the French) has proved particularly difficult to resolve.

One feature of the Commission's strategy to push for a CEP has been the use of external events as leverage for more integration (see Haaland Matlary 1997). This was seen most clearly in the reaction to the Gulf War in 1990–1. DG XVII very quickly responded to the invasion of Kuwait and the subsequent raising of oil prices by suggesting first that the EC become a full member of the IEA, and then a much more ambitious oil-sharing mechanism. This latter proposal also came to include EC intervention to stabilise oil prices. Needless to say, the Member States strongly opposed this, despite the apparent advantages it offered, primarily because of the power it would have given the Commission during non-crisis periods. Similarly, the increased public consciousness about the environment gave the Commission a chance to raise energy's importance on the EC's agenda and a way into merging energy and environmental goals, partly through increased use of the environmental provisions of the Treaty.

Perhaps this use of external events to further integration is most clearly seen in the case of the collapse of communism. The resultant energy problems in the CEECs and the CIS saw the development of the European Energy Charter Treaty (see box 1).

The Commission will undoubtedly continue to pursue its policy options on the development of a CEP. Its new approach was most clearly laid out in the White Paper of 1995. The objectives which the Commission sought to fulfil have been mentioned above (see II). Already by this time a considerable array of formal and informal competences could be claimed (see box 2). What is interesting is the way in which the Commission foresees their achievement, namely through a primacy of Member States' interests rather than supranationalism. The aim is then 'establishing confidence between Member States via transparency, dialogue and the exchange of information' (1995 White Paper). At the same time, Member States' interventions in energy policies have impacts on EC actions in the IM and competition. As such, it is necessary to have an EC level to promote effectiveness at the Member States' level. Proportionality and minimum regulation by the EC will be the watchwords.

The Commission had hoped that this new approach would be acceptable to the Member States at the 1996 IGC, but even this more modest proposal was ignored. The persistence of national interests is still a considerable force to be reckoned with.

BOX 1
European Energy Charter Treaty

First proposed at the Dublin European Council of June 1990 by Dutch Prime Minister Lubbers, a non-binding Charter was signed in December 1991. This was superseded by the binding Treaty, signed three years later in Lisbon by the EU, CEECs, all CIS states and some other OECD members (USA, Canada, Japan), which came into force in April 1998.

It has as an aim the introduction of market economy principles across the whole of Europe in the field of energy. Areas covered include energy resources and use; transport; transit; investment; dispute settlement. This represents a *de facto* extension of the IM across Europe.

The strong role of the Commission in the negotiation process reflects the coincidence of its work in the development of the internal energy market at the time. Nevertheless, one should not forget that (as with the ECSC) the political motivations for the Charter Treaty (i.e., stabilising the CEECs and the CIS) were at least as important as the question of energy supply.

A supplementary treaty, on national treatment for foreign investors in the pre-investment stages of development, is due to be adopted during 1998.

BOX 2
EC Competences at the time of the 1995 White Paper

Formal competences:

(a)   Infrastructure development (105 million ECU for the period 1995-99).

(b)   Aid for general energy development in cohesion Member States.

(c)   Restructuring of coal production.

(d)   Merging of energy and environmental policy.

(e)   Prevention of monopolistic practices.

(f)   Acting for EU in the IEA and the United Nations Conference on the Environment and Development (UNCED).

Informal competences:

(a)   Establishment and administration of control on some parts of gas and electricity transmission.

(b)   Implementation, management and ensuring adherence to the European Energy Charter until the setting up of the permanent secretariat in December 1995.

VII. FURTHER READING

Literature is not easily found for energy policy, especially pieces of academic analysis. However, the books which do exist are of a generally high quality. The book by Haaland Matlary stands out as a key work in this respect, analysing the subject from an actor-based perspective. The two Commission documents provide both a good overview of the scope of the EU's energy policy and a justification of its extension. Padgett is more concentrated on the developments in the wake of the SEA.

EUROPEAN COMMISSION: *An Energy Policy for the European Union*, White Paper, COM(95)682, 13 December 1995, Brussels.

EUROPEAN COMMISSION: *An Overall View of Energy Policy and Action*, Communication, COM(97), 21 April 1997, Brussels.

HAALAND MATLARY, Jane: *Energy Policy in the European Union*, London, Macmillan, 1997.

PADGETT, Stephen: 'The Single European Energy Market: the politics of realization', *Journal of Common Market Studies*, vol. 30, 1992, pp. 53–75.

Website

| DG XVII (Energy) | http://europa.eu.int/en/comm/dg17/dg17home.htm |

9 TRANSPORT POLICY

Julian Vassallo

I. RATIONALE

A functioning Internal Market (IM) requires an efficient and effective transport system that satisfies the economic, environmental and social aims of the Union. The absence of such a system would make the physical free movement of goods, persons and services little more than an aspiration.

The transport industry represents 7% of total EU employment and 7% of total EU GNP. The clear disadvantages of organising transport links between Member States only at a national level, together with the strong environmental implications of most significant transport projects makes it an ideal area for decision-making at a European level.

The policy also aims to facilitate and increase transport links with the EU's trading partners particularly to the East and to a lesser extent to the South, while seeking to allow access of EU operators to other transport markets.

II. LEGAL BASIS, PRINCIPLES, OBJECTIVES

II.1 Legal Basis

The establishment of a common transport policy is based on TEC Arts. 3.e, 74 and 75. TEC Arts. 61 and 76–84 refer to several aspects of transport policy while Arts. 129b–d provide the legal basis for Trans-European Networks (TENs).

II.2 Principles

On the basis of the Commission's 1992 White Paper, on *The Future Development of the Common Transport Policy*, the guiding principles in this area can be defined as:

(a)   balancing the need for an effective transport system for the EU with protection of the environment, leading to a situation of *sustainable mobility*;

(b)   the defence of the needs and interests of individual citizens as consumers, transport users and people living and working in areas of transport activity.

II.3 Objectives

(a)   The elimination of the considerable anomalies and missing links in the European transport network that prevents the IM from producing maximum benefits.

(b)   The creation of an effective, efficient, safe and accessible transport system that supports the free movement of goods, persons and services.

(c)   The fostering of competition in the transport industry, the restraining of state aids and the removal of barriers which impede EU enterprises from operating in other Member States.

The Common Transport Policy Agenda 1995–2000, entitled *An Action Programme towards Sustainable Mobility in Europe*, outlines the EU's strategy in pursuing these objectives and puts emphasis on three areas:

(a)   improving quality by developing integrated and competitive transport systems based on advanced technologies which also contribute to environmental and safety objectives;

(b)   improving the functioning of the single market in order to promote efficiency, choice and a user-friendly provision of transport services while safeguarding social standards;

(c)   broadening the external dimension by improving transport links with third countries and fostering the access of EU operators to other transport markets.

III. Key Actors

European Commission
DG VII gives direction to the common transport policy. The Commission is the initiator of all Community transport legislation and oversees all spending from the Community budget on transport policy. Given the vast funds involved in Trans-European Transport Networks (which represents only part of TENs) the Commission has taken an active role in attracting private enterprise involvement in their financing.

European Parliament
Transport is one of those policy areas which still fall under the cooperation procedure which allows the EP only limited powers (see chapter 3). The Treaty of Amsterdam (ToA) provides for co-decision in transport policy.

The use of the co-decision procedure in the definition of Trans-European Transport Network Guidelines means that here the EP is almost on the same footing as the Council of Ministers.

Council of Ministers
Unless it rejects the Commission's original proposal, the Council can adopt most transport policy decisions by qualified majority voting (QMV) under the cooperation procedure. This is not the case, however, when defining TENs guidelines, as mentioned above.

Economic and Social Committee and Committee of the Regions
ECOSOC is consulted during the legislative process. The Committee of the Regions will be consulted in the same manner after the coming into force of the ToA.

National, regional and local administrations
The very nature of the policy requires the close involvement and cooperation with administrations in the Member States in both the planning and implementation stage.

IV. POLICY INSTRUMENTS

IV.1 Legislation

The largest part of legislation, in the form of regulations and directives, is aimed at increasing competition in the transport industry through the harmonisation of technical, fiscal and social provisions in the Member States.

IV.2 Financial Support

The financing of transport policy initiatives takes place through:
(a)   direct financing from the European Regional Development Fund with planned expenditure of ECU 15 billion (see chapter 13);
(b)   direct financing from the Cohesion Funds (half of which are dedicated to transport) to the tune of ECU 8 billion;
(c)   low-interest loans from the European Investment Bank (EIB) for major TENs projects;
(d)   loan guarantees from the European Investment Fund;
(e)   financing of feasibility studies, loan guarantees and interest rate subsidies for TENs of at least ECU 1.8 billion.
Meanwhile on the basis of Agenda 2000 an ever-greater part of PHARE funds will be spent on direct investment in the upgrading of transport infrastructure in the applicant CEECs.

IV.3 Research and Technical Development

The declared aim of making European transport more environmentally friendly, easier and safer led the EU to spend over 900 million ECU on research in this area between 1994–98. Many of the larger programmes focused on the use of new information technologies for all forms of transport. Other funds went to research into materials technology, energy efficiency, electric vehicles research and the introduction of black boxes for ships.

IV.4 Guidelines

This includes the mapping of European transport infrastructure in order to illustrate missing links and expose the clear absence of a coherent European transport network. As examples the Commission points to the incompatible power and signalling systems of European railways, motorways which come to a sudden end at frontiers and the 52 separate air traffic control centres using 20 different operating systems and 70 programming languages.

IV.5 International Agreements

International agreements with the EU's neighbours to the East and South seek to rationalise the transport links between them. Most of the investment goes to the CEECs and includes projects such as support for the development of Estonian port facilities, which cater for an ever-greater proportion of EU-Russian trade flows.

V. TRANS-EUROPEAN TRANSPORT NETWORKS

The Trans-European Transport Networks are an attempt to rationalise the often incompatible national transport networks on a European level by improving the links between the existing systems (through inter-operability) and filling in the missing links. These gaps increased in number with the 1995 enlargement and promise to increase further with the forthcoming eastern enlargement.

The Commission expects these costly projects:

(a)   to create a more vigorous, competitive economy capable of creating many more new jobs;

(b)   to embody the concept of sustainable mobility by improving the quality of today's environment and preserving tomorrow's natural resources without sacrificing today's economic growth;

(c)   to guarantee higher personal safety and a decline in traffic congestion and pollution;

(d)   to offer travellers and goods a wider choice of transport means and deliver them to their destination more quickly;

(e)   to establish better connections between regions on the periphery of the Union and those at its centre;

(f)   to include links with partner countries in Central and Eastern Europe moving towards membership of the Union.

Several projects are already underway while others are still awaiting final approval by the Council and EP. If the Commission's proposals are adopted, transport TENs until the year 2010 will involve an expenditure of 400 billion ECU on 70,000 km of railway (of which 22,000 km on new and upgraded track for high-speed trains), 15,000 km of new roads, combined transport corridors and terminals, networks of inland waterways and a remarkable 267 airports of common interest.

According to the Commission, these projects will:

give Europe an operating network of high-speed trains, much more efficient air traffic control systems, airports and ports which connect well with the territories they serve, motorways in regions which have few or none at all and some new and redeveloped inland waterways. State-of-the-art transport telematics are woven into the network to allow us to make the best possible use of its capacity.

The 1994 Essen European Council approved 14 priority Trans-European Transport Networks (see box). They support the idea of shifting the transport balance away from its dependence on road transport, with its environmental and congestion implications, in favour of intermodal transport. As its name suggests intermodal transport involves the use of several means of transport. In many cases this implies seeking to combine the flexibility of road transport with the advantages of other forms of transport by making the switch from one to another easier. Thus 80% of the investment goes to rail links, a further 8% goes to road/rail links and only 10% is set aside for the construction of new roads.

Priority Trans-European Transport Networks

1. High-speed train (Paris — Brussels — Cologne — Amsterdam — London)
2. High-speed train/Combined Transport North-South (Berlin — Nuremberg, Munich — Verona)
3. High-speed train South (Barcelona — Perpignan, Valladolid — Vitoria)
4. High-speed train Paris — Eastern France — Germany (including Metz — Luxembourg branch)
5. Conventional rail/combined transport Betuwe line
6. High-speed train/combined transport France — Italy (Lyon — Turin, Turin — Milan — Venice — Trieste)
7. Greek motorways PATHE and Via Egnatia
8. Lisbon — Valladolid motorway
9. Conventional rail link (Cork — Dublin — Belfast — Larne — Stranraer)
10. Malpensa Airport, Northern Italy
11. Fixed rail-road link between Denmark and Sweden — Øresund fixed link
12. Nordic Triangle
13. Ireland — United Kingdom — Benelux road link
14. West Coast Main Line (UK)

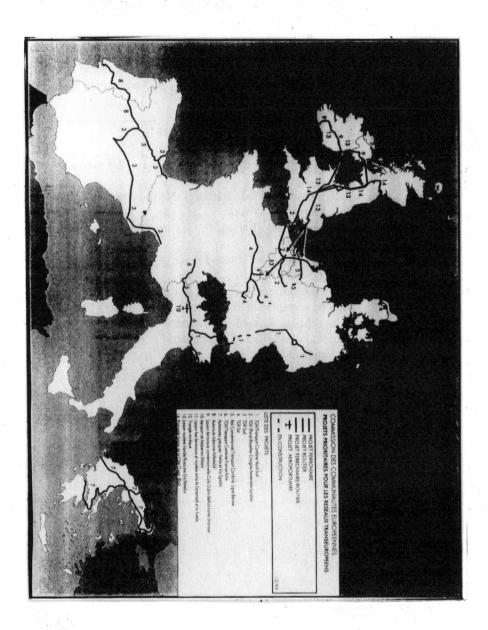

The EU's continuing concern with promoting and facilitating combined transport and rebalancing the use of different modes of transport is apparent in this area. In 1993 a Council decision was adopted aiming to create a trans-European combined transport network consisting of rail, inland-waterway, sea and road links by 1999. Intermodal termini and investment in special rolling stock will form the second phase of the project, to be completed by 2005.

VI. COMMON TRANSPORT MARKET

Apart from seeking to ensure a more effective transport system, the EU has also sought to complete the IM in the business of transportation itself. Much legislation has been put in place to allow for a real free movement of services and the right of establishment in this area so that the nationality of the operator does not prevent it from entering the transport market of another Member States. By 1993, the basic legislation necessary for the creation of the Common Transport Market had been put into place. This is a remarkable feat in itself when one considers that transport has always been a notoriously monopolistic and state-dominated industry. However, the multi-faceted nature of the industry means that while road transport is largely liberalised, developments relating to other means of transport lag behind.

But full liberalisation and harmonisation with competitive transport markets in each industry was never going to be enough to develop an efficient and cost-effective industry. In the past the flexibility of road transport led to a dominance of this environmentally unfriendly form of transport at the expense of rail transport in particular. There is a clear need to find a better balance between road, rail, sea and air transportation. This, together with the fact that many journeys are best carried out through several forms of transportation, has led the EU to encourage the setting up of transport chains and the establishment of competing transport operators offering a combination of different forms of carriage.

To this end the EU (since 1992) has been financing PACT (Pilot Actions for Combined Transport) which has had some success in bringing about a more balanced intermodal transport system. Nevertheless a suggestion that intermodal transport operators should be allowed derogations from competition provisions was given the red light in December 1997, from the 'group of wise men' set up under DG IV.

VII. HISTORICAL DEVELOPMENT

Transport policy was identified as an important and natural area for action on the European level already in the TEC in 1957. Nevertheless for many years

Member States continued to view transport policy as a predominantly national tool for the protection of local employment and the propping up of symbols of national pride such as state-owned airlines and railways. International transportation was based on a maze of multilateral and bilateral agreements, which, together with extensive border controls, created a bureaucratic headache for its users.

The situation only started to change after 1985 when the ECJ upheld a claim by the EP against the Council for infringing the Treaty's rules on the freedom to provide international transport services. It was also at this time that the slow process of liberalisation started to gain momentum. The emphasis on national symbols shifted to more rational considerations such as the need for easy movement across borders, safety, costs, environment, workers' interests and access to transport. The elimination of border controls, which came with the establishment of the IM, added new impetus to the developments in this area.

VIII. RECENT DEVELOPMENTS AND FUTURE PROSPECTS

The liberalisation of the transport industry is an ongoing process which has been taking place in parallel to the emergence of side interests including the environment, the avoidance of congestion and safety.

The various sectors have reached different levels of progress.

Road transport
The full liberalisation of international road transport of goods with full freedom to operate services in other Member States only came into force in 1998.

Rail Transport
In July 1996 the Commission issued a White Paper outlining its strategy for revitalising the Community's railways, by rationalising their financial situation, ensuring freedom of access to all traffic and promoting the integration of national systems. The Commission has also proposed the introduction of an operating licence in order to provide uniform access to infrastructure.

The emphasis on rail in transport TENs, and particularly on high-speed rail links, is certain to have a significant impact on this form of transport as more projects are concluded.

Maritime transport
The three priorities of the Commission's White Paper approved in December 1996 were safety, maintenance of open markets and enhanced competitiveness.

Recent accidents have added impetus to the first priority and have led, amongst other things, to EU initiatives on safety on roll-on roll-off ferries and the obligation for the registration of ferry passengers.

Inland waterway transport

Cabotage for internal waterway transport was liberalised on 1 January 1993, allowing users of these services a free choice of carrier. The market should be fully liberalised by 1 January 2000.

Air transport

The liberalisation of air transport, in terms of market access, capacity control, fares and the issuing of operating licences came into effect in 1993. The liberalisation is slowly leading to a real IM in air services — a process which is being fostered by the introduction of several legislative measures harmonising technical standards, common standards for airworthiness, and mutual recognition of civil aviation personnel licences, together with competition rules for air transport undertakings.

Meanwhile 'open skies' negotiations to create an air zone common to the EU and the US continue, with the division between an enthusiastic Commission and a reluctant Council remaining apparent.

Amsterdam and the Consolidation of the Treaties

ToA Art. 71 provides for transport policy and TENs to fall under the co-decision rather than the cooperation procedure giving more power to the EP (see chapter 3). Otherwise the table below shows that all other ToA changes were cosmetic.

Current TEC provisions	Provisions after Amsterdam
Art. 3f (Objectives of the EC)	Unchanged
Art. 61 (Freedom to provide transport services)	Art. 51 — unchanged
Art. 74 (Cohesion with other policies)	Art. 70 — unchanged
Art. 75 (Decision-making)	Art. 71 — co-decision replaces cooperation legislative procedure, except where regulatory measures have serious standard-of-living or employment repercussions
Art. 76 (Interim measures)	Art. 72 — unchanged
Art. 77 (State aids)	Art. 73 — unchanged
Art. 78 (Measures on transport rates)	Art. 74 — unchanged
Art. 79 (Prohibition of discrimination on basis of nationality of carrier)	Art. 75 — unchanged
Art. 80 (Prohibition of state support and protection)	Art. 76 — unchanged
Art. 81 (Reduction in border charges)	Art. 77 — unchanged
Art. 82 (Qualified exemptions for Federal Republic of Germany)	Art. 78 — unchanged
Art. 83 (Advisory Committee)	Art. 79 — unchanged
Art. 84 (Application of Title to different forms of transport)	Art. 80 — unchanged
Art. 129b (Objectives of TENs)	Art. 154 — unchanged
Art. 129c (Instruments of TENs)	Art. 155 — unchanged
Art. 129d (Decision-making procedure for adoption of TENs guidelines)	Art. 156 — unchanged

IX. FURTHER READING

The ideas and basic materials for this chapter came from several official publications of the Union together with the analysis and insight of the following recommended publications.

BAUCHET, Pierre: *Les transports de l Europe: La trop lente intégration*, Paris, Economica, 1996.
DEHOUSSE, Franklin and GALER, Benoit: *La Politique Européene du Rail*, Centre de recherche et d'information socio-politique.
EUROPEAN COMMISSION: *Towards a Common Pan-European Transport Policy*, DG VII, Luxembourg, EUR-OP, 1997.
HAVEL, Brian F.: *In Search of Open Skies: Law and Policy for a New Era in International Aviation: a Comparative Study of Airline Deregulation in the*

United States and in the European Union, The Hague, Kluwer Law International, 1997.

OECD: *Transport — New Problems, New Solutions: Introductory Reports and Summary of Discussions*, International Symposium on Theory and Practice in Transport Economies, European Conference of Ministers of Transport, Paris, 1996.

TRINNAMAN, John: *Crisis or Opportunity? Trans-European Networks*, University of Hull, Centre for European Union Studies, Discussion Papers, Jean Monnet Group of Experts, 1995.

Websites

EU Transport Policy	http://europa.eu.int/pol/trans/en/trans.htm
DG VII (Transport)	http://europa.eu.int/en/comm/dg07/index.htm

10   COMMON COMMERCIAL POLICY

Simon Usherwood

I. RATIONALE

The Common Commercial Policy (CCP) has been a common policy of the EC since the Treaty of Rome in 1957. Given that it is one of only three common policies agreed at the time (along with agriculture and transport), one might ask why Member States have chosen to give it such importance.

Trade is of vital importance to the EC. Even before the 1995 enlargement, the EC accounted for 20% of global trade (39% when intra-EC trade is included). This, coupled to the 370 million people who live in the EC (the world's largest single market), gives trade a key economic role. Some 10–12 million jobs depend directly on exports, making up about 9% of EC GDP.

But what are the advantages of a CCP ?

(a) *Logical consequence of a customs union.* The creation of the customs union in the Treaty of Rome required that a common external tariff (CET) be imposed at the EC's external frontier. It implies some kind of supranational management of the application of that CET and the custom union's relationship with other trading partners (see chapter 6).

(b) *Greater bargaining power at a global level.* Member States felt that they could enhance their bargaining power in international fora (such as GATT/WTO) if they spoke and acted as one, rather than individually.

(c) *A substitute for a Common Foreign Policy.* The Treaty of Rome followed the failure of the EDC Treaty in 1954. Foreign policy was thereafter treated primarily in the transatlantic relationship, rather than a European one.

Consequently, it was felt that it would be easier to integrate commercial policies (low politics) than foreign or defence policies (high politics). Although this dynamic was more relevant in the 1950s, it still plays some role today, as witnessed by the continuing problems of creating an effective CFSP (see chapter 20).

II. LEGAL BASIS, OBJECTIVES

II.1 Legal Basis

(a) CCP is one of the main activities of the EC (TEC Arts. 3b, 18, 110).

(b) Common Customs Tariff (TEC Arts. 18–28).

(c) Genuine CCP Articles (TEC Arts. 110–15):

TEC Art. 110: aims for the 'harmonious development of world trade, the progressive abolition of restrictions on international trade and the lowering of customs barriers'.

TEC Art. 112: provides for a harmonised system in the granting of aid for exports to third countries.

TEC Art. 113: is the central legal provision in CCP. Due to the vagueness of its wording it has been the subject of much conflicting interpretation. It refers to a CCP without defining its scope. The main points are:

— Principle of uniformity: trade policy common to all Member States.

— Non-exhaustive list of subjects included in CCP (tariff rates, conclusion of trade agreements, measures to protect trade, etc.).

— Commission has the sole right to initiate legislation on the basis of TEC Art. 113. Council acts by qualified majority.

— The Commission negotiates agreements with third countries or international organisations on the authorisation of the Council. Commission conducts negotiations in consultation with the 113 Committee of civil servants, appointed by the Council (see III). The Council concludes the agreements. Relevant provisions of TEC Art. 228 apply.

TEC Art. 115: is a safeguard clause in case of economic difficulties in one or more Member State. It allows *temporary* restrictions on the import of products originating outside the EC, under the Commission's authorisation. Since the establishment of the Internal Market (IM) in 1993, TEC Art. 115 has been completely disapplied, despite its continued presence in the Treaty.

(d) Other relevant provisions:

TEC Art. 228. The EC has the power to conclude international agreements, in areas within its sphere of competence. The procedure for making such agreements is the same as for TEC Art. 113, with the Council acting by QMV, unless the relevant internal Treaty provision requires unanimity, in which case the Council uses unanimity.

TEC Art. 229. The Commission maintains 'all appropriate' relations with UN, GATT/WTO and other international organisations.

TEC Art. 238. Association Agreements. These create an association with reciprocal rights and obligations between the EC and the third state. They often act as a stepping stone to accession to the EU (as in CEECs).

The EC has *exclusive* competence in CCP — Member States are no longer competent to act on their own with regard to commercial policy measures (see ECJ *Opinions 1/75, 1/78* and *1/94*), unless they have express authorisation from the Commission (see also VI).

II.2 Objectives

CCP revolves around two basic objectives. On the one hand, the EC aims to *promote an open multilateral trading system.* On the other, it aims to *defend EC interests* in relations with trading partners. In so doing, the EC has worked within the framework of the 1947 General Agreement on Tariffs and Trade (GATT).

III. KEY ACTORS

Commission
Under TEC Art. 113, the Commission makes proposals to implement the CCP; it recommends to the Council to open negotiations; it negotiates international agreements; and it represents and/or observes for the EU in international trade bodies. Furthermore it permits Member States to adopt safeguard measures under TEC Art. 115. In consequence, it is the Commission which sets much of the tone of CCP, both internally and externally, and has proved to be a key means of displaying the benefits of a concerted European action internationally.

Primary responsibility for CCP rests with DG I (Commercial Policy and Relations with North America, the Far East, Australia and New Zealand), supported by the two other external relations DGs — DG IA and DG IB — and, to a lesser extent DG III (Industry), DG VII (Transport) and DG XV (Internal Market and Financial Services).

Council
The Council is the other key actor in CCP, alongside the Commission. While the Commission negotiates, it is the Council which gives the former its negotiating mandate and it is the Council which actually signs agreements with

third countries, regional blocs and organisations. In short, while the Commission proposes, the Council decides, and this relationship has shaped the way that CCP has developed. As the representative of Member States' interests, the Council often holds a different view of the options and possibilities than the Commission, and so attempts to use its powers to full effect: this is seen in the use of tightly phrased negotiating mandates and the 113 Committee (see below).

European Parliament
One of the results of the fight for supremacy between Commission and Council has been a continuing weak role for the EP. Even Amsterdam has done little more than formalise current practices of information of progress before and during negotiations (the so-called Luns–Westerterp procedure). The only point where the EP has a substantial leverage is in its right of assent to agreements made under TEC Art. 228.3 para. 2 (agreements establishing an institutional framework, or with important financial implications, or amending an act agreed by co-decision) and TEC Art. 238 (association agreements). Beyond this power, the EP has only limited consultation rights (TEC Art. 228.3).

European Court of Justice
The ECJ's role is, like the EP's, rather limited. The Court can give its opinion on the compatibility of agreements with the Treaties under TEC Art. 228.6, as it did with the Uruguay Round (see IV).

113 Committee
As already discussed above, the Council tries to control the Commission as much as it can and the 113 Committee is a prime player in this. Made up of high-level Member States civil servants, and named after TEC Art. 113, it acts as a political watchdog (it is also known as the *Comité des belles-mères*), overseeing the Commission in negotiations. While it is supposed to support the Commission in its capacity as a consultative body, all too often it is a competitor, especially in the many grey areas of negotiating competence. The net result is an obvious problem of coherence and flexibility in the EU's overall position, and increased tensions between all involved.

IV. POLICY SCOPE

The scope, both instrumentally and materially, of CCP has been highly contested between the EC and Member States.

IV.1 Instrumental Scope

Measures to be included in CCP: changes in tariff rates, conclusion of tariff and trade agreements, etc., as in TEC Art. 113. Two interpretations:

(a)   *Commission interpretation (instrumental approach)*: the inclusion of a measure in CCP should be made according to its specific character as an instrument regulating international trade. For example, the General System of Preferences (GSP), even if used in development policy, is nonetheless a trade instrument and thus should fall under the scope of CCP (i.e., TEC Art. 113 — Council votes with QMV).

(b)   *Council interpretation (finalist approach)*: only measures which have the sole purpose of influencing the volume or flow of trade should fall within CCP. Since the purpose of GSP is development through trade, the measures of the GSP should not fall in the scope of CCP and therefore should be adopted according to TEC Art. 235 (i.e., Council votes with unanimity).

ECJ Ruling on GSP (March 1987). The ECJ gave a pragmatic interpretation: trade policy is a concept which has evolved and therefore the legal basis of GSP is TEC Art. 113, and QMV applies in the Council, to the Commission's advantage.

IV.2 Material Scope

The areas that CCP can cover. Originally, CCP only related to trade in merchandise goods. However, world trade has become considerably more diverse than simple trade in goods, with trade-related issues of services, trade-related aspects of intellectual property rights and investments that are not purely financial.

There is no definition of the material scope of CCP in the Treaty, so it is important to determine what falls under the scope of TEC Art. 113, as this will determine whether the EC has exclusive competence to act in the area in question or not.

Negotiations prior to the TEU swung between the restrictive interpretation of the Council and the much more inclusive and broad viewpoint of the Commission.

The resolution came with ECJ *Opinion 1/94*, following the Commission request to the ECJ to confirm the exclusive competence of the EC to conclude the major parts of the WTO Agreement. The Opinion of the Court was more in line with the views of the Council (namely a restrictive interpretation) and the majority of Member States. The Court ruled:

(a) The EC has sole exclusive competence, under TEC Art. 113, to conclude the multilateral agreements on trade in goods. This also includes agriculture.

(b) One aspect of GATS — the cross-frontier supplies of services — is covered by TEC Art. 113 (commercial presence, consumption abroad, and presence of natural persons do not fall within the scope of CCP).

(c) Apart from provisions of the conclusion of international agreements concerning border measures to prevent the release for free circulation of counterfeit goods, the TRIPS Agreement does not fall within the scope of CCP.

Thus, the EC and the Member States are jointly competent to conclude both GATS and TRIPS.

The Treaty of Amsterdam has modified TEC Art. 113 to take account of these rulings. However, the new ToA/TEC Art. 300 does not solve the problem of competence (see VI).

V. POLICY INSTRUMENTS AND AGREEMENTS

V.1 Instruments

V.1.1 Regulatory Framework for Imports and Exports

Common External Tariff (CET) and Most Favoured Nation (MFN)
The CET, established in July 1968, is a key regulatory instrument of CCP. It decides the common EC tariff to be levied on imports into the Community. The CET is inextricably linked to GATT/WTO and the MFN Clause (which provides for the same treatment to be replicated for all third countries).

Import Regulation 3285/94 of 22 December 1994
This regulation provides common rules for imports into the EU. Normally there is unrestricted market access, which means a ban on any quantitative restrictions and thus customs duties. Exceptions to this include safeguard and surveillance measures; products from state trading countries and non-GATT members; some textile products; agricultural products covered by Common Market Organisations (see chapter 7).

Export Regulation 2063/69 of 26 December 1969
Exports from EU to third countries are in general unrestricted.

General System of Preferences
Provides duty-free access for industrial products and for some 400 agricultural products to the EC market within certain quantity limits (see chapter 14).

V.1.2 Trade Protection/Defence Measures

Safeguard and surveillance measures: Regulation 3285/94
These protect EC producers against a boost of imports not resulting from
subsidies or dumping. Such measures may only be taken if the producer suffers
serious injury (for safeguard measures) or a threat of serious injury (surveillance measures). Measures can be applied on a regional basis: the Commission,
subject to review by the Council, is entitled to impose these measures, but
without hindering the IM. Safeguard measures may take the form of
quantitative restrictions. TEC Art. 115 also allowed for safeguard measures
between Member States, authorised by the Commission. Since 1993, no new
TEC Art. 115 measures have been authorised.

Quantitative Restrictions (TEC Art. 36)
For imports circulating in the EC, quantitative restrictions may also be applied
in case of a TEC Art. 36 exception (public morality, public policy, public
security, protection of health, etc.) or of a 'mandatory requirement' (see
chapter 6).

Voluntary Export Restraints (legal basis TEC Art. 113)
Poorly defined. Reflect a grey area and thus difficult to evaluate. VERs are often
applied on an informal level, on the basis of informal gentlemen's agreements
to limit exports of certain products. VERs are to be phased out over a period of
four years following the conclusion of the Uruguay Round (with the exception
of the Japan–EU agreement on automobiles which lasts until 1999).

*Anti-dumping duties (Regulation 384/96), countervailing measures (Regulation
3284/94)*
Dumping means that a product is sold below its normal value. Normal value
refers to the price at which the product is sold in the home market of the
exporter or elsewhere or the full cost of production with a minimum margin for
profit. GATT has tightened this definition, reducing the EC's discretion.
    Countervailing duties are aimed at curbing export subsidies or export
premiums. Regulation 3284/94 tackles subsidies both by national and
sub-national levels of government.
    The Commission receives complaints from Member States or industries
which consider themselves injured or under threat. The Commission carries out
the investigation in both anti-dumping and countervailing duties cases and the
Council adopts protective duties. Voting in the Council is by simple majority.

The new trade policy instrument, Regulation 3286/94
Instrument used to retaliate against unfair competition or illicit practice with regard to EC exports in third markets. It can be invoked by persons representing a Community industry or by individual enterprises and it is directed against illicit trade practices by third states. Any commercial policy measures can be taken, on the condition that it is done in compatibility with existing international obligations, e.g., suspension or withdrawal of concessions, raising of customs duties, quantitative restrictions.

The Commission conducts the investigation and the Council decides on the nature of retaliation. If the Community decides to activate dispute settlement mechanisms, these should normally be through the dispute settlement procedures of the WTO.

V.2 Agreements with Third Countries and Regional Blocs

V.2.1 Types of Agreements

Simple trade agreements — TEC Art. 113
Agreements of this type deal exclusively with *commercial* matters, normally import and export issues.

Trade and cooperation agreements — TEC Arts. 113, 235 and 228
These are usually called 'Agreements for commercial and economic cooperation' and involve more than just trade regulations. They also provide for consultations in various fields: economic, industrial, technical, scientific, transport and environmental. Usually there are joint committee meetings and exchanges of views on a regular basis. May be either reciprocal or non reciprocal.

Association agreements — TEC Arts. 113, 228 and 238
These agreements create strong ties between the partners and involve genuine trade elements and political elements that enrich the trade relation. These give preferential access.

Two types of association agreements exist: those with an evolutive clause — seen as a stepping stone to EU membership (although this is not automatic, e.g., Turkey) — and those without, used for development purposes.

Interim agreements
An established practice whereby trade provisions of association or trade and cooperation agreements can come into force in advance of other provisions by way of interim agreements, concluded by the EC alone without the need for Member States' ratification, since TEC Art. 113 is an exclusive competence of the EC.

V.2.2 External Trading Relations by Area

European Economic Area
Provides for free movement of goods, capital, services and even persons throughout the EEA on the basis of the relevant EC *acquis*. Also includes the application of EC competition rules. Essentially this will lead, with a few exceptions (e.g., agriculture), to the extension of the IM to the participating EFTA countries (see chapter 6).

Central and Eastern Europe
Before 1988, there were no formal relations between the EC and CEECs. For the most part, these countries were considered state-trading countries and thus were not even granted MFN treatment under GATT. CEECs' exports faced considerable trade obstacles often in the form of national or Community quantitative restrictions.

There were almost no attempts to liberalise trade between the EC and CEECs, apart from some restrictive sectoral agreements in agriculture, steel and textiles. Following the EC–Comecon Declaration of 1988, the situation went from no cooperation at all to rapid progress towards trade liberalisation. First-generation trade and cooperation agreements were signed with Hungary and Poland and Czechoslovakia. GSP was progressively introduced from 1990 onwards.

Second-generation agreements consisted of association 'Europe Agreements', which were signed in December 1991 with Poland, Hungary, and Czechoslovakia. At a later stage, Europe Agreements were also concluded with Romania and Bulgaria, and two separate agreements were renegotiated for the Czech and Slovak Republics.

Country	Date signed	Date of entry into force
Poland	16 December 1991	1 February 1994
Hungary	16 December 1991	1 February 1994
Czechoslovakia: Czech Republic Slovakia	16 December 1991 4 October 1993 4 October 1993	 1 February 1995 1 February 1995
Romania	1 February 1993	1 February 1995
Bulgaria	8 March 1993	1 February 1995
Estonia	12 June 1995	1 February 1998
Latvia	12 June 1995	1 February 1998
Lithuania	12 June 1995	1 February 1998
Slovenia	15 June 1995	1 January 1997

The main trade provisions of the Europe Agreements are:

(a)   establishment of a free trade area over a period of 10 years: gradual elimination of quotas and duties on both sides, with more rapid liberalisation on the EC side;

(b)   granting of very *limited* trade concessions in agriculture and fisheries;

(c)   liberalisation of services (with special arrangements for transport); free movement of capital and payments related to free movement of goods and foreign direct investment;

(d)   application of competition rules (including anti-dumping) similar to the EC's;

(e)   political conditionality.

At the Essen European Council of December 1994, a pre-accession strategy was agreed (see chapter 23).

A Europe Agreement has also been signed with Slovenia (June 1996). An interim trade agreement entered into force 1 January 1997.

In July 1997, the Commission proposed a system of pre-accession aid in Agenda 2000, which accompanied its *avis* on enlargement, to develop transport and environment infrastructures, beginning in 2000.

Baltic states
Individual free trade agreements were signed with Estonia, Latvia and Lithuania in July 1994 (replacing trade and cooperation agreements), covering two-way free trade in industrial products. These were renegotiated into full Europe Agreements in 1995. All three countries are also included in the pre-accession strategy.

Commonwealth of Independent States
Non-preferential partnership and cooperation agreements were signed with CIS members in 1994. These agreements replace the 1989 trade and cooperation agreement with the former Soviet Union and will be wider in scope. These agreements basically abolish EU quantitative restrictions on imports of most products from these countries. Some interim trade agreements have been signed in advance of full ratification of partnership and cooperation agreements.

Mediterranean Countries
The Mediterranean participants at the Barcelona Conference, November 1995: Cyprus, Malta, Turkey, Algeria, Egypt, Morocco, Tunisia, Israel, Palestinian Autonomous Territories, Jordan, Lebanon and Syria. *EU–Mediterranean Partnership* — ambitious aim of creating a free trade area by 2010 (see chapter 6).

Cyprus, Turkey and Malta already have associate status with the EU. Cyprus is in the process of planning a customs union. Turkey signed its association agreement in 1963 and has been in a customs union with the EC since 1996. Since freezing its application to join the EU in 1996, Malta started to negotiate a Free Trade Area in 1998.

African, Caribbean and Pacific Countries (ACP)
These countries have been provided very preferential liberal treatment under the framework of the Lomé Conventions (see chapter 14). Commercial elements of Lomé include:

(a) almost complete duty-free entry of industrial exports into the EU without any quantitative restrictions;

(b) agricultural products are also almost duty-free, though there are some quantitative restrictions;

(c) preferential treatment in trade, financial support (export earnings) and technical assistance (aid projects) is provided.

Other less developed countries, not falling under the Lomé Convention or the Mediterranean agreements, may be granted GSP status by the EU.

Asia
Non-preferential agreements signed with Sri Lanka (July 1994), India (entered into force August 1994), being negotiated with Vietnam. Framework trade and cooperation agreement has been negotiated with South Korea. Main aims of the agreements to improve conditions for trade and investment, stress protection of the environment and strengthen political environment.

Latin America
All covered by GSP. 14 countries covered by specific regional trade and cooperation agreements. December 1995, EU–MERCOSUR (Argentina, Brazil, Paraguay, Uruguay) meeting with the aim of political dialogue and an eventual free trade agreement. Efforts to establish closer commercial ties with Mexico and Chile.

South Africa
Cooperation agreement EU–South Africa (October 1994). Partial membership of Lomé since 1997, but outside the Convention's general trading system, given its economic size and development. Instead, a bilateral FTA agreement is being negotiated.

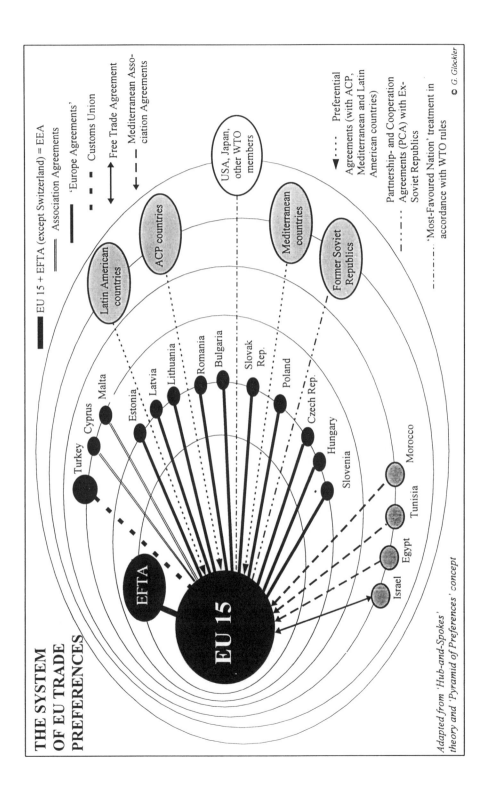

THE SYSTEM
OF EU TRADE
PREFERENCES

━━━ EU 15 + EFTA (except Switzerland) = EEA
Association Agreements

· · · · 'Europe Agreements'

╍ ╍ Customs Union

↕ Free Trade Agreement

╌ ╌ Mediterranean Association Agreements

▼ · · · · Preferential Agreements (with ACP, Mediterranean and Latin American countries)

╌ · ╌ Partnership- and Cooperation Agreements (PCA) with Ex-Soviet Republics

╌ · · ╌ 'Most-Favoured Nation' treatment in accordance with WTO rules

© G. Glöckler

Latin American countries

ACP countries

USA, Japan, other WTO members

Mediterranean countries

Former Soviet Republics

Turkey
Cyprus
Malta
Estonia
Latvia
Lithuania
Romania
Bulgaria
Slovak Rep.
Poland
Czech Rep.
Hungary
Slovenia
Morocco
Tunisia
Egypt
Israel

EFTA

EU 15

Adapted from 'Hub-and-Spokes' theory and 'Pyramid of Preferences' concept

VI. RECENT DEVELOPMENTS

VI.1 The Conclusion of the Uruguay Round and the WTO

With the conclusion of the Uruguay Round of the GATT at Marrakesh in April 1994, after some eight years of negotiations, the final pillar of the post-war international economic system was finally put in place. The World Trade Organisation (WTO) stands next to the World Bank and the IMF as a key institution on the global level.

The WTO's main functions are:

(a)   to administer and implement the multilateral and plurilateral trade agreements which make up the WTO;

(b)   to act as a forum for multilateral trade negotiations;

(c)   to seek to resolve disputes;

(d)   to oversee national trade policies;

(e)   to cooperate with other international institutions involved in global economic policy.

Main Elements of Uruguay

(a)   Reduction of average tariffs for industrialised countries from 5 to 3.5%.

(b)   *Extension of GATT to include textiles and agriculture.* Multi-Fibre Agreements (MFAs) in the textiles sector are to be phased out over 10 years, while non-tariff measures in agriculture are to be replaced by tariffs (the so-called tariffication; see chapter 7).

(c)   *General Agreement on Trade in Services (GATS).* Trade in services is incorporated for the first time into international trade rules, based on the principle of progressive liberalisation. A GATS Council has been established.

(d)   *General Agreement on Trade-related Aspects of Intellectual Property Rights (TRIPS).* Setting of minimum standards of protection for: patents, trademarks, copyrights, design rights, etc. Many of the rules taken from existing international conventions. Flexibility has been allowed for LDCs and state-trading countries in transition. A TRIPS Council has been established.

(e)   *Dispute Settlement Understanding.* Establishment of a Dispute Settlement Body with the authority to establish panels to decide on complaints and disputes arising between members of the WTO. This marks a big step forward for the juridical control of world trade, while still leaving room for common understandings between disputing parties.

(f)   *Programme of work.* The 1994 Marrakesh Accords laid out a comprehensive programme of negotiations to be completed before 2000, in all areas of the WTO's competence. Until another comprehensive round of negotiations is agreed upon, this will ensure continuing progress in trade liberalisation. In

March 1998 the Council and Commission declared their support for opening a 'Millennium Round' in 2000 to continue tariff reductions. This would also deal with issues such as trade and competition and investment and competition.

The First Ministerial Conference of the WTO was held in Singapore in December 1996. Here members' commitment to the multilateral system was confirmed in the Ministerial Declaration. New areas will be looked at (trade and investment; trade and competition policy; public procurement). Agreement was reached on IT products, and the pharmaceutical products list was extended. A subsequent agreement on telecommunications was reached in February 1997, after renewed post-Singapore negotiations (see chapter 18).

VI.2 Treaty of Amsterdam

At Amsterdam, the provisions on CCP were both extended and clarified. Old provisions, relating to the initial transitional period of the Treaty of Rome, were removed and all remaining Articles were renumbered:

Current TEC provisions	Provisions after Amsterdam
Arts. 18–28 (CET)	Repealed
Art. 110 (Principles)	Art. 131 — unchanged
Art. 112 (Harmonised system for export aid)	Art. 132 — references to transition period removed
Art. 113 (CCP functioning)	Art. 133 — unchanged, apart from a new 133.5, which allows the use of the article to conclude agreements in services and intellectual property rights. This requires unanimity in the Council and EP
Art. 115 (Temporary restrictions)	Art. 134 — unchanged
Art. 228 (International agreements)	Art. 300 — new 300.2. This allows for provisional application of an agreement before it comes into force. The same procedure (QMV, unless a unanimity policy or an ToA Art.310 agreement) can be used to suspend application of an agreement, or to form Community positions in a ToA Art.310 body, when that body has to adopt decisions with legal effect (but not for modification of the institutional framework). The EP is now to be immediately and fully informed of any decisions taken under ToA Arts. 300 or 310
Art. 229 (UN and GATT relations)	Art. 302 — unchanged
Art. 238 (Association agreements)	Art. 310 — unchanged

VI.3 The Transatlantic Marketplace

In March 1998, the Commission approved a plan by Commissioners Brittan, Bangemann and Monti on a Transatlantic Marketplace. This proposal is intended to create a legally binding New Transatlantic Market (NTM). To achieve this, the Commission suggests negotiations in four key areas:

(a)   abolition of all customs duties on industrial products by 2010, in accordance with MFN rules and conditional upon other trading partners also participating;

(b)   a free trade area for services;

(c)   continued removal of technical barriers to trade in goods;

(d)   liberalisation in the areas of public procurement, intellectual property and investment.

The proposal would not cover the controversial sectors of agriculture or audiovisual industries.

Reaction from Member States and the US was somewhat muted. France rejected the proposal almost immediately, saying it preferred to use the WTO route to achieve trade liberalisation. Other Member States have also expressed concern about the compatibility of the NTM with WTO rules. The US has shown some interest, but would appear to be waiting for a decision by the Council. In April 1998, the Council put the proposal on hold, both because of the opposition of Member States and because of the ongoing problems of the US Helms–Burton and d'Amato laws (which fine companies trading in the US who also trade with 'rogue states'). This means the NTM was not be discussed at the May 1998 EU–US Summit in London.

VII. FURTHER READING

BARNES, Ian and BARNES, Pamela: 'The European Union and the world trading system', in Barnes, Ian and Barnes, Pamela: *The Enlarged European Union*, London, Longman, 1995, pp. 358–85.

MESSERLIN, Patrick: *La Nouvelle Organisation Mondiale du Commerce*, Paris, IFRI, 1995.

TSOUKALIS, Loukas: *The New European Economy: The Politics and Economics of Integration*, Oxford, OUP, 1993.

WOOLCOCK, Stephen and HODGES, Michael: 'EU policy in the Uruguay Round', in Wallace, Helen and Wallace, William (eds), *Policy Making in the European Union*, Oxford, OUP, 1996, pp. 301–23.

Website

| DGI (Common Commercial Policy) | http://europa.eu.int/en/comm/dg01/dg1.htm |

11 COMPETITION POLICY

Gabriel Glöckler

I. RATIONALE

EC competition policy can be conceived as following the *functional logic* of 'common rules for a common market'. Historically, competition policy was a central element of the political economy of the original EC. In a single market, national trade policy instruments of Member States in their dealings with each other became obsolete; a common competition policy reassured Member States against 'unfairness' from their partners.

Competition policy at EC level is needed because a market of the size of the EC means that decisions have to be taken at the appropriate level, i.e., for the entire EC (application of subsidiarity). Moreover, given the different (economic and social) impact of market integration in the Member States, a supranational, neutral enforcement mechanism for competition rules was needed to foster acceptance and credibility of the IM as a whole. *Regulatory efficiency* justifies EC competition policy. Companies prefer a 'one-stop shop' in EC-wide competition disputes, e.g., for cross-border mergers where firms avoid multiple dealings with national competition authorities in the Member States.

Finally, EC competition policy is an *instrument for achieving the objectives of the EC*. It is based on the conviction that market forces produce efficient allocation of resources, more effective supply structures, resulting in better quality products and services at lower prices to the consumer. Moreover, a truly competitive market provides incentives for initiative and innovation which render the EU economy as a whole more competitive in the global market. Thus, competition within the IM is seen as a means to achieve 'harmonious and balanced development of economic activities, sustainable and non-inflationary growth respecting the environment, a high degree of convergence of economic performance, a high level of employment and of social protection, the raising of the standard of living and quality of life, and economic and social cohesion' (TEC Art. 2).

This broad statement of the beneficial effects of competition rests on a whole set of philosophies, ideologies and economic theories:

(a)   A non-economic interpretation of the merits of competition asserts that competition guarantees openness, freedom of choice and initiative in society. Competition policy therefore has the objective of diffusing economic power, because large economic concentrations might undermine the democratic policy process and obtain privileges and protectionism.

(b)   The economic arguments rest on two divergent philosophies which prescribe rather different objectives of competition policy (see Williams, Pelkmans):

Harvard School	Austrian/Chicago School
stresses merits of competition per se. Free markets may be incompatible with competitive industrial structures because they produce — if uncontrolled — concentration and dominant market position. Intervention is needed to ensure that competition is maintained. Main concern is thus *avoidance of anticompetitive structures*. Dominated 1950–70.	rests on premise that free markets will lead to best outcomes, even if unfettered market forces lead to concentration and dominant positions. Key concept: *potential competition*. Efficient firms will always prevail, while inefficient firms — however large and dominant — will sooner or later face more efficient new entrants. Main concern is to avoid barriers to entry for new competitors.

II. OBJECTIVES, LEGAL BASIS, PRINCIPLES

II.1 Objectives

Combining elements of these two divergent philosophies, '*EC competition policy is geared towards the prevention of market power and other distortions to competition and thereby helps to make the market function properly*' (Pelkmans). The EC has thus opted for a policy which aims at *workable competition* (as opposed to perfect competition), in which the pursuit of competition is balanced with wider goals such as:

(a)   *Social and redistributive objectives*:
  (i)   maintenance of high levels of employment;
  (ii)   avoidance of social hardship, e.g., by allowing *crisis cartels* where competitors are permitted a coordinated scrapping of capacity in order to facilitate adjustment and restructuring to lower sector-wide capacity;
  (iii) industrial policy as an alternative EC instrument to fulfilling these objectives conflicts with competition policy in many instances (see III).

(b)   *Market integration*: related to creation and proper functioning of a true IM by encouraging cross-border trade, even if this is not necessarily economically desirable.

(c)   *Protection of small and medium-sized enterprises (SMEs)*: SMEs contribute to a competitive environment, thereby assuring a diffusion of economic power.

(d)   *Consumer protection*: competition policy is conducted with a view to ensuring the greatest possible benefit to the consumers (see chapter 16).

Some anti-competitive practices, e.g., joint purchase by firms of raw materials at cheaper prices, are admissible for as long as the cost advantage is passed on to the consumer of the final product.

In practice, EC competition policy is committed to the ideal of a European economy without internal barriers. In the pursuit of this ideal, the Commission has — despite a fair degree of political sensitivity — earned the reputation of an 'ayatollah' for its placing of competition before either national interests or EC 'competitiveness'.

II.2 Legal Basis

Competition policy broadly covers two areas: (a) enterprise conduct (regulated by TEC Arts. 85, 86 and 91; Arts. 65 and 66 Treaty on ECSC) and (b) state intervention (TEC Arts. 37, 90, 92–4 TEC; Arts. 4 and 95 Treaty on ECSC).

TEC Title V, Chapter 1 'Rules on Competition'
— TEC Art. 85.1 prohibits agreements between firms and other concerted practices which might affect trade or distort competition.
— TEC Art. 85.3 regulates exemptions from above prohibition (either by exempting a whole category of agreements, through so-called *block exemptions*, or individual Commission decisions granting exemptions).
— TEC Art. 86 prohibits abuse of a dominant market position to distort competition and affect trade (also used by Commission for *ex post* control of mergers).

— TEC Art. 92.1 states incompatibility of state aids which distort competition with the IM.

— TEC Art. 92.2 and 3 list conditions for exceptions, i.e., state aids compatible with the IM.

— TEC Art. 90 stipulates that rules on competition policy apply also to public enterprises and utilities.

— TEC Art. 37 prohibits national monopolies of commercial nature to discriminate among Member States' nationals regarding its suppliers or outlets.

— Reg. 17/62 endows the Commission with far-reaching powers to enforce the EC's competition rules, to become 'policeman, prosecutor, judge and jury' in competition disputes (Wilks and McGowan).

— Reg. 19/65 empowers the Commission to establish a regime of block exemptions.

— Reg. 4064/89 establishes EC competence for control of corporate mergers and acquisitions (reformed in 1997; see VII).

— Art. 66 Treaty on ECSC endows High Authority/Commission with power to control mergers in the coal and steel sector.

II.3 Principles

Rather than giving an exhaustive list of prohibited practices or regulating competition through case-by-case decisions, EC competition policy rests on *universal prohibitions of anti-competitive behaviour* (e.g., restrictive agreements, abuse of dominant position, competition-distorting state subsidies, discriminatory behaviour of public undertakings).

However, a responsive regulation of a dynamic market requires some flexibility and the wider policy objectives of the EC and the Member States demand some differentiation of this otherwise very static regime. This is done through a system of *block exemptions* set out in the Treaty and which are being revised and applied by the Commission and interpreted by the ECJ.

Extra-territoriality implies that EC competition rules are applicable to non-EC firms if they conduct their business within the IM; moreover if the effect of restrictive practices (even if formulated by non-EC firms) is felt in the EC, these firms are liable under EC competition rules.

III. HORIZONTAL LINKAGES OF COMPETITION POLICY

Competition policy forms part of a wider regime of EC policies and provisions. Competition policy can complement, partly substitute or even conflict with other EC policies.

III.1 Industrial Policy

Traditional industrial policy and competition policy are fundamentally opposed since they follow two very different philosophies. Whereas competition policy relies on market forces to bring about efficient outcomes, industrial policy attempts to remedy perceived 'market failures' through government intervention. For the sake of social, political and economic objectives (e.g., low unemployment, avoidance of regional disparities, international competitiveness) governments intervene in the economy by means of:

(a)   state-directed restructuring of industries (e.g., through state aids, subsidies, protectionist measures, benefits for 'infant industries');

(b)   promotion of 'national' (or, at EC level, 'European') champions by allowing mergers that damage competition and deliberately exempting firms from competition;

(c)   discriminatory public procurement;

(d)   technology policy, e.g., state-financed R&D programmes.

Whereas some general and horizontal measures (i.e., affecting the economy as a whole and all sectors equally) are less distorting and even economically justifiable, sectoral measures (affecting only a particular sector) are in clear conflict with the aims and objectives of competition policy.

Since the 1980s, the EC industrial policy has lost its interventionist, anti-competitive ambitions and focused — in line with the prevailing neo-liberal paradigm — more on the maintenance of general conditions favourable to economic development. The 1993 White Paper on *Growth, Competitiveness and Employment* stresses a stable macroeconomic framework, efficient and flexible labour markets, TENs, R&D, as well as 'open and fair competition'. In this sense, competition policy now forms the centrepiece of industrial policy (see chapter 12).

III.2 Commercial Policy

Open trade policy represents a highly effective form of competition policy, because it exposes EC businesses to actual or potential competitive pressures; in fact, external exposure tends to exercise greater competitive discipline than intra-EC competition.

Anti-dumping duties, quantitative restrictions, etc. are trade policy instruments which directly affect intra-EC competition (see chapter 10).

Vice versa, application of competition policy within the EC affects trade relations with the EC's partners, the extraterritoriality principle greatly extends the reach of EC competition policy, e.g., Commission objections to Boeing–McDonnell Douglas merger (1997) had repercussions for US–EU relations.

III.3 Transport/Energy/Telecommunications Policy

Under the premise that regulation is only second-best to genuine competition, the application of competition policy may render unnecessary a number of regulatory requirements in those sectors, once they are liberalised and opened in the IM (see chapters 9 and 18).

Insistence upon more complete removal of barriers to a genuine EC energy market refocuses EC energy policy from its preoccupation with security of supply (perpetuating the cosy setting of national monopolies) to more competitive, consumer-oriented structures (see chapter 8).

III.4 Agricultural Policy

TEC Art. 42 exempts agricultural products from the EC's competition regime and Common Market Organisations are to be established (TEC Art. 43). The resulting market and price distortions for agricultural products can be seen as a vindication of a competition-based market order. Recent reforms aim at re-orienting agricultural production towards market mechanisms (see chapter 7).

IV. KEY ACTORS

European Commission
Conducts competition policy, acting either on its own initiative or following complaints by Member States, companies or individuals. Direct powers to investigate, decide, set fines, to implement and enforce its decisions ('policeman, prosecutor, judge and jury'); decisions within the Commission are taken by simple majority; DG IV deals with Competition, the Commissioner responsible for competition is Karel van Miert (Belgium).

European Parliament
Assesses the Commission's actions in an annual report and also issues observations on major developments in competition policy.

Council of Ministers
Limited to authorising block exemptions; sets and revises the legal basis on merger control.

European Court of Justice
Ultimate adjudicator of competition disputes, rules on matters of principle, i.e., checks whether Commission decisions infringe a Treaty provision; has

unlimited jurisdiction to modify certain fines (TEC. Art. 172). So far, the Court has usually confirmed the Commission's decisions on penalties.

Court of First Instance

To alleviate workload of the ECJ it also investigates factual content of competition disputes.

Enterprises

As policy-takers, enterprises are directly affected by the Commission's far-reaching powers. In case of objections to Commission decisions, enterprises can appeal against decisions in competition disputes and thus set in motion the review process before the ECJ (see chapter 5).

V. POLICY INSTRUMENTS

V.1 Anti-collusion Policy

TEC Art. 85 prohibits — and declares automatically void — all agreements which may (as objective or in effect) prevent, restrict or distort competition within the IM, such as price-fixing, quantitative restrictions on production, market sharing, control or limitation of R&D and investment, etc. Restrictive agreements can be:
— horizontal, e.g., price cartels;
— vertical, e.g., exclusive distribution or purchase agreements, e.g., between breweries and public houses, or oil companies and petrol stations;
— of other nature, e.g., agreements on short lifetime of a product.
However, certain kinds of cooperation are judged to be positive, and therefore do not fall under the TEC Art. 85 prohibition, e.g., when they contribute 'to improving the production or distribution of goods or to promoting technical or economic progress'.

The decisions for such exemptions are taken by the Commission either on a case-by-case basis, or under category exemptions, so-called *block exemptions*, which:
— are granted for some distribution systems, including franchising, R&D collaboration, transfer of technology and certain specialisation agreements (e.g., motor vehicle distribution and servicing agreements);
— are generally restricted to low (joint) market share and SMEs with a turnover ceiling.

V.2 Anti-monopoly Policy

TEC Art. 86 prohibits abuse of dominant position within a substantial part of the IM. Such abuse includes unfair prices (too high, too low, predatory pricing), unfair trading conditions, or discrimination among suppliers or consumers.

However, the application of TEC Art. 86 faces formidable problems of definition:

(a)   What is a dominant position? Dominant position is defined by the firm's ability to prevent competition and its power to behave independently from competitors and customers (ECJ in *United Brands*, 1978). Evaluation on basis of a number of criteria, e.g., market share.

(b)   How to define the relevant market? The relevant market is defined in two dimensions: the product market and the geographical market; definition is continuously revised by the Commission (most recently in 1997).

(c)   What is the relationship between existence and abuse of dominant position? In the past, the Commission and ECJ considered that the dominant firm's power to behave independently suffices to constitute an abuse; consequently, efforts to strengthen a dominant position, e.g., by taking over a rival, are also considered to be abuses and thus unlawful (see *Continental Can* ruling 1972). Only since the 1979 *Hoffmann–La Roche* case (85/76) has the Court defined 'abuse' as an 'objective concept' whereby 'competition is weakened with recourse to methods different from those which condition normal competition'. More recently, a clearer distinction has been made between 'dominant position' and 'abuse' (see *Tetra Pak II* ruling 1997).

TEC Art. 86 is no basis to divest or break up monopolies; ECJ and Commission can only condemn abuse and fine the abusers.

TEC Arts. 85/86 Proceedings

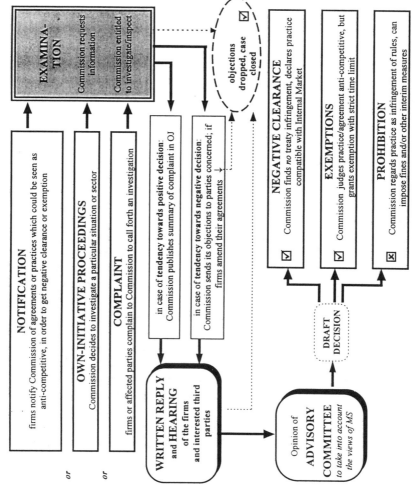

NOTIFICATION
firms notify Commission of agreements or practices which could be seen as anti-competitive, in order to get negative clearance or exemption

or

OWN-INITIATIVE PROCEEDINGS
Commission decides to investigate a particular situation or sector

or

COMPLAINT
firms or affected parties complain to Commission to call forth an investigation

EXAMINA-TION
Commission requests information
Commission entitled to investigate/inspect

objections dropped, case closed ☑

in case of **tendency towards positive decision**:
Commission publishes summary of complaint in OJ

in case of **tendency towards negative decision**:
Commission sends its objections to parties concerned; if firms amend their agreements →

WRITTEN REPLY and HEARING of the firms and interested third parties

Opinion of **ADVISORY COMMITTEE** *to take into account the views of MS*

DRAFT DECISION

NEGATIVE CLEARANCE
☑ Commission finds *no* treaty infringement, declares practice compatible with Internal Market

EXEMPTIONS
☑ Commission judges practice/agreement anti-competitive, but grants exemption with strict time limit

PROHIBITION
☒ Commission regards practice as infringement of rules, can impose fines and/or other interim measures

The great weakness of the procedure was the lack of clear time limits (some notifications take a number of years to reach the clearance stage). To remedy this untenable business condition, the Commission issues informal 'letters of comfort/discomfort' which, however, fail to deliver the legal certainty required by the undertakings because they are not enforceable before national courts.

V.3 Merger Control

The 1957 TEC contained no stipulation on merger control (in 1950s, cross-border mergers were rare and legally very difficult; also, merger control was seen as too sensitive to be 'communitarised'):
— over two decades, the Commission slowly established competence for mergers with a 'Community dimension';
— the ECJ's 1973 *Continental Can* ruling opened the way to *ex post* control of mergers, continued support for EC merger control through judgments;
— '1992 programme' led to rapid increase of cross-border mergers; with business favouring a 'one-stop shop', i.e., merger clearance from EC only.

The *1989 Merger Control Regulation* gave the Commission the power of *ex ante* merger control, i.e., to establish whether a planned takeover will lead to dominant position. With this competence, the Commission can block an agreement altogether or require companies to change it or dispose of assets so as to avoid dominant positions.

Up to 1995, there were only three refusals of mergers:

(a)   1991 ATR takeover of De Haviland (politically controversial, seen as undermining Europe's global competitive advantage);

(b)   1994 joint venture MSG by Bertelsmann, Deutsche Telekom and Taurus (uncontroversial, prevented blatantly obvious dominance).

(c)   1998 projected establishment of a German Digital Pay-TV conglomerate owned by Bertelsmann/Kirch/PREMIERE and Deutsche Telekom/Betaresearch (controversial within Germany).

Most mergers are influenced by DG IV's 'Mergers Task Force' during the negotiation stage; eventual approval of a merger is conditioned to fulfilment of conditions set by the Commission (e.g., set of conditions for approval of 1997 Boeing–McDonnell Douglas merger).

In 1997, a *revised merger regulation* was agreed upon. Since March 1998:

(a)   The regulation covers all structural joint ventures (i.e., merging companies have joint control, over the 'full function' and on a 'lasting basis').

(b)   New (i.e., reduced) turnover thresholds were introduced to cover deals which might otherwise lead to multiple national filings:

(i)   the threshold for aggregate worldwide turnover of the companies involved has been reduced to 2.5 billion ECU;

(ii)   the threshold for individual turnover within EC of at least two of the companies concerned was reduced to 100 million ECU (before 250 million) unless each firm derives more than two thirds of its EU-wide turnover within one Member State;

(iii)   in a new provision, the Commission considers *combined* aggregate turnover of merging companies in *at least three* Member States.

(c)   the method of calculating the turnover of credit and financial institutions was altered;

(d)   procedures and timetables were renewed.

Merger Control Proceedings *(as revised in 1997)*

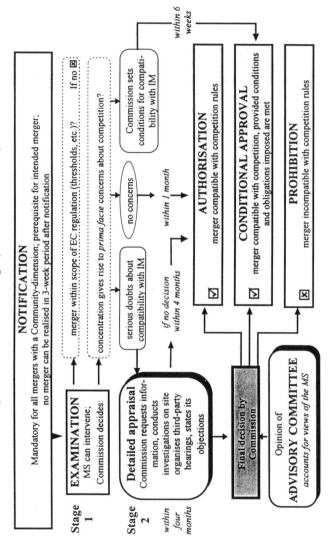

Most importantly, and to the satisfaction of the business community, a clear time frame was set for the completion of merger control proceedings.

V.4 Control of State Aids

TEC Arts. 92 and 93 prohibit state aids, i.e., public subsidies to private undertakings which threaten competition in trade between Member States. Exemptions are made. The conditions under which state aids are compatible with the IM are:

(a)   when aid promotes a development in the interests of the Union as a whole;

(b)   when the realisation of a project is entirely dependent on aid being available;

(c)   when the type and volume of aid are appropriate for the objectives which are hoped for.

In general, permissible aids should be linked to sectoral or regional objectives.

Taking stock: *Fifth Survey on State Aid in the European Union 1992–1994*

Overall state aids 1992–94: 95 billion ECU with slight downward trend since 1990–92; falls in cohesion countries (Greece, Spain, Portugal, Ireland), notable increases in Germany (new *Länder*):

— state aid to industry in 1992-94: 43 billion ECU or 1400 ECU per person employed, with downward trend, most aid concentrated in shipbuilding;

— state aid to non-manufacturing sectors (around 59% of total aid) particularly to railways and other transport; coal, steel, agriculture, fisheries.

State aids have long enjoyed major exceptions from the EC's otherwise strict and effective competition policy regime — at the price of heavy distortions to the IM. Whereas aid for R&D is acceptable and economically sensible, Member States' and the Commission's pursuit of wider objectives (than just competition) have made this relaxed practice possible.

The high politicisation of state aids reduces effectiveness of EC's surveillance system (e.g., subsidies to Air France in 1994–5); but EMU fiscal constraints and general convergence on pro-market policies have contributed to a gradual decrease of state aids.

Proceedings for New State Aids (similarly: Review of Existing Aids)

NOTIFICATION
MS have statutory duty to inform
Commission of plans to grant aid

Standstill position; MS
cannot pay out grants
until Commission has
reached decision

ASSESSMENT
Commission forms opinion on
compatibility of state aid with IM

NO formal investi-
gation necessary

Questions
raised

**FORMAL INVESTIGATION
PROCEEDINGS**
formal opening of procedure by
publication of notice in OJ
invitation of third parties' comments

Final decision by
Commission

APPROVAL
positive decision by Commission,
state aid judged compatible with IM

REFUSAL
Commission orders Member State to abolish or alter aid,
can demand recovery of aid already paid out

V.6 Utilities and Public Enterprises

TEC Art. 90 requires Member States to respect the competition rules in their policies for public undertakings to which they have granted special or exclusive rights. Member States must disclose their financial dealings with these undertakings and supply the necessary information on request from the Commission.

A number of problems arise with the application of TEC Art. 90:

(a)   The enterprises concerned are utilities or networks which pursue (or have to pursue) other than purely economic objectives; e.g., 'universal service' for telecoms and mail.

(b)   Main argument: economic burdens of 'universal service' (e.g., uniform price for letters even in remote areas) justify existence of exclusive rights or monopolies to the detriment of competition and the workings of the IM.

However, advancing privatisations of the utilities and network sectors in the Member States (e.g., Telefónica, Deutsche Telekom) have brought about increased willingness to allow competition into these sectors, e.g., 1998 liberalisation of telecoms market, proposed opening to competition of postal services (see chapter 18).

VI. HISTORICAL DEVELOPMENT

Competition policy at EC level had to combine very *different state traditions*. The UK has had a tradition of anti-trust and monopoly legislation, even though it was sometimes weakly enforced. However, France has had a strong tradition of interventionism and '*dirigisme*'. Germany's policy contained liberal strands and a general preference of '*Ordnungspolitik*' over '*Interventionspolitik*', not least because US administrators post-1945 put strong emphasis on anti-trust rules.

The *1952 ECSC Treaty* included competition (and even merger) rules. French acceptance of these was justified by the argument that strict anti-trust rules would avoid concentration and contain German economic power. Yet the economic context was very particular with the coal and steel sectors being essentially heavily regulated industries.

In the *1958 Rome Treaty on EEC*, the competition rules were strongly influenced by liberal bias of German notions of competition, but less strict than ECSC rules with more scope for intervention of Community authorities.

Before 1962, TEC Art. 85 remained virtually unenforced, owing to very different attitudes in the Member States. This was remedied by 1962 Council Resolution 17/62 empowering the Commission to enforce competition rules based on a uniform interpretation. The Commission thereby received *exclusive competence* for competition issues. The Commission's power was further enhanced in 1967 when the Council conferred the power to exempt by category (block exemptions).

Throughout the development of the EC, every step in completion of the IM has been accompanied by attempts of private and public actors in Member States to mitigate the competitive effects of market integration, *inter alia*, through collusive arrangements, mergers and state aids. The Commission and the ECJ have responded flexibly to these challenges, whilst retaining essentially the legal basis of the EEC Treaty.

Decisive rulings of the ECJ in the area of competition policy

1966 *Consten and Grundig* (56 and 58/64): ruled unlawful partitioning of the IM between supplier and distributor, guaranteeing the free movement of goods within the IM (as required by Member States — TEC Art. 37) also applies to private undertakings.

1972 *ICI* (48/69): in oligopoly, there is a thin line between explicit cooperation and implicit cooperation, ECJ ruled also implicit cooperation unlawful.

1973 *Continental Can* (6/72): defined that mergers can reinforce dominant position; ruling opened the way to *ex post* control of mergers by application of TEC Art. 86.

1978 *United Brands* (27/76): first explicit ECJ definition of 'dominant position'.

1993 *'Woodpulp'* (89 et al./85): if restrictive agreements are formulated outside EC (e.g., by non-EC firms) but they affect the IM, such agreements can be reviewed by the ECJ.

1996 *Tetra Pak II* (C-333/94): after investigating 'dominant position' in one relevant market, 'abuse' was found in another market where the undertaking was not actually dominant.

1998 *Kali und Salz* (C-68/94 and C-30/95): The ECJ confirmed the applicability of the Merger Reg. to 'collective dominance', i.e., when proposed concentration leads to oligopoistic market structures.

The *1989 Merger Control Regulation* granted the Commission the power to examine a planned merger or takeover with 'Community dimension' *before* it takes place and to demand alterations during the merger negotiations.

VII. RECENT DEVELOPMENTS

VII.1 Proposal for a European Cartel Office

— Predominantly German proposal, deriving from the wish for the purest possible application of competition rules.

— Rationale lies in German experience of independent bodies charged with the regulation and maintenance of market order (e.g., Bundesbank, Federal Cartel Office).

— Competition policy is strongly influenced by the views and dynamism of the relevant commissioner (e.g., P. Sutherland and L. Brittan regarded competition as aim in itself, K. van Miert more as a means to a series of other objectives) as well as by the political sensitivities within the Commission. Taking competition policy out of the Commission's hands would make it truly independent.

— Discussions so far within DG IV as well as between Member States, but no decision at Amsterdam.

VII.2 Revision of the 1989 Merger Regulation

In 1997, the Council agreed to modernise the legal basis for the EC decisions on mergers, as a consequence of a long battle between the Commission (supported by business), which was pressing for an extension of its own jurisdiction, and the Member States attempting to retain some competence for their national competition authorities. Overall, the revised regulation extends the Commission's jurisdiction — reflecting business people's desire for regulatory efficiency and a 'one stop-shop' — while adding complexity.

VII.3 The Amsterdam Summit and the Consolidation of the Treaties

Current TEC provisions	Provisions after Amsterdam
Art. 85 (Distortion of trade)	Art. 81 — unchanged
Art. 86 (Abuse of a dominant position)	Art. 82 — unchanged
Art. 87 (Supporting regulations)	Art. 83 — references to transition period removed
Art. 88 (Member State compliance)	Art. 84 — unchanged
Art. 89 (Implementation of ERDF)	Art. 85 — unchanged
Art. 90 (Public undertakings)	Art. 86 — unchanged
Art. 91 (Dumping)	Repealed
Art. 92 (State aids)	Art. 87 — removal of shipbuilding from possible exemptions
Art. 93 (State aids procedure)	Art. 88 — unchanged
Art. 94 (State aids decision-making)	Art. 89 — unchanged

VIII. FUTURE PROSPECTS

VIII.1 Reforming Competition Policy

The current rules, dating from the 1950s are incapable of dealing with the increased workload. In fact the system has become almost unmanagable, due to:
— increased number of cases as IM integrates (e.g., backlog of some 1300 cases of TEC Arts. 85 and 86 proceedings in 1996);
— long delays (e.g., up to 10 years before formal clearance); legal uncertainty (e.g., for cases of informal clearance through letter of comfort);
— cases becoming more complex and politically controversial.
DG IV has only limited resources, and is thus less and less capable of handling this workload.

Proposals for Internal Reform

— Decrease workload by filtering out cases which do not require EC attention, e.g., raise thresholds, exempt more types of agreements.
— Consequently, more cases are to be left to Member States' competition authorities.
— Establish legally binding deadlines (e.g., new merger regulation).
— Depoliticise state aid procedures by making investigations more transparent and inviting third-party opinions.

Competition and Globalisation

EU competition policy is primarily concerned with maintaining competition *within* the EU. Yet as globalisation increasingly integrates the world economy, some of the EU's competition rules — and the Commission's strict interpretation of them — might actually undermine the competitiveness of the EU firms vis-à-vis international competitors. This is the underlying debate within the EU, between Member States and the Commission; a conflict which, in the longer term, could find a solution in a global approach to competition rules.

VIII.2 Towards a Global Competition Order?

Worldwide operations of multinational firms require a global perspective on competition issues. In an attempt to establish some form of global governance structure for adjudication of competition disputes, the EC has:
— *concluded an EC–US anti-trust cooperation agreement* (1991) — fruitful discussion, but problems with confidentiality of companies' business information and lack of real conflict resolution mechanism in case of substantive differences;
— joined multilateral cooperation efforts, such as the OECD proposals on convergence of national competition rules and procedures (e.g., regarding enforcement, time delays);
— proposed the WTO as the appropriate body not only to deal with trade-related competition issues (including anti-competitive practices) but also to identify core competition rules and procedures which could be adopted at international level.

The 1997 WTO Basic Telecommunications Agreement can be seen as a first success. It binds 69 countries to common regulatory principles including competition rules (similar to TEC Arts. 86 and 90). Moreover, in June 1998, the EU and US signed an agreement on application of positive comity. This would allow one party to ask the other to investigate a merger in the latter's territory.

IX. FURTHER READING

ALLEN, David: 'Competition policy: policing the Single Market' in WALLACE, Helen and WALLACE, William (eds): *Policy Making in the European Union*, Oxford, OUP, 1996, pp. 157–83.

BULMER, Simon: 'Institutions and policy change in the European Communities: the case of merger control,' *Public Administration*, vol. 72, 1994, pp. 423–44.

EUROPEAN COMMISSION: *XXVIth Annual Report on Competition Policy in the European Community 1996*, Luxembourg, EUR-OP, 1997.

NEVILLE, David et al.: *Merger in Daylight: the Economics and Politics of European Merger Control*, London, Centre of Economic Policy Research, 1993.

PELKMANS, Jacques: *European Integration: Methods and Economic Analysis*, Harlow, Longman, 1997 (especially pp. 183–205).

WILKS, Stephen and McGOWAN, Len: 'Disarming the Commission: the debate over a European Cartel Office', *Journal of Common Market Studies*, vol. 33, 1995, pp. 259–73.

OXFORD REVIEW OF ECONOMIC POLICY, issue on competition policy, vol. 9, No. 2 Summer 1993, especially articles by WILLIAMS, Mark E.: 'The effectiveness of competition policy in the United Kingdom' and HAY, Donald: 'The assessment: competition policy'.

Website

| DG IV (Competition) | http://europa.eu.int/en/comm/dg04/dg04home.htm |

12 INDUSTRIAL POLICY AND RESEARCH AND DEVELOPMENT POLICY

Lie Junius

INDUSTRIAL POLICY

I. DEFINITION AND RATIONALE

I.1 Defining Industrial Policy

There is no generally accepted definition of industrial policy. But here it is understood to cover all government intervention in the economy to correct market failure and to steer the economy in order to realise certain economic (e.g., competitiveness through structural adjustment), political (e.g., protection and/or promotion of certain industries) and social objectives (e.g., employment, redistributive goals). This definition of industrial policy covers a wide range of policies such as competition policy (guarantee a competitive environment), deregulation policies (to remove obstacles to the Internal Market (IM)), social policy, regional policy and research and development policy.

Government intervention can take the form of (Nicolaides, 1992):

(a) *Active or negative policy:*

—active policy: a policy which tends to shape the industrial structure and intends to improve performance (*Interventionspolitik*);

—negative policy (passive): a policy which corrects market failures and removes barriers to enhance a stable economic environment (*Ordnungspolitik*).

(b) *Horizontal or general/sectoral policy*:

—horizontal policy: a policy which affects all sectors of industry at the same time;
—sectoral policy: a policy which focuses on particular sectors.

I.2 Rationale for Industrial Policy

Generally, there is a debate between economic schools and political traditions. Three economic schools can be identified (McDonald and Daerden, 1991):

(a) *Market-based or negative industrial policy*: relies on the conviction that market mechanisms on their own are able to produce an efficient industrial structure. Government intervention is exceptionally allowed in *significant* cases of market failure, e.g., underprovision of R&D expenditure. We can call this kind of intervention a negative policy since this policy limits itself to the prevention of abuse of market power and the removal of obstacles to free trade.

(b) *Interventionist or positive industrial policy*: this school claims that there is a need for intervention to correct market failures and to allow the development of a dynamic industrial base. Social and regional factors especially justify intervention. This school tolerates intervention in a wide range of sectors and industries (declining and rising industries).

(c) *Selective intervention or strategic industrial policy*: in this school industrial policy should be focused on new rising industries to help them overcome difficulties they are confronted with when entering or participating in the market.

Member States' industrial polices are normally a mix of different schools of industrial policy — even though a bias towards one of the schools could be discernible. The UK and Germany, for instance, have a more liberal market-based approach, while France and Italy are known to be more interventionist; but both groups have elements of both approaches in their industrial policies. Today a general tendency towards a more market-based policy (McDonald and Daerden) is noticeable. This dichotomy is reflected in EC policy, with a constant tension between the interventionist DG III (Industry) and the liberal, market-oriented DG IV (Competition) as well as inside the DGs themselves.

Why Should the EC Conduct Industrial Policy?
Industrial policy at EC level can be justified on *functional* grounds (*subsidiarity*):

— policy coordination on EC level promotes efficiency and effectiveness (e.g., R&D);
— Member States' industrial policies become less efficient and effective as integration progresses (consequence of IM and EMU; Nicolaides, 1993);
— non-harmonised industrial policy tends to distort competition (e.g., state aids).
Yet political objectives also enter the argument. EC industrial policy:
— helps the EC to stay competitive in comparison with other trading blocks (Japan, US);
— could be used to achieve redistributive objectives, to promote adjustment and convergence.

These arguments, however, are questioned at the national level. One can find, for instance, objections against interventionism per se, which means also a rejection of EC interventionism.

II. LEGAL BASIS, PRINCIPLES, OBJECTIVES

II.1 Legal Basis

ECSC and Euratom Treaties:

— ECSC Treaty contains explicit provisions on industrial policy in the coal and steel sectors (market regulation and structural policies).
— Euratom Treaty includes provisions for an industrial policy in the field of atomic energy.

The current legal basis was fully established at Maastricht with Title XIII dedicated explicitly to 'Industry' (TEC Art. 130).
— TEC Art. 130.1: weak acceptance of the principle of intervention (conditions for competitiveness of industry must be ensured).
— TEC Art. 130.2: Member States to coordinate action under encouragement of the Commission.
— TEC Art. 130.3: interconnection with other policies (competition, vocational training, etc.).

The EC has an explicit and concurrent but *not an exclusive competence* in industrial policy.

In a wider definition of EC industrial policy, the legal bases for EC intervention into the economy can be found in:
— Title VIII: Social Policy (TEC Arts.123–5 on the European Social Fund);
— Title XII: Trans-European Networks (TEC Arts. 129b–d);
— Title XV: Research and Development (TEC Arts. 130f–p).

II.2 Objectives

TEC Art. 130 sets out the objectives of EC industrial policy:
— the adjustment to structural changes;
— business creation and development, especially SMEs;
— inter-firm cooperation;
— commercial application of research results and innovations.

III. KEY ACTORS

Council
Any specific EC action to be taken in the Member States in support of the Treaty's industrial policy objectives has to be decided unanimously (TEC Art. 130). Under TEC Article 100a, the Council decides on harmonisation with QMV, as a co-legislator with the EP.

European Parliament
The EP gives its opinion on TEC Art. 130 initiatives. It co-legislates with the Council, for TEC Art. 100a under the co-decision procedure.

Commission
The Commission initiates policy and legislative proposals, manages and administers industrial policy instruments and initiatives. Although several DGs are involved in different aspects of industrial policy, overall responsibility for the policy rests with DG III. The Commissioner responsible for industrial policy is M. Bangemann (Germany).

IV. POLICY INSTRUMENTS

EC action can be classified into budgetary and regulatory instruments (Buigues and Sapir, 1993).

IV.1 Budgetary Instruments

(a)   R&D policy.
(b)   Encouragement of economic activities in depressed or backward regions. Structural Funds (ERDF, EAGGF), the 'European Social Fund (ESF), loans from the EIB, and the Cohesion Fund are used for infrastructural development, training, incentives for productive investment etc. (see chapter 13).

(c)   Sectoral policies: especially for the three 'crisis sectors':
(i)   *steel*, e.g., RESIDER programme (1988) to help to ease the social and economic costs of the steel industry in the poorest regions of the Community;
(ii)   *shipbuilding*, e.g., RENAVAL programme to help regions which are affected by the decline of shipbuilding and ship repair activities (1988);
(iii)   *textiles*, e.g., RETEX programme to help regions depending highly on textiles and clothing industry.
And to a lesser extent for telecommunications, aeronautics, data-processing etc.

IV.2 Regulatory Instruments

(a)   Policies for completion of IM (harmonisation, liberalisation, mutual recognition, common legal statute, public procurement regulation, etc.).
(b)   Trade policy (see chapter 10):
(i)   quantitative restrictions (TEC Art. 115);
(ii)   anti-dumping policy (TEC Art. 91).
(c)   Competition policy (see chapter 11).
(d)   Enterprise policy: Action Programmes for SMEs, cooperation initiatives (e.g., BCNet is a business cooperation network that provides information to undertakings).

V. HISTORICAL DEVELOPMENT

V.1 Before Maastricht: an 'ad hoc' Industrial Policy

The original 1957 TEC, in contrast to the ECSC Treaty, did not mention industrial policy. The Member States felt that only they themselves should have control over their national active, even interventionist, industrial policies. As a result there were no dispositions on industrial policy at the EC level. At the EC level, a liberal *laissez-faire* policy ruled. Nevertheless, early elements of an industrial policy can be detected in competition policy (TEC Arts. 85, 86 and 92–94; see chapter 11), as well as in commercial policies (see chapter 10). Consequently, tensions arose between relying on the market mechanisms in the IM and the interventionist programmes of governments.

In the late 1960s, the Member States were still the masters of the game. In the light of the rising and overwhelming competition from the US, Member States reacted with the promotion of *national champions* by offering a wide range of measures such as subsidies, fiscal reductions, etc. The outcome was unsuccessful and ineffective: for example, the high subsidies for these national champions resulted in rent-seeking situations where no structural adjustments were made to improve competitiveness and rivalries were created between national champions. At EC level only a passive policy was conducted in the framework of the establishment of the customs union, and competition policy existed mainly through 'negative integration' measures.

The 1970s, however, saw a tendency towards horizontal measures on the EC level. This initiative was diluted by the protectionist reaction of the Member States to the 1973–4 oil crisis.

The Commission produced a memorandum, the Colonna Report (1970) which advocated the setting up of an industrial policy based on a macro-industrial/horizontal approach. The report promoted the completion of the IM and the restructuring of European industry through the creation of 'Euro-champions' (through promotion of transnational mergers, the creation of a European company statute, the harmonisation of company laws and the creation of a European identity in research and development).

At the 1972 Paris summit and after a new Commission memorandum, an action plan was adopted in 1973 by the Council, containing harmonisation and liberalisation measures, export support measures as well as defensive policies for declining sectors. This was a weak reflection of the Colonna report.

The 1973 crisis stimulated protectionist reactions of Member States and resulted in a stagnation of industrial policy actions at EC level.

The 1980s saw a new impetus on an EC level for actions as Member States realised the shortcomings of national industrial policies resulting in a decline of industrial competitiveness. Therefore, Member States looked to the EC level for a remedy.

European action in the field of information technology was launched by the European Strategic Programme for Information Technology (ESPRIT, 1984). After ESPRIT similar programmes at EC level meant the start of an explicit R&D policy (see the second part of this chapter).

One of the main focal points of the 1980s was the completion of the IM. This was realised in 1985 with the launching of the 1985 White Paper on completion of the Internal Market (see chapter 6). One of the objectives of this white paper was the creation of a European Industrial Area. To attain this goal, the Commission proposed:

(a)   to remove obstacles to trade (e.g., harmonisation of standards);

(b)   to create a common legal environment (e.g., proposal for common licences);

(c)   to promote cooperation between undertakings;

(d)   to develop multi-annual R&D framework programmes;

(e)   to use competition policy as a liberal instrument of industrial policy.

The resulting 1986 Single European Act introduced a legal basis for R&D policy (TEC Art.130f).

V.2 The Maastricht Era: Birth of a New Policy?

In the 1990s, new factors determine the competitiveness of European industry. In this new setting emphasis is put on:
— training and human resources;
— the degree of involvement in R&D;
— the integration of objectives of environmental protection etc.
— efficiency of industrial organisation;
— the ability to use competitive networks;
The wider context of European industry is also relevant:
— size of EC industries: 99% of the industrial output is made by SMEs;
— increase of mergers: search by industry for the optimal size to compete in the world;
— reduction of employment in industry.
The EC developed a new, more coherent approach to industrial policy with the 1990 Bangemann Proposal. The Council adopted the Commission's Paper on *EC Industrial Policy in an Open and Competitive Environment*, aiming at:

(a)   Phasing out direct support to firms and setting up of horizontal measures. A coherent use of all policies that have an influence on industry is necessary.

(b)   An increase in visibility of public policies for undertakings (especially for SMEs), and the setting up of a partnership between private business and public policy makers.

(c)   An emphasis on the three main stages of structural adjustment: prerequisites, catalysts and accelerators. A catalyst for structural adjustment acts on the willingness of business to undertake adjustments in reply to pressures and opportunities, e.g., the implementation of the IM and the prospect of opening this market to third countries. Accelerators further develop structural adjustment through R&D, training and development of human resources and the development of services and industrial cooperation networks. Prerequisites required for structural adjustment are respect for competition, a stable economic context, a good educational level, economic and social cohesion and environmental protection.

Yet the temptations of sectoral intervention also appeared again: sectoral interventionism for strategic reasons or for political sensitivities (e.g., shipbuilding in the RENAVAL programme, textiles in the BRITE programme, steel etc.); rent seeking situations.

The conclusions of the Bangemann Proposal were more or less institutionalised in TEU provisions on industry (Title XIII; TEC Art. 130).

VI. RECENT DEVELOPMENTS

VI.1 White Paper on Growth, Competitiveness and Employment (1993)

The Commission's White Paper contains an analysis of the problems facing European economies. It is the benchmark for action taken by the EU and its Member States to tackle the early 1990s crisis, characterised by cyclical and structural unemployment, and proposes responses to challenges and ways forward into the 21st century for European economies, e.g.:

(a) creating a healthy, open, decentralised and more globally competitive European economy;

(b) action on jobs: to invest in lifelong education and training, fostering internal and external business flexibility, reduction in relative cost of low-qualified work, thorough overhaul of national employment policies, efforts to meet new needs;

(c) investment in trans-European networks: transport, energy and information highways;

(d) changing society and new technologies: information, biotechnology, audio-visual sector.

VI.2 Commission Communication, *An Industrial Competitiveness Policy for the European Union* (1994)

This report recalls the new global conditions for European industry:

— mounting international competition;

— emergence of the information society;

— need for industrial change in the new less-developed regions;

— inadequacy of major European networks;

— combinations of technological innovations have led to intangible investment growing faster than capital investment.

It proposes guidelines and practical measures to face up to these new conditions:

— promote intangible investment (e.g., improvement of vocational training);

— develop industrial cooperation (e.g., support organisation of Round Tables);

— ensure fair competition (external and internal measures e.g., reduction of state aids);

— modernise the role of public authorities (e.g., setting up of a working party to simplify legislation and administrative procedures).

VI.3 Action Programme and Timetable Announced in the Communication *An Industrial Competitiveness Policy for the European Union* (1995)

The Action Programme includes measures of various types:
— action already under way which contributes to industrial competitiveness (e.g., organisation of Round Tables);
— action requiring more detailed political guidelines (e.g., Adoption of Green Paper on the promotion of innovation);
— action requiring the adoption of legislative proposals.

The Communication also provides for the setting up of a series of research/industry task forces to establish closer links between all actors involved and to help to make EC action more effective and increase the spin-offs from Europe's research for citizens, consumers and taxpayers.

VI.4 Green Paper on the Promotion of Innovation (1995)

This Green Paper explains the many obstacles to innovation which are a handicap for European business. These obstacles reduce competitiveness, e.g., an inadequate and dispersed R&D input, difficulty to translate results into new products, bad administration, etc. The proposed actions include:
— the development of economic intelligence;
— the promotion of the mobility of students and research;
— the improvement of funding;
— simplifying administrative procedures;
— the setting up of a fiscal regime.

VI.5 Amsterdam and the Consolidation of the Treaties (1997)

Current TEC provisions	Provisions after Amsterdam
Art. 130 (Industrial policy — Title XIII)	Art. 157 — unchanged (Title XVI)
Art. 130f (Research and Technological Development — Title XV)	Art. 163 — unchanged (Title XVIII)
Art. 130g (R&D activities)	Art. 164 — unchanged
Art. 130h (R&D coordination with Member States)	Art. 165 — unchanged
Art. 130i (Multi-annual Framework Programme (MFP))	Art. 166 — unchanged
Art. 130j (Implementation of MFPs)	Art. 167 — unchanged
Art. 130k (Supplementary programmes)	Art. 168 — unchanged
Art. 130l (EC involvement in Member States R&D)	Art. 169 — unchanged
Art. 130m (R&D cooperation with third countries)	Art. 170 — unchanged
Art. 130n (Joint undertakings)	Art. 171 — unchanged
Art. 130o (Procedure for implementation of MFPs and joint undertakings)	Art. 172 — Co-decision for MFPs; Council uses QMV for joint undertakings
Art. 130p (Report on R&D)	Art. 173 — unchanged

For the renumbering of other EC activities in the economy:
— Trans-European Networks — see chapters 8 and 9;
— Social Policy — see chapter 17;
— Employment policy — see chapter 17.

VII. FUTURE PROSPECTS

VII.1 Agenda 2000

Agenda 2000 reiterates the objectives of an EU industrial policy, as stated in the Treaty on European Union in the light of enlargement. Competitiveness of EU industry should be enhanced, which should lead to rising living standards and high employment rates. These objectives should be realised through a policy which is horizontal by nature and by using instruments from a variety of policy domains (competition policy, trade policy, etc.). This horizontal approach is the best way forward with enlargement, but it would come under pressure as sectoral and regional aspects will probably receive high political attention. It is expected that the *acquis* on the IM will be adopted by the acceding countries at the end of any transition period. In this context, Agenda 2000 points out the problem of shortcomings of the public administration of the acceding countries in the implementation of the *acquis*. A reference is made to the topic of modernisation of the role of public administration with regard to industry as mentioned in the Commission Communication, *An Industrial Competitiveness Policy in the European Union* (1994).

The integration of industries from the candidate countries with both their strengths and weaknesses will present a challenge to the EU. In particular the use of the acceding countries as low-cost production sites for industrial activities will bring sectoral and regional adjustment strains in both present and new members. The same goes for the imperative of alignment to EU environmental and social norms. Agenda 2000 promotes industrial cooperation as one of the mechanisms for achieving integration and for alleviating sectoral constraints.

* * *

RESEARCH AND DEVELOPMENT POLICY

I. RATIONALE and OBJECTIVES

R&D: an Answer to Different Challenges

EC intervention in R&D activities derives from the rationale that:
— a duplication of research in the different Member States should be avoided;
— coordination on the EC level means economies of scale and learning;
— joint research may result in spill-over effects and the development of common standards.
Consequently, TEC Art. 130f sets out the basic objectives of R&D policy at the EC level as:
— strengthening of the *scientific and technological base* of EC industry;
— the development of Europe's *competitiveness*;
— the promotion of all *research activities* deemed necessary by virtue of other chapters of the Treaty.

II. A BRIEF HISTORY OF R&D POLICY

Whereas the EEC Treaty did not mention R&D, the Euratom Treaty (concluded at the same time) provided for the first steps in the field of R&D, notably regarding nuclear power. In 1957, a Joint Research Centre (JRC) at Ispra (Italy) was created.

In 1967, a DG XII for science, research and development was established and a Working Group on R&D was created — PREST (politique de recherche scientifique et technique).

1970s

During the 1970s, R&D is already explicitly mentioned in different reports and communications of the Commission. In 1974, the creation of CREST (Comité de la recherche scientifique et technologique) was aimed to assist the Commission in its R&D activities. During the 1970s Europe witnessed a shift from 'sunset' to 'sunrise' industries, from sectoral to horizontal policies. In this decade the 'first generation' of sectoral R&D programmes came to the fore in areas of energy, environment and raw materials.

1980s (Davignon Era)

In the 1980s there was a greater readiness of the Member States to cooperate in R&D because of the technological gap with the United States and Japan. Etienne Davignon, then Commissioner for industry, took the initiative to focus attention on actions in the field of information technology (IT). He brought the heads of the 12 leading European IT industries together to discuss an action plan. These gatherings became known as the 'Big Twelve' Round Table Discussions.

The result of these efforts was the 1983–4 pilot phase of a European Strategic Programme for R&D in Information Technology (ESPRIT). This pilot programme proved to be so successful that the first ESPRIT programme was launched in 1984. Other ESPRIT programmes followed. ESPRIT coordinates and stimulates European research in the pre-competitive phase by associating companies, research centres in universities and European research centres. 15 sectors are covered: micro electronics, software technology, information processing, informatics and system development, office systems and computer-integrated manufacturing (see chapter 18).

At the same time large-scale pan-European interventionist programmes were set up outside the EC framework — Airbus, European Space Programmes (ESA, European Space Agency, Ariane, Hermes, Columbus), EUREKA (1985): e.g., JESSI (semiconductors), HDTV (high-definition television). EUREKA was designed as a counterweight to the American 'Star Wars' programme.

The 1987 Single European Act codified R&D policy at EC level (TEC Arts. 130f–q).

R&D was implemented through the adoption of Multi-annual Framework Programmes (1984–7; 1987–91; 1990–4; 1994–8) and main Community

Programmes. Examples of Community Programmes are RACE (to develop the technological base for an integrated broad-band communications network), EURAM (European Research on Advanced Materials), BAP (Biotechnology Action Programme), FAST (Forecasting and Assessment in Science and Technology).

The TEU (Title XV) extended the EP's influence over EC policy in this area by introducing the co-decision procedure.

III. POLICY INSTRUMENTS AND DECISION-MAKING

Multi-Annual Framework Programmes (MFPs) are the basic policy instrument (TEC Arts. 130i–m). An MFP:

(a)   lays down the major scientific and technical objectives of the Community, defines the respective priorities and establishes the maximum overall amount for all activities envisaged and its breakdown between the various activities;

(b)   is founded on the principle of 'rolling scientific research' (this means overlapping in time and financial carry-overs to new programmes) and the principle of EC financial co-participation (between EC and other participants).

R&D programmes are an example of the principle of subsidiarity, i.e., EC actions are concentrating more on generic key technologies which have an interest for the whole EC.

MFPs are executed through (see Moussis, 1994):

(a)   Direct actions: EC R&D activities implemented in its research establishments (Joint Research Centres — JRCs), and financed from the community budget.

(b)   Concerted actions: the Community defines the framework for action. In this setting, researchers from the Member States act independently. EC funding is limited to coordination costs of national activities.

(c)   Indirect actions: shared cost-research where the Community pays 50% of the total cost of the research work. This research is conducted in research centres, universities or Community undertakings.

(d)   Joint undertakings (TEC Art. 130n, e.g., JET: Joint European Torus).

The basic conditions for project eligibility stipulate that projects must be of a 'pre-competitive' nature and require cross-border research cooperation (involvement of at least two mutually independent partners established in two different Member States).

The decision-making procedure is set out in TEC Arts. 130i and 130o:

(a)   Adoption of MFP: Council by unanimity throughout co-decision procedure with EP and after consultation of ECOSOC (TEC Art. 130i.1).

(b) Adoption of specific programmes: Council by qualified majority after consultation of EP and ECOSOC (TEC Art. 130i.4).

(c) Implementation of MFP (TEC Arts. 130j–l — supplementary programmes, participation): Council using cooperation procedure, after consulting ECOSOC (TEC Art. 130o.2).

(d) Commission Annual Report presented to Council and EP (TEC Art. 130p).

VIII. FURTHER READING

BIANCHI, Patrizio: *Industrial Policies and Economic Integration. Learning from European Experiences*, London, Routledge, 1998.

McDONALD, Frank and POTTON, Margaret: 'Industrial policy in the EU', in McDONALD, Frank and DEARDEN, Stephen, *European Economic Integration*, London, Longman, 1991, pp.116–35.

MOUSSIS, Nicolas: *Access to the European Union*, Rixensart, EuroConfidential, 1994.

NICOLAIDES, Phedon: *EC Industrial Policy*, EIU European Trends, No. 2, 1992.

NICOLAIDES, Phedon: *Industrial Policy in the European Community: a Necessary Response to Economic Integration?*, Maastricht, EIPA, 1993, especially the chapter by Pierre BUIGUES and André SAPIR.

REVUE DU MARCHÉ COMMUN ET DE L UNION EUROPÉENNE: *La Politique industrielle de la Communauté européenne*, Special issue, No. 396, March 1996.

SAUTER, Wolf: *Competition Law and Industrial Policy in the EU*, Oxford, Clarendon Press, 1997.

WOOLCOCK, Stephen: 'European industrial policy in the 1990s' in FURLONG, Paul and COX, Andrew (eds): *The European Union at the Crossroads: Problems in Implementing the Single Market Project*, Boston, Earlsgate Press, 1995, pp.187–205.

Websites

DG III (Industry)	http://europa.eu.int/en/comm/dgiii/dgiiiint.htm
DG XII (Science, R&D)	http://europa.eu.int/comm/dg12/index.html
Joint Research Centre	http://www.jrc.org/jrc/

13 REGIONAL POLICY AND COHESION

Gabriel Glöckler and Lie Junius

I. DEFINITION AND RATIONALE

I.1 The Meaning of Cohesion and Regional Policy

Economic and social cohesion could be defined as the reduction of socio-economic disparities within the Union by aiding regional development (Nanetti 1996). The goal is not regional development in absolute terms, but rather a strengthening of internal cohesion within the Union. The policy of cohesion embodies the idea of solidarity within the Union, for it aims to reduce — by way of redistribution — the impact of relative gains and losses due to market integration.

EU regional policy is the central instrument of cohesion, for it addresses the economic and social factors which sustain regional disparities. A 'catching up' of the Union's poorest regions demands a reconversion and restructuring process in the fabric of their economic activity. EU regional policy can help to improve the competitive positions of backward regions through developing infrastructure (motorways, telecoms) and human resources endowments (vocational training, education, etc.). This means in practice a financial redistribution system on a continental scale.

I.2 The Rationale of EU Regional Policy

Generally, EU regional policy is justified on grounds that the EU must intervene in some way to rectify the process for which it has been, or would be, a catalyst. By creating a large European common market, the EU has set in motion an economic adjustment process with far-reaching social and welfare implications.

I.2.1 Economic Justification

Economic integration and competition in the Internal Market (IM) invariably brings about adjustment needs for the regions. As different regions manage the restructuring processes more or less successfully, regional disparities, in terms of income, productivity and employment levels may deepen, or newly appear. Regional economic theory — in stark contrast to pure neoclassical predictions — shows that regional imbalances will not be eliminated by market forces alone. Active regional policy is thus a recognition that reliance on a philosophy of 'the rising tide lifts all boats' is insufficient. If regional imbalances persist, the longer-term dynamic effects could be polarised growth with an economically vibrant and highly competitive core and a periphery which continually lags behind. Sooner or later such a lopsided economic pattern would generate massive labour migration and political instability.

Yet migration is low in the EU (due to language and culture differences) and lower costs for labour and land in the peripheral regions are likely to avoid the emergence of permanently depressed regions. Nevertheless, the economics of market integration provides substantive justification for a regional policy to accompany economic adjustment processes of the IM, to soften the impact of declining industries and to boost the competitive position of less-favoured regions.

I.2.2 Political Rationale

Tackling regional disparities has a wider political rationale:

(a)   Regional imbalances may form a *barrier to integration*. If deeper integration systematically disadvantages certain regions, the 'regime support' needed for further integrative steps will fail to materialise — the EU's very legitimacy is at stake. A certain benefit from the integration project has to be apparent (e.g., the UK — missing out on the financial transfers of CAP — wanted its *'juste retour'* of EC funds through regional policy).

(b)   Each Member States has a vested interest in avoiding excessive regional disparities; a depressed region in another Member States is, after all, a depressed market for exports.

EU regional policy is an application of the subsidiarity principle: redistributive mechanisms in a market the size of the EU have to be assigned to the European level of governance to avoid suboptimal (i.e., narrow national) policy choices. Policy efficiency is increased by ensuring that regional spending is concentrated in the most needy areas (e.g., if 'poor' regions are concentrated in certain Member States, national instruments and financial resources are clearly insufficient). Organisationally, regional policy at the EC level coordinates otherwise distinct national regional policies of the Member States.

Summing up, the Member States have stipulated as an objective of the EC 'to promote throughout the Community a harmonious and balanced development of economic activities ... and economic and social cohesion and solidarity among Member States' (TEC Art. 2).

II. LEGAL BASIS, PRINCIPLES, OBJECTIVES

II.1 Legal Basis

TEC Art. 2 states the objective of balanced economic development, to be achieved through 'the strengthening of economic and social cohesion' (TEC Art. 3).

TEC Title XIV is concerned with *Economic and Social Cohesion*:
— TEC Art. 130a: EC action is to be aimed at 'reducing disparities between the levels of development of the various regions and the backwardness of the least-favoured regions, including rural areas'.
— TEC Art. 130b: enumerates the various financial instruments (see V) and provides for the Cohesion Report.
— TEC Art. 130c: spells out objectives of ERDF funding.
— TEC Art. 130d: stipulates procedures and sets up the Cohesion Fund.
— TEC Art. 130e: regulates implementation.

II.2 Principles

II.2.1 Concentration
Funds must be concentrated on a set of priorities/objectives, i.e., where they are most needed:
— Regions are classified in NUTS (*Nomenclature des unités territoriales statistiques*).
— Funds can be obtained if the region qualifies under one of the six objectives (see II.3.1).
Thus the concentration principle brings about a financial and geographical concentration.

II.2.2 Programming
Programming means the elaboration of strategic plans, rather than piecemeal projects:

—Establishment of Community Support Framework or Single Programming Document.
—Take into account the totality of a region's economic and social situation.

II.2.3 Partnership
Regional policy decisions should be taken by a partnership of actors, i.e., Commission, Member States, representatives of regional and local level, socio-economic partners.
—The partnership principle concerns preparation and financing, advance appraisal, monitoring, *ex post* evaluation of projects and programmes.
—By insisting on partnership, EU regional policy has helped the establishment and/or extension of activities of sub-national, regional authorities in Member States with otherwise centralist state traditions (e.g., France, Ireland or planning regions in England).
The mobilisation of those actors for projects funded by the Community thus represents a very significant impact of 'Europe' on the political systems and power relations within the Member States.

II.2.4 Additionality
Community spending should add to, rather than substitute for, Member States' spending:
—Projects awarded EU finance must also be part financed by the Member States; for all objectives (except No. 1) there is a 'matching-funding' requirement so as to reduce dependency and promote responsible financial management.
—Community action must impart an added value to national initiatives.
—No additionality requirement for Cohesion Fund projects.

II.2.5 Monitoring
All regional policy activities are appraised, then monitored during the operation and finally evaluated after completion:
—Each November, the Commission reports to EP and the Council.
—Every three years, publication of the Commission's *Report on Economic and Social Cohesion* (latest from 1996).

II.3 Objectives

> *In order to promote its overall harmonious development, the Community shall develop and pursue its actions leading to the strengthening of its economic and social cohesion. (TEC Art. 130a).*

In particular, this means 'reducing disparities between the levels of development of the various regions and the backwardness of the least-favoured regions, including rural areas'. In attaining this general goal, EC regional policy follows a twin-track approach, through (a) the *Objectives Policy* and (b) *Community Initiatives*, both of which follow a specific set of objectives and rationales.

II.3.1 Objectives Policy
Under this section, projects in the Member States are financed under the heading of a specific objective, and regions are eligible for funds depending on their particular economic situation:

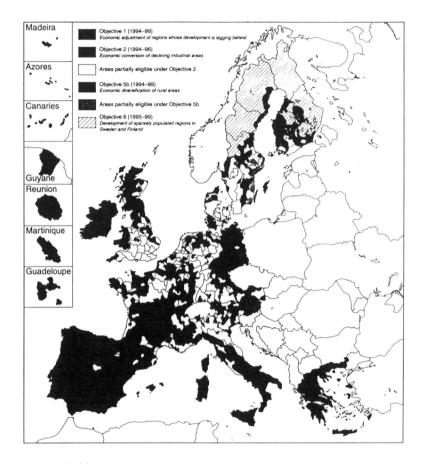

Areas eligible under the regional Objectives of the Structural Funds (1994—99)

Objective 1	93.972 billion ECU
Objective 2	15.360 billion ECU
Objectives 3 and 4 (non-regional)	15.180 billion ECU
Objective 5(a) (non-regional)	6.916 billion ECU
Objective 5(b)	6.862 billion ECU
Objective 6	0.697 billion ECU

(Source: European Commission)

Objective No.	Content	Funds
1	To promote the development and structural adjustment of *regions whose development is lagging behind*: • Eligible regions: NUTS whose GDP/capita < 75% EC average; • List drawn for six years by the Council by QMV; • Funding maximum 75%, minimum 50% of total; • For region in cohesion country, funding up to 80% (85% outermost regions).	ERDF ESF EAGGF FIFG EIB
2	To convert regions, frontier regions or parts of regions which are seriously *affected by industrial decline*. Regions are eligible if three criteria are fulfilled: (a) the three-year average unemployment > EC average; (b) The share of industrial employment in total employment $\geq$ EC average since 1975; (c) affected by an observable fall in industrial (or fisheries) employment since 1975. Funding maximum 50%, minimum 25% of public expenditure.	ERDF ESF FIFG EIB
3	To *combat long-term unemployment* and facilitate the integration into working life of young people and those socially excluded from labour market.	ESF EIB
4	To facilitate the *adaptation of workers to industrial change* and to changes in production systems (objective added in 1993).	ESF EIB
5a	To promote rural development by speeding up the *adjustment of agricultural structures* in the framework of the reform of the CAP.	EAGGF EIB
5b	To *promote rural development* and structural adjustment of rural areas. Funding intended for those regions not covered under objective 1. Regions have to satisfy two of the following criteria: (a) high share of agricultural employment in total employment; (b) low level of agricultural income, in particular in terms of agricultural added value per agricultural work. (c) low population density and/or a significant depopulation trend.	EAGGF ESF ERDF EIB
6	To promote the development and structural adjustment of extremely low populated areas. Added in the 1995 enlargement to cover the sparsely populated Arctic regions of Sweden and Finland, mainly located in Lapland.	EAGGF ERDF ESF EIB

II.3.2 Community Initiatives

This branch of regional policy operates under the direct supervision of the Commission and the objectives are therefore broader and more 'integrationist':

(a) Trans-border, trans-national and inter-regional cooperation and networks.

(b) Rural development and assistance to the outermost regions.

(c) Promoting employment and human resource development.

(d) Management of industrial change.

III. THE HORIZONTAL DIMENSION OF REGIONAL POLICY

III.1 Environmental Policy

— Regional imbalances frequently manifest themselves in diverging environmental conditions; the Cohesion Fund thus provides for transfers for environmental projects.

— Community initiatives (e.g., ENVIREG encouraging efficient use of resources, respecting the environment — see chapter 15).

III.2 Competition Policy

— TEC Art. 92 allows Member States to give state aids to promote development of areas lagging behind.

— Derogations from the rules of competition policy by allowing state aids to promote the economic development of areas with serious underemployment and abnormally low standard of living (see chapter 11).

III.3 Common Agricultural Policy and Common Fisheries Policy

— Objective 5a is basically the structural part of the MacSharry reform (see chapter 7).

— Objective 2 is also designed for areas dependent on the fishing industry.

III.4 Social policy

— Objectives 3 and 4 are not regional objectives in the strict sense. Any region is eligible for objectives 3 and 4 — the actions under those objectives could thus be part of social policy.

— In practice, most of the objective 1 — regions also qualify for objectives 3 and 4, in the sense that high unemployment and social problems are often concentrated in economically backward regions. Objectives 3 and 4 are thus de facto regionalised objectives.

IV. KEY ACTORS

Commission
Main policy initiator; approves programmes submitted for financing by the Member States; monitoring tasks (tri-annual Cohesion Report); DG XVI responsible for regional policies and cohesion; related policy initiatives from DG V (Employment, Industrial Relations, Social Affairs); DG VI (Agriculture) and DG XIV (Fisheries). The Commissioner primarily responsible for regional policy is M. Wulf-Mathies (Germany).

The Commission has a crucial role throughout the policy cycle: 'Brussels' provides the money, contributes to the elaboration of the Community Support Framework and controls the implementation and administration of the funds. Such extensive Commission involvement regularly meets with opposition from regional and local authorities, on grounds of subsidiarity. Yet compared to the inefficiency and/or corruption of the often weak administrations, the Commission has a justified engagement on the ground, and frequently accelerates the much needed modernisation of local administrations.

Council
The Council defines the tasks, objectives and organisation of the ERDF as well as the rules applicable to it; at unanimity; principal locus of intergovernmental bargaining on the 'financial perspectives' and Member States' *'juste retour'* from the system (also in European Council).

European Parliament
The EP has to assent to definition of tasks, objectives and organisation of Structural Funds; cooperation procedure for implementing ERDF decisions; is consulted by the Commission on the Community Initiatives.

Committee of the Regions
Consultative role in regional policy matters affecting local and regional authorities, e.g., Structural Funds.

Administrations (national, regional, local)
Extensive role in developing Regional Development Plans (see V); principal actors in implementing and assessing EC-supported programmes and projects; since mid 1980s proliferation of representation offices of regions and municipalities in Brussels to support efforts to attract EC funds ('state lobbying').

V. POLICY INSTRUMENTS

V.1 The Structural Funds

V.1.1 European Regional Development Fund (ERDF)
— Set up in 1975, main instrument of EC regional policy.
— To date, some 800 programmes have been co-financed by ERDF.
— Constant struggle between Commission and Council.
— Current budget of approximately 13 billion ECU.

V1.2 European Social Fund (ESF)
— Set up originally in the Treaty of Rome.
— Originally, paid 50% of the costs of *re-employing* workers by means of *retraining* and resettlement.
— Granting of aid to workers whilst their *undertaking is being converted* to the production of a more viable product.
— Today the ESF finances objectives 3 and 4. It is the second largest structural fund, with roughly 7.5 billion ECU.

V.1.3 European Agricultural Guidance and Guarantee Fund (EAGGF), Guidance Section
15 per cent of EAGGF (4.0 billion ECU) is earmarked for structural measures of CAP. The 1992 CAP reform was accompanied by structural measures to soften the implications for the farmers (see chapter 7).

V.1.4 Financial Instrument for Fisheries Guidance (FIFG)
Created in 1994; used to be a part of the EAGGF, but recognition that backward fishing regions have very distinct problems.

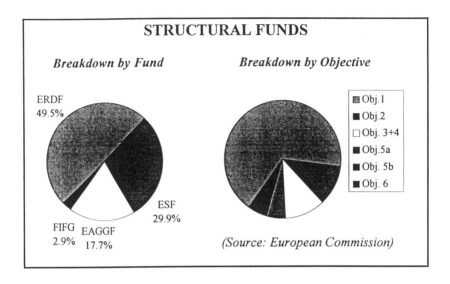

STRUCTURAL FUNDS

Breakdown by Fund   *Breakdown by Objective*

ERDF 49.5%

ESF 29.9%

FIFG 2.9%   EAGGF 17.7%

- Obj.1
- Obj.2
- Obj. 3+4
- Obj.5a
- Obj. 5b
- Obj. 6

(Source: European Commission)

V.2 The Cohesion Fund

The goal of the cohesion fund is convergence of the national economies in the run-up to EMU, rather than regional development. It finances projects in the fields of environment and transport infrastructure.

— Funds are focused on national governments, and *not* on regional or local partners.

— Threshold for eligibility is set by *national* GDP per capita at < 90% of EU average, thus covering Ireland, Greece, Spain and Portugal.

— A further requirement is the presentation of a programme leading to economic convergence and sound government finances (decreasing overall public debt and avoiding excessive deficits; see EMU).

— Fund provides assistance of up to 80% (general) and 85% (most peripheral regions) of the total costs of projects, on condition that these projects are not already financed by the EC structural funds.

— 15.1 billion ECU are available in total for 1993 to 1999.

V.3 Other Instruments

European Coal and Steel Community
Arts. 54 and 56 of the ECSC Treaty provide for financial measures for re-employment of workers in coal and steel industries.

European Investment Bank
Offers non-profit making loans and loan guarantees.
—The EIB's very high credibility provides for good financial conditions.
—Original tasks of regional development within the EU enlarged to pre-adhesion policy in the CEECs.

New Community Instrument (NCI)
Created by Commissioner X. Ortoli in 1977 (Ortoli facilities), specific loans to SMEs, managed by the EIB.

Integrated Development Operations
EC aid for socio-economic development and renewal in depressed areas, geographically limited, e.g., 1979–84: Belfast and Naples inner cities.

Integrated Mediterranean Programs (IMPs)
EC aid packages destined for social and economic development in the Mediterranean; focus on France, Italy and Greece. At the time, it was seen as a side-payment to those countries in return for their acceptance of the 1986 Southern Enlargement (Spain, Portugal). Great deal of local administrative input.

IV.4 Implementing Regional Policy

Regional Policy is one of the few policy areas where the Commission is directly and extensively involved in the implementation phase, which is otherwise left to Member States (see Hooghe).

IV.4.1 Regional Development Plans
Under the objectives policy, Member States whose regions fall under one of the six objectives (see II.3.1) submit to the Commission their regional development plan containing:
—a description of the current situation in the area;
—description of an appropriate strategy;
—an overall financial table of EC and Member States funding;
—an appraisal of the environmental situation.

The Commission, in cooperation with the Member States, on the basis of national plans, then goes on to establish the *Community Support Framework (CSF)* for each region, which comprises:
—the operations to be undertaken with support from the structural funds;
—the forms of assistance to be given;

— a finance plan;
— the duration of the assistance.

Community Initiatives
The 13 present Community initiatives benefit from 9% of the structural funds. They are not solely the responsibility of the Commission. Comitology applies, namely the management committee, giving Member States a greater say. Nevertheless, Community Initiatives are a prime action field in which the Commission directly intrudes into otherwise exclusively national action in the regions.

VI. HISTORICAL DEVELOPMENT

Before 1975, supporting depressed areas was almost entirely a national affair. Regional policy at the European level was fragmented and of very limited extent. The ECSC and the EAGGF offered financial help in depressed regions only in so far as it concerned the industries they were designed to assist. The EIB was also involved in making loans to projects in depressed areas. EC competition policy had become involved in a fairly weak manner in attempting to regulate how Member States used their own regional subsidies (see chapter 11).

In 1967, the Commission presented a proposal for Community action regarding regional development and a communication on EC regional policy. In the EC's first attempt at EMU (1971; see chapter 19), the Member States accepted the need for structural and regional actions to prepare for monetary union — including the necessity of a financial mechanism. The 1974 Paris Summit endorsed the idea and a 1975 Council regulation established the European Regional Development Fund and its related financial provisions. A genuine EC regional policy was thus instituted. Clearly, the entry of the UK into the EEC provided another crucial push factor: given the negligible benefit of CAP to the UK, an EC regional policy could provide a '*juste retour*' for the UK while building on the British tradition of regional policy.

The initial EC regional policy had a threefold structure: a financial instrument (ERDF) was complemented by other EC funds and institutions operating with regional bias as well as measures to improve coordination between the EC, Member States, regional and local authorities. Member States exerted a very strong influence over how the money was spent and who received assistance. The money was distributed according to specific *shares* and *negotiated quotas*, following the Council's deliberations, with very little input from the Commission. Moreover, the help given from the EC funds was *narrow in scope*, essentially limited to grants for infrastructure and industry investments, with no support for other instruments such as tax incentives, loans, advice, or provision of industrial premises. Finally, the financial resources were meagre: 0.04% of combined EC GDP or 4.8% of the EC budget (1976).

Very soon after its inception, Member States and the Commission felt a need to reform the provisions on regional policy. In the *1979 reform*, 5% of the Fund was made into a non-quota section, over which the Commission had more control. This 5% could be spent by the Commission as it saw fit, regardless of whether the recipient region had been designated 'in need' by its national government. However, 95% of the fund remained under the control of the Member States and the quotas still applied.

In the *1984 reform*, the quota/non-quota division was abolished and replaced by Project and Programme assistance. The quota system changed into *'fourchettes'* or indicative ranges (e.g., the UK's indicative range in 1984 was 21.42–28.56% of the Fund). The lower figure is guaranteed, but in order to be given more of its indicative share, the Member State would need to persuade the Community to finance more projects.

The successive *enlargements to Greece (1981), Spain and Portugal (1986)* made the need for a more substantial regional policy all the more clear. The Southern entrants, most with backward economies, brought with them serious problems of inadequate economic structures and high unemployment. With the relaunch of the integration process in the Single Market project, greater competition (the four freedoms) was coupled with cooperation (social, environment, research) and solidarity (opportunities for all regions). Thus, in the *Single European Act*, regional policy was set on a firm legal basis with a new title (Title V Economic and Social Cohesion). This codified the *acquis communautaire*, and stated a clear objective for regional policy (see II.2).

Having ratified the SEA, the Member States also agreed on a financial package (*Delors I*) organising the 'financial perspectives' of the EU for the period 1988–92. By doubling the resources for structural funds, economic and social cohesion became the second largest expenditure item of the EC, just behind the CAP. Once the financial means were made available, a more detailed judicial framework had to be established. The *reform of 1988* established principles which still govern the regional policy nowadays (see II.1). This marked an important shift in including regional authorities into the policy process; in a sense, development policy *for* the regions became to a greater extent a development policy *by* the regions (Nanetti 1996).

The *1991 Treaty on European Union* introduced further modifications, providing, inter alia, for tri-annual *progress reports on economic and social cohesion* to be submitted by the Commission. It also stipulated exact procedures for the EU's regional policy activities, e.g., regarding the tasks, priority objectives and the organisation of the Structural Funds, implementation issues, or actions outside the framework of the structural funds. The Council's decisions thereby have a strong consultative input, from the EP, the ECOSOC and the newly created Committee of the Regions.

Most importantly, the TEU set up the *Cohesion Fund* which was seen by many observers as a side-payment to the 'poorer' Member States in return for their agreement to EMU — which was seen as creating yet another adjustment shock. This added another 15 billion ECU to the EU-financed structural policy, but national, rather than regional, governments gained control over these funds.

In 1991, a second package of 'financial perspectives' (*Delors II*) was agreed upon (1992–9). It envisaged 141 billion ECU for the structural funds over six years — a quadrupling of funds compared to 1987 levels. 96.3 billion ECU of this amount was earmarked for the most needy areas (objective 1 regions). There is no longer any form of quotas or *fourchettes* in the strict sense of the word, rather the Member States negotiated their 'returns' when bargaining over the entire package.

Throughout the 1990s, structural funds and policies were 'fine-tuned' to account for changes of the political and economic environment. For example, the East German *Länder* were counted as objective 1 regions, and a new objective 6 (Arctic regions) was included to provide 'returns' from regional aid to the new entrants of the 1995 enlargement. In the run-up to EMU, Member States' tight public-sector budgets and their keen interest to keep Community expenditure under control have increased the pressure to make EC regional assistance more efficient and to concentrate funds on the most needy regions.

> **The impact of regional policy** (Begg et al.)
>
> EU regional policy has a mixed record. In some beneficiary areas (e.g., Ireland, parts of Spain) EU regional aid has been a success story, with a real 'catching up' of the local economies to the EU average. All cohesion countries (bar Greece) qualified for EMU — manifesting their (nominal) convergence with the core European economies. The financial impact in those countries is considerable, with EU transfers amounting to up to 4% of GDP, thus raising local incomes and improving economic infrastructure.
>
> These Member States apart, EU regional policy spreads a small amount of money too thinly over numerous aid schemes, despite the concentration principle. And even then, administrative deficiencies in the Member States hamper a full exploitation of the funds provided. There has been some convergence of national living standards, but income gaps are widening within Member States. Italy's Mezzogiorno and Germany's New *Länder* provide evidence that even transfers of a far larger scale than EU funds fail to create a competitive and developed economic structure in the backward regions. In such a context, an even modest contribution of EU regional policy to balanced economic development in the EU is remarkable.

VII. RECENT DEVELOPMENTS

VII.1 Amsterdam and the Consolidation of the Treaties

Current TEC provisions	*Provisions after Amsterdam*
Art. 130a (Objectives)	Art. 158 — unchanged
Art. 130b (Instruments)	Art. 159 — unchanged
Art. 130c (ERDF)	Art. 160 — unchanged
Art. 130d (Decision-making)	Art. 161 — references to transition period for Cohesion Fund removed
Art. 130e (Implementation of ERDF)	Art. 162 — co-decision procedure replaces cooperation

VII.2 The Reform of Structural Funds — Agenda 2000

In early 1998 the Commission put forward its proposals to reform the structural funds for the period 2000–6. The reform proposals are designed around three general principles:

(a) greater concentration;
(b) simplification and decentralisation;
(c) a clarification of responsibilities.

VII.2.1 Concentration
At four different levels, to increase the effectiveness of the policy:
(a) A concentration by *theme* to Community priorities for each objective.
(b) A *geographical* concentration: currently 51% of the EU population benefits from the support of objectives 1 and 2, to be brought down to 35–40% by 2006.
(c) A *financial* concentration: two thirds of the resources of the structural funds are to be allocated to objective 1 regions
(d) A concentration of the *objectives* and Community initiatives. The Commission proposes to enhance the structural funds' efficiency and visibility by reducing the seven objectives to three (all regions will be re-evaluated in this light).

Objective No.	Content	Funds
1	For regions whose *development is lagging behind*, i.e., per capita GDP < 75% of EC average. Also the most remote regions (currently covered by objective 6) with the same GDP percentage will be covered. Two thirds of the resources of the structural funds will be devoted to this objective, such that 20% of the population will benefit from it. The Commission insists on stricter enforcement of the qualifying criterion in future. If put into effect, a number of regions in Western Europe (e.g., all of Ireland, Scottish Highlands, Lisbon, Sardinia) are set to lose their objective 1 status. Since this entails a real loss of financial transfers, it is certain to meet with fierce resistance in the Council. Assistance for current objective 1 regions that no longer qualify will be phased out in a six-year transition period.	ERDF ESF EAGGF FIFG
2	For areas *undergoing economic and social conversion* or areas with structural problems, including those in the wealthier Member States. These are industrial, rural, urban and fisheries-dependent areas facing structural problems of socio-economic restructuring, including restructuring of services. Not more than 18% of the EU population is to be covered by the new objective 2. Assistance for areas currently eligible for objectives 2 and 5b that no longer qualify for the new objective 2 will be phased over a four-year period.	ERDF ESF EAGGF FIFG
3	To support the *adaptation and modernisation of education, training and employment* policies and systems. Only areas not covered by objective 1 and 2 are eligible for objective 3.	ESF

Community initiatives
The Commission proposes a limitation to three initiatives aimed at:
(a) rural development;

(b)   trans-national, cross-border and inter-regional cooperation to stimulate regional economic development and encourage a balanced regional planning; as well as

(c)   trans-national cooperation to fight discrimination and inequality which prevents access to employment. Five per cent instead of the current 9% of the structural funds will be allocated.

VII.2.2 Simplification and decentralisation
The Commission proposes to simplify and decentralise the management of the structural funds by means of a new partnership between the Commission, the Member States and the regions and other sub-national authorities. A simplification of the financial management is also proposed.

VII.2.3 Clarification of responsibility
Responsibilities of the Commission and the Member States should be clarified whereby the Commission should focus on the strategic aspects of programming (defining the intervention priorities, the budgetary allocations etc.) and would be responsible for setting the Community priorities. The Member States would be responsible for the implementation of the programmes. A counterpart of this increase in responsibilities for the Member States would be more financial control and evaluation on the part of the Commission.

In the light of improving the cost-effectiveness of the policy, the Commission is proposing to set up a reserve fund in which 10% of the budget is placed, which would be allocated after the mid-term evaluations to the most efficient programmes.

Within the overall package of the reform of structural policy, a number of controversies are still to be resolved:

(a)   Should beneficiaries of the Cohesion Fund continue to receive transfers once they have achieved the original aim — i.e., qualifying for EMU?

(b)   Should there be a certain volume of reserved credit available to the newly admitted members from Eastern Europe — or should they just be included in the normal system?

VIII. FUTURE PERSPECTIVES

VIII.1 Regional Policy in Economic and Monetary Union

The impact of EMU (set to start in 1999) is likely to exacerbate the current restructuring pressure for the regions; a single currency with common macroeconomic policy-making would thus speed up the convergence process (e.g., 1990 German–German monetary union).

Yet EMU also deprives less-developed regions of their current adjustment mechanisms intended to preserve local incomes:

— a monetary stimulus through lower interest rates by the national central bank becomes very muted with a centralised policy-setting by the ECB;

— a devaluation of the local currency is impossible with a common currency;

— increased public spending is restricted by the 'Stability and Growth Pact' (see chapter 19).

Economic theory suggests that a large-scale EU-wide redistribution mechanism ('fiscal federalism') is required to cope with 'asymmetric shocks' (e.g., a sudden drop in demand and resulting high unemployment in a particular region or Member States). For the time being, such a costly transfer system (30% of EU GDP) appears politically inconceivable (the current EU resources amount to 1.27% of EU GDP). Indeed, the Stability and Growth Pact, EMU's 'no bail out' clause (TEC Art. 104b) as well as the coordination of economic policy in the informal 'Euro-11' Council (see chapter 19) are instruments with a clear intention of avoiding monetary union becoming a transfer union.

VIII.2 Regional Policy in an Enlarged Union

With the coming rounds of enlargement to 10 CEECs (and Cyprus), the EU will take in countries whose per capita GDP is substantially below the EU average. This is set to increase regional disparities within the Union vastly and stretch the existing financial transfer system to the limits of, if not beyond, the acceptable.

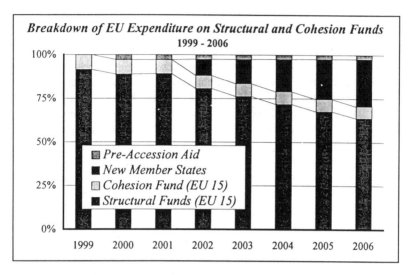

in billion ECU/€	1999	2000	2001	2002	2003	2004	2005	2006
Structural Funds (EU 15)	31.4	31.3	32.1	31.3	30.3	29.2	28.2	27.3
Cohesion Fund (EU 15)	2.9	2.9	2.9	2.9	2.9	2.9	2.9	2.9
New Member States	0.0	0.0	0.0	3.6	5.6	7.6	9.6	11.6
Pre-Accession Aid	0.0	1.0	1.0	1.0	1.0	1.0	1.0	1.0
TOTAL	34.3	35.2	36.0	38.8	39.8	40.7	41.7	42.8

in 1997 prices   *Source: European Commission*

The Commission's Agenda 2000 proposes to retain the financial upper ceiling of 1.27% of EU GDP on the Union's budget. The cake will not grow any more, and has to be divided between a greater number of Member States, of which the CEECs have the most legitimate claims. Agenda 2000 thus proposes a comprehensive reform of the existing structural policy (see VII.2) and a formula to gradually increase transfers to the prospective Member States whilst keeping the overall expenditure constant. At the time of writing, the debate is in full swing between net contributors (Germany, the Netherlands) — who would like to see their contributions decrease but who are also likely to be the greatest beneficiaries of Eastern enlargement — and net recipients (Spain, Portugal, Greece), who are determined to cling on to their share of the cake, and who are likely to lose out economically in the coming enlargement (see chapter 23).

IX. FURTHER READING

ALLEN, David: 'Cohesion and structural adjustment' in WALLACE, Helen and WALLACE, William: *Policy-Making in the European Union*, Oxford, OUP, 1996.

HOOGHE, Liesbet and KEATING, Michael: 'The politics of European Union Regional Policy' *Journal of European Public Policy*, vol. 1, pp. 367–93.

NANETTI, Raffaella Y.: 'EU cohesion and territorial restructuring in the Member States' in HOOGHE, Liesbet (ed.): *Cohesion Policy and European Integration: Building Multi-level Governance*, Oxford, OUP, 1996.

OXFORD REVIEW OF ECONOMIC POLICY, issue on Regional Policy, vol. 11, No. 2 Summer 1995, in particular BEGG, Iain et al.: 'The assessment: Regional Policy in the European Union'.

TSOUKALIS, Loukas: *The New European Economy Revisited*, Oxford, OUP, 1997, pp.187–222.

Websites

DG XVI (Regional Policies and Cohesion)	http://europa.eu.int/en/comm/dg16/dg16home.htm
European Structural Fund Information	http://194.70.69.3/ethos/tap/sfguide.htm
Information on ERDF and Cohesion Fund	http://www.inforegio.org/

14 DEVELOPMENT COOPERATION

Simon Usherwood

I. RATIONALE

Development cooperation has grown out of a variety of factors, which have changed over time. Indeed, the policy did not have a proper legal basis in the Treaty before the TEU. Even today, there is still much discussion of the merits and demerits of development cooperation, given its wider implications (e.g., the question of conditionality).

Historically, the driving force behind development cooperation has been the Member States' colonial past. This was true in 1957, with France, Belgium and the Netherlands, and became even more so with the accession of the UK in 1973. All of these countries had privileged and preferential relationships with their (former) colonies and so wished to preserve their economic and political ties.

Strategically, increasing globalisation has led to ever more interdependence between the regions of the world. The North depends upon the South's raw materials, the South on the North's processed goods. If the South falters in its consumption of the North's goods, then the North will suffer too. Therefore, the best way to ensure this does not happen is to help the South to develop. Furthermore, such development will hopefully help to stem the negative interdependence between South and North — drugs, immigration, etc.

Morally, the humanistic tradition in Europe and the belief in the equality of man has proved to be a somewhat secondary motivation. Through development cooperation, Europeans can assuage their consciences by feeling that they are helping people around the globe to enjoy their lives with more freedom and comfort than would be otherwise the case.

II. LEGAL BASIS, PRINCIPLES, OBJECTIVES

II.1 Treaty of Rome

In the Treaty of Rome there was no specific legal basis for development cooperation. Instead, cooperation was based on provisions for Overseas Territories and for the Common Commercial Policy (CCP).

Treaty of Rome, Part IV Association of the Overseas Territories and Countries

— TEC Art. 131 (Purpose of association). Promotion of economic and social development of the countries and territories, and the establishment of close economic relations between these regions and the Community.
— TEC Art. 132 (Association objectives). This guarantees the same trade treatment as that accorded to Member States and helps with the investment required for the progressive development of the countries and territories.

Explicit external relations competences used to foster development purposes
— TEC Art. 238: Conclusion of agreements establishing an association with third states involving reciprocal rights and obligations, common action and special procedures (Council unanimity and EP assent).
— TEC Art.113: Simple trade agreements (Council QMV: no EP consultation; see chapter 10).
— TEC Arts.113 and 235: Framework and cooperation agreements with the 'non-associates' i.e., with Latin American and Asian countries (Council QMV for trade issues, unanimity for the rest: EP not consulted for trade; consultation for the rest)
— TEC Art. 235: Unilateral aid or trade actions, i.e., co-financing of development with non-governmental organisations (NGOs; Council unanimity and EP consultation).

II.2 Treaty on European Union

The TEU inserted in the TEC a new Title XVII, Development Cooperation.

Objectives

— TEC Art.130u.1 — *socio-economic*:

- 'sustainable economic and social development of the developing countries, and more particularly the most disadvantaged' among the less-developed countries (LDCs);
- 'smooth and gradual integration of the developing countries into the world economy';
- 'campaign against poverty in the developing countries'.

— TEC Art.130u.2 — *political*: Consolidation of democracy in the developing countries within the framework of political stability.

— TEC Art.130u.3 — *consistency with other international organisations' objectives*: Consistency with objectives approved in UN context or within other international organisations (such as for structural adjustment).

Principles

These have been explained further in the Commission's *Communication on Development Cooperation in the Run-up to 2000* (SEC (92)915 final):

— *Complementarity*: development cooperation policy 'shall be complementary to the policies pursued by the Member States' (TEC Art. 130u.1).

— *Coordination*: between Member States and Community policies (TEC Art. 130x), especially in international organisations (stress on Commission's role).

— *Coherence*: the EC has to take into account effects on development in other policies (TEC Art. 130v).

— *Geographical weighing*: as a priority, support should be given to the LDCs.

— *Political conditionality*: aid should be conditional upon the development of democratic structures of governance and societal relations in recipient states.

Procedure

— TEC Art.130w: Cooperation procedure (TEC Art. 189c), so the EP has an important role. However, this article applies only when other provisions of the Treaty do not cover decisions — future conflicts on legal basis could arise.

— TEC Art.130w.3: Guarantees the particular nature of the Lomé convention and its financing.

— TEC Art.130y: Contractual dimension of development policy: reference to TEC Art. 228.

III. KEY ACTORS

Given that development cooperation is partially communitarised, it is not surprising that there is some friction both between and within EU institutions and between the EU and Member States. The EU gives 15% of total Member States' aid.

Commission
Responsible for proposing legislation, negotiating agreements with third states and managing cooperation programmes. DG VIII (Development) is responsible for Lomé and some other specific programmes, and DG IB (External Relations) is responsible for the Mediterranean, Asia and Latin America. Humanitarian aid is under the control of the European Community Humanitarian Office (ECHO), an organisationally distinct body within the Commission. DG VIII is relatively well integrated, with an allocation policy which aims to reconcile the differences of the 15 Member States' policies; this means relatively little Member State intervention in the Commission's operations. At the same time, it has shown an increasing concern for its own interests, over those of recipient governments, as witnessed by the development of conditionality.

European Parliament
The main legislative lever is the assent required for international agreements, including Lomé. Since the European Development Fund (EDF) is not part of the EC budget, the EP cannot control expenditure from that fund, and so is forced to use its overall political control over the Commission to express itself. With Amsterdam, decision-making will be conducted under co-decision, instead of cooperation, further increasing the EP's weight.

Council
The key decision-maker in development cooperation. Decisions are by QMV, apart from financial provisions, which fall under unanimity.

Member States' Development Agencies
In financial terms, these represent the prime movers. Despite the increasing coordination with each other and the Commission, there is still substantial divergence between individual agencies. Scandinavian agencies, for example, tend towards a policy of aid distribution based on objective criteria of poverty, while former colonial powers often retain a more preferential system for their former territories.

Interest Groups and Lobbies
These play a relatively weak role in the policy cycle, as they speak either for groups without their own voice (the poor or the persecuted) or for more abstract ideas of maximising the benefits of development aid. Of the latter, the European Centre for Development Policy Management, in Maastricht, provides both monitoring and lobbying work to improve cooperation.

IV. POLICY INSTRUMENTS

IV.1 Aid Instruments

Aid instruments are either contractual (i.e., negotiated with the third party), as with Lomé and Mediterranean countries, or are unilaterally granted by the EC, as for the rest of the developing world.

Financing is split between the European Development Fund (EDF), which is primarily concerned with Lomé; loans by the EIB; and specific lines within the EC budget.

Aid can be broken down into various parts, each with its own particularities:
— Emergency aid and refugee aid are dealt with separately within the Commission, under the competence of ECHO.
— Decentralised cooperation moves aid away from potentially inefficient and corrupt donee governments to NGOs working on the ground.
— Financial and technical cooperation has been provided to ACP states since Lomé IV.
— Food aid.

IV.2 Trade Instruments

The *objectives* of trade instruments are somewhat different from aid, being more concerned with preferential access for LDCs' goods to the EC market, security of export income for LDCs (many of whom are dependent on a single product), and promotion of trade and investment by EC industry in LDCs.

Preferential access is instrumentalised through agreements with the Mediterranean and Lomé, and through the GSP system for other regions (see chapter 10).

Security of export income is guaranteed by the STABEX and SYSMIN programmes (see VI) for ACP states.

Trade promotion comes through logistic support for EC exports to LDCs and the stimulation of cooperation between economic operators in the private sector, while *investment* is promoted by the European Community Investment Partners Scheme.

V. HISTORICAL DEVELOPMENT

The history of development cooperation has been characterised by tensions between regionalism (in the sense of keeping cooperation concentrated on a few select areas) and globalism.

The *Treaty of Rome* in 1957 included a section on the 'Association of the Overseas Countries and Territories' (see IV). This was imposed by France as a condition for the conclusion of the Treaty, since it was concerned about its relationship with its territories in Africa. The section covered the French and Belgian colonies of Africa. The main elements of the 'association package' (which had been unilaterally decided by the EC) were free trade in both directions and economic aid.

Part IV of the Rome Treaty lost its binding character with the decolonisation process, but the newly independent countries wished to maintain preferential access to the EC market. This was to lead to the negotiation of the *Yaoundé Convention* (1964, Yaoundé I; 1969, Yaoundé II). The agreement covered both trade and aid relations between the EC and the Associated African and Malagasy States (AAMS). However, the AAMS did not enter into a free trade area between themselves as was initially wished by the EC. The novelty of the approach lay in the negotiated nature of the agreement and the creation of common institutions to facilitate dialogue among EC and AAMS.

The 1950s and 1960s were characterised by the 'regional approach', namely the tendency to concentrate development cooperation towards specific privileged geographical areas. But gradually there was a move towards globalisation. The key turning points in this were the OPEC oil crisis of 1973–4, which was both an economic and a psychological shock, and the UK's accession in 1973. This latter event required that the English-speaking developing countries from the Pacific and the Caribbean become included in the development cooperation 'policy'.

In 1971, the EC set up the *Generalised System of Preferences (GSP)*. This was based on the principles of *non-reciprocity* and *autonomy* (whereby the granting country may unilaterally remove the benefit), and of *graduation* (which allows the removal of the most 'competitive' countries from the list of GSP beneficiaries on a product-by-product basis). In the beginning only industrial products were covered, although some agricultural products were included later. The GSP covers all developing and transition countries: in addition for LDCs there is a system of 'super GSP'. This exempts them from all the quantitative limitations of the industrial GSP scheme, provides a positive list for agriculture and fisheries products, and is almost equivalent to the provisions for Lomé states.

The original GSP functioned firstly by partial or total tariff suspensions or reductions on certain industrial and agricultural products. This preferential treatment ranged from a total suspension of the normal duty under the CET to the charging of a lower rate. Secondly, predetermined quotas were fixed, establishing the value or volume limits for preferential treatment. This worked through *tariff ceilings* (whereby after exhaustion of the quota, duties could be reintroduced by the Commission at the request of a Member States) and *duty-free amounts* (after this amount is reached, duties were automatically re-established for more sensitive products). The principle of *graduation* meant that the granting of duty-free quotas was on a country–product basis (albeit with the exclusion of certain combinations), rather than by universal provisions.

In 1995, the GSP system was reformed. This saw the replacement of both tariff ceilings and duty-free quotas by another system of protection: *modulated preferential duties*. Whilst the exclusion of certain country–product combinations has been retained, two new indicators have been introduced, namely the *development index* and the *industrial specialisation indicator*. These make it easier to assess states' economic performance and to adjust GSP levels accordingly.

The Commission produced a *Memorandum* in 1972 on the need to transform EC policy towards the Third World into a comprehensive development policy. As a consequence, the *Paris Summit* of the same year suggested three main guidelines: first, there should be an evolution towards 'an overall policy of cooperation in development on a world scale', while maintaining the advantages given to those countries with whom 'special relations existed'. Secondly, EC and Member States' development policies should be coordinated. Thirdly, there should be the development of new policy instruments for financial and technical cooperation.

In 1974, the Commission's document on the *Fresco of Community Aid Action* endorsed a 'basic needs' approach for food sufficiency, emergency aid and regional integration. By 1975 the first *Lomé Convention* had entered into force between the EC and the African, Caribbean and Pacific (ACP) states (see VI), replacing the Yaoundé system.

The next big step was the 1982 *Pisani Memorandum*. This tried to formulate a global development strategy, while simultaneously keeping the amount of aid at the same level. Emphasis was put on predictability and security in trade relations and also on the application of a case-by-case approach. The memorandum stated some of the guiding principles of EC development cooperation, but failed to provide a clear set of priorities or to define the appropriate means of implementing those principles.

The 1970s and 1980s saw the first agreements in the *Mediterranean, Asia and Latin America (ALA)* and with the *Association of South East Asian Nations (ASEAN)* (see IV).

By the 1990s, the mid-term revision of Lomé IV had highlighted the changes in the EU's priorities. There is now a new emphasis on the human element, with a concordant increase in the importance of human rights and sustainable development. Clauses making development cooperation dependent upon the fulfilment of certain political and social criteria (the so-called 'political conditionality') have been introduced into all agreements since 1991, after a resolution of the Council in November of that year. Dealing with regional groupings still prevails, even if the scope of development cooperation has become global.

VI. DEVELOPMENT COOPERATION BY REGION

VI.1 Lomé Convention (ACP)

Conventions were originally concluded for five-year periods (1975–80, 1980–5, 1985–90), with the exception of the last agreement (Lomé IV), which runs for 10 years (1991–2000) with a mid-term review in November 1995. There are now some 70 ACP countries.

Lomé is a group-to-group agreement with an institutional framework to regulate relations. In legal terms it is a mixed agreement, with both the EC and Member States represented in dealings with the ACP, and with non-budgetarised financing by the EDF and the EIB. Trade preferences granted by the EC are not reciprocal: almost all ACP exports are granted access to the Community at zero custom duties.

Since Lomé III (1984), there has been a new focus on the 'human dimension' and structural adjustment:
— Human rights dimension and political conditionality.
— Emphasis on participation of decentralised actors (regions, rural collectivities, local NGOs).
— Environmental concerns.
— Aid is given for technical assistance, for import schemes and for the social dimension in structural adjustment.

In terms of *trade provisions*, Lomé provides for market access and financial intervention for export revenue.

Market access:
— All raw materials and industrial products originating in the ACP are imported into the EC free from custom duties and quotas.
— Some 40 CAP products have either a total or partial exemption from customs duties.
— A protocol on rum and bananas is kept to protect traditional ACP suppliers.

STABEX and SYSMIN are instruments aimed at guaranteeing a certain security of exports for the products coming from ACP states.

STABEX:
— System compensating loss of export revenues due to production drops or price falls in products on which the ACP states are dependent. Covers over 50 agricultural products.

— The dependency threshold is 5% of total export revenues of the previous year and the loss of revenue must be at least 4.5% of the average total of a reference period;

— Before Lomé IV, compensatory transfers did not need to be reimbursed.

SYSMIN: facility for mining products, used to offset loss of earnings due to temporary disruptions in the mining sector and to aid export diversification.

The Mid-term Review — Lomé IV B

— Second Financial Protocol — aid commitments: 12.9 billion ECU (8th EDF) and 1.6 billion ECU in loans from the EIB.

— Trade and related issues: concessions with regard to market access for certain agricultural products; rules of origin: higher percentages allowed for some non-ACP LDCs.

— Cooperation financing: introduction of phased programming for the execution of national programmes.

— Strengthening of the Human Rights and Democracy Clause: reinforcement of conditionality of aid; increased political dialogue.

— South Africa's accession: became a qualified member of Lomé in 1997, via a 'fast-track' procedure. The general trade regime does not apply, with a bilateral FTA currently under negotiation instead.

Prospects for the ACP–EC Relationship — Main Issues
The ACP group is highly artificial: it brings together states which have little or nothing in common with each other, apart from their colonial pasts. This raises questions about the efficiency of Lomé, as a single convention for such a diverse group will tend towards a lowest common denominator. This said, the Community's 1998 proposals for Lomé IV's replacement, with three separate agreements (one for each region), was met with much displeasure by the ACP, who perceive strength in unity. There has also been a tendency, despite the rhetoric, to impose the EU's values and interests on the ACP (conditionality being the classic example), rather than approaching the convention as a partnership of equals.

Preferential trade access for the ACP states has also lost much of its value, with the global liberalisation of trade and, more particularly, the new agreements between the EU and the CEECs. This latter move has raised fears that the EU is no longer committed to the ACP and that in any case CEEC imports will compete with ACP imports.

In terms of the Lomé programme itself, there are ongoing problems of aid management and of inefficiency in the administrative process for the approval, monitoring and assessment of interventions. Coupled to difficulties of accountability and major financial bottlenecks, the ongoing negotiations for Lomé IV's replacement are set to produce substantial changes to the current system.

VI.2 Mediterranean Policy

Origins of the EC Mediterranean Policy

— Non-preferential trade agreements with Israel (1964) and Lebanon (1965).
— Commercial agreements with Morocco and Tunisia (1969).
— Commission's proposal for an Overall Mediterranean Policy accepted by the 1972 Paris Summit.
— 'Overall cooperation agreements' signed between 1975 and 1977 with Israel, Tunisia, Algeria, Morocco, Egypt, Jordan, Syria and Lebanon. Concluded under TEC Art. 238, these agreements cover all fields of technical, financial and economic cooperation.
— However with southern enlargements in the early 1980s, the EC had to review its strategy and the Protocols of 1986–8 led to a political commitment to maintain trade advantages, to increase aid and to foster regional integration.

New Mediterranean Policy and Guidelines for the Future

Events in Central and Eastern Europe led to a renewal of the EU's commitment to the Mediterranean and the creation of a New Mediterranean Policy in 1990. This is currently being implemented through the 4th Financial Protocol concluded in 1992 which triples previous aid.

Priority Areas

— Protection of global Mediterranean interests such as environment protection.
— Decentralisation of cooperation and interventions of regional relevance, especially in research and education (e.g., Med Campus).
— A specific financial envelope has been created for support of economic reforms and structural adjustment.

Current Developments

— Agreements with Tunisia and Morocco.
— Customs union with Turkey.
— Middle East peace process: the EU is the largest donor to the region, including support to the development of the Occupied Territories.

Euro-Mediterranean Partnership

—Launched at Barcelona in November 1995, with a follow-up conference in Malta in April 1997, the EMP provides a general framework to regional relationships, bringing together the 15 EU Member States and 12 Mediterranean countries with the long-term objective of establishing a free trade area by the year 2010 (see chapters 6 and 10).
—Areas covered include: financial and economic cooperation; political relations and security dimension; social and human resources.
—Progress has been stalled by the current breakdown in the Middle East peace process.

VI.3 Asia and Latin America

Historical Developments

—1960s and 1970s: simple trade agreements and unilateral measures (food and emergency aid).
—1980s: broader framework agreements (second-generation agreements).
—Early 1990s: third-generation agreements.

Current Policy Framework
Implementation of third generation agreements, with emphasis on:
—Involvement of decentralised actors.
—Regional cooperation.
—Environment.
—Rural development.
—Accompanying measures for structural adjustments.
—Political conditionality clause.
—Regional cooperation agreements: Mercosur, Andean Pact, the Central American Common Market, and ASEAN.

VII. RECENT DEVELOPMENTS

VII.1 Treaty of Amsterdam

Since most of development cooperation is based upon secondary instruments, it was not felt necessary to make any substantial modification of the current TEU provisions. Amsterdam, therefore, limited itself to tidying up the numbering, and to extending the EP's power by moving from cooperation to co-decision.

Current TEC provisions	Provisions after Amsterdam
Art. 130u (Objectives)	Art. 177 — unchanged
Art. 130v (Cohesion with other policies)	Art. 178 — unchanged
Art. 130w (Decision-making)	Art. 179 — co-decision replaces cooperation legislative procedure
Art. 130x (Coordination of Member States)	Art. 180 — unchanged
Art. 130y (Relations with third countries)	Art. 181 — unchanged

VIII. FURTHER READING

HOFMEIER, Rolf: 'Political Conditions attached to development aid for Africa', *Intereconomics*, May/June 1991, pp. 122–7.
MARANTIS, Demeterois: 'Human rights, democracy and development: the European Community model', *Harvard Human Rights Journal*, vol. 7, 1994, pp. 1–24.
STEVENS, Christopher: 'The EC and the Third World', in DYKER, David (ed.): *The European Economy*, London, Longman, 1992, pp.221–9.

Websites

DG VIII (Development)	http://europa.eu.int/en/comm/dg08/dgviii.htm
ECDPM, Maastricht	http://www.ecdpm.org/

15 ENVIRONMENTAL POLICY

Nicola Notaro

I. RATIONALE

For the Internal Market (IM) to function properly, distortions of an otherwise level playing field have to be avoided. Differing environmental standards, entailing different costs for companies locating within the IM, represent such a distortion and thus require a certain degree of harmonisation. Environmental policy is thus a necessary complement of the IM, functionally accompanying its establishment and functioning.

In most cases environmental problems are of a trans-boundary nature, which renders narrow national remedies and policy actions insufficient and makes a joint approach more attractive. Indeed, the global dimension of many environmental questions calls for international solutions and negotiated conventions. A unified EU stance thus appears as the best way to defend a common position and to 'export' European standards in order to achieve a high global level of environmental protection.

Among the European publics environmental awareness has risen significantly during the past three decades, the 1986 Chernobyl disaster marking a high point in this ongoing development. Through action in the environmental field, the EC can respond directly to citizens' concerns, thus adding a 'human face' to the otherwise purely economic nature of the European integration process (see also chapter 16).

II. LEGAL BASIS, OBJECTIVES AND PRINCIPLES

II.1 Legal Basis

Before the Single European Act
No specific provisions; TEC Arts. 100 and 235 served as legal basis for European environmental policy.
— TEC Art. 100 provides for the harmonisation of Member States laws. The European Court of Justice (ECJ) held that environmental provisions could be validly based on TEC Art. 100, provided that they were linked to the setting up or the operation of the IM.
— TEC Art. 235 authorises Community action in areas which are not expressly provided for in the Treaty 'to attain, in the course of the operation of the common market, one of the objectives of the Community'.
Both articles require unanimity in the Council and consultation of the EP.
   Several other provisions were also used on occasions as legal basis for EU environmental measures: e.g., TEC Art. 39 (Common Agricultural Policy); TEC Art. 99 (harmonisation of indirect taxes); as well as Arts. 30–4 of the Euratom Treaty.

SEA, new Title 'Environment' TEC Arts. 130r–t

— TEC Art. 130r lists the principles of Community environmental policy.
— TEC Art. 130s identifies the legislative procedures to be adopted.
— TEC Art. 130t allows Member States to adopt more stringent standards.
— New TEC Art. 100a also relates to environmental measures. The new cooperation procedure for harmonisation allows a greater say for the EP, which has traditionally held 'greener' attitudes than the Council. Moreover, in its proposals concerning environmental protection, the Commission should take as a base a high level of protection. The derogation clause (TEC Art. 100a.4) allows Member States, after a harmonising measure, to apply national provisions, *inter alia*, to protect the environment or the working environment (see chapter 6).
   The distinction between TEC Arts. 100a and 130s is not always an easy one, but the resulting differences in the voting procedures and the role of the EP are important. The adoption of legislation on the incorrect legal basis, on several occasions, has been challenged before the ECJ as an abuse of the principle of institutional balance (see chapter 3).

Treaty on European Union
Major changes to the legal basis:
—Co-decision applicable to harmonisation measures (TEC Art. 100a).
—TEC Art. 130s now provides for three different voting procedures:
- QMV in the Council and cooperation procedure with the EP. This is of general application.
- QMV in the Council and co-decision procedure with the EP for 'general action programmes'.
- Unanimity in the Council and consultation of the EP for provisions of a primarily fiscal nature; measures concerning town and country planning, land use (except waste management and measures of a general nature) and management of water resources; measures significantly affecting a Member State's choice between different energy sources and the general structure of its general supply.

Moreover, the TEU gives the Member States several opportunities to apply different national standards:
—TEC Art. 130s.5: if the costs of an environmental measure are prohibitive for a Member State, the Council may grant temporary derogation and/or financial help from the Cohesion Fund.
—TEC Art. 130t: Member States are free to maintain, or introduce, more stringent national standards, as long as they are compatible with the Treaty. The TEU reinforced the powers of the Commission by stating that these measures must be notified.
—TEC Arts. 100a.5 and 130r.2: provide for the inclusion in harmonisation measures of a safeguard clause allowing Member States to adopt provisional measures for non-economic purposes subject to an EC inspection procedure.

While the SEA had introduced the concept of *subsidiarity* to define the limits of EC competence in the environment field (TEC Art. 130r.4); the TEU removed the reference and replaced it by the general rule of TEC Art. 3b.

II.2 Objectives

Objectives of the EU environmental policy (TEC Art. 130r.1):
—preserving, protecting and improving the quality of the environment;
—protecting human health;
—prudent and rational utilisation of natural resources;
—promoting measures at international level to deal with regional or worldwide environmental problems.

The phrasing used is quite wide and gives much leeway to the institutions to act in this field.

II.3 Principles (TEC Art. 130r.2)

Preventive Action Principle
This starts from the assumption that 'prevention is better than cure'. Present in all Environmental Action Programmes (EAPs — see IV), it was the main focus of the third EAP. The Environmental Impact Assessment Directive is an example of its application.

Rectification of Environmental Damage at Source
The source principle requires, for example, that preference is to be given to emission limits over quality standards.

Polluter-pays Principle
The polluter-pays principle aims to encourage polluters to find less-polluting products and technologies, by imposing charges or environmental standards that are costly to comply with (linked to the source principle).

Integration Principle
Environmental protection requirements must be integrated into the definition and implementation of other Community policies.
    This does not mean that environmental protection should always prevail in case of clashes with other policy areas. Clashes should be solved by applying the principle of proportionality: if an objective can be achieved in a variety of ways, the integration principle requires opting for the environmentally least harmful.

Precautionary Principle
Added by the TEU and stems from German environmental law where it is known as the *Vorsorgeprinzip*. The principle is that whenever there is a strong suspicion that a certain activity may have environmentally harmful consequences, it is better to act before the damage occurs rather than wait for incontrovertible scientific evidence.

High Level of Protection Principle
This was inserted by the TEU into TEC Art. 130r. 2 and is the only instance where qualitative requirements are imposed on the Commission in the preparation of its proposals. However, the practical effect of this appears to be minimal.

Other Criteria
The EC shall take account of the following criteria when preparing its environmental policy (TEC Art. 130r.3):

— availability of scientific and technical data;

— different environmental conditions in the various regions of the EC and their balanced economic and social development.

III. KEY ACTORS

European Council
The European Council has always paid particular attention to the environmental situation of the Community. Indeed, the very creation of an EC competence for the environment was the work of the 1972 Paris Summit. In 1978, the European Council decided on a specific Community action on sea pollution; the 1983 Stuttgart European Council stressed the danger threatening European forests and decided that environmental protection should become a priority; and in 1985, at Brussels, it encouraged the integration of environmental objectives into other European policies.

Commission
Key actor in European environmental policy, DG XI (Environment and Nuclear Safety), is responsible for the legislative initiative. Numerous consultative committees, composed of experts from the Member States, give advice to the Commission during the preparation of its proposals. The Commission not only starts the legislative process but also monitors the correct implementation of legislation by the Member States and it does so, in particular, by using its discretionary power to start an infringement procedure, under TEC Art. 169 (see chapter 5). Moreover, under TEC Art. 171, if the Commission considers that a Member State has not complied with an ECJ judgment, it can refer the matter back to the ECJ, asking for it to impose a fine or penalty on the Member State concerned.

While these powers are not specific to the environment sector they are particularly important in this area: of the complaints and cases investigated by the Commission every year, environmental matters hold the first position. This is why the Council, in its resolution adopting the fourth EAP, called upon the Commission to send it and the EP regular reports on the application of EC environmental law in order to assess environmental policy.

Council
Main legislator, Council of Environment Ministers meets several times a year.

European Parliament
The EP is involved in policy-making through cooperation and co-decision procedures, especially the EP's Committee on Environment, Health, Consumer Protection. Otherwise provides consultative input.

Economic and Social Committee
ECOSOC gives non-binding opinions on the Commission's proposals.

Ad hoc Dialogue Groups
Formed since the fifth EAP, these three groups are:

(a)   The General Consultative Forum on the Environment, to guarantee a better consultation and exchange of information between industry, business, regional and local authorities, professional associations, trade unions, environmental and consumer organisations and the Commission.

(b)   The Implementation Network (IMPEL), composed of representatives of national authorities and the Commission, to develop common approaches on a practical level.

(c)   The Environment Policy Review Group, including high-level representatives of the Commission and the Member States, to further a better understanding and an exchange of views.

Member States
Member States perform a double role as legislator, in the Council, and implementing actor, at the national level. Some of them (Denmark, Germany, the Netherlands), are traditionally more sensitive to environmental issues and have been very active in promoting European environmental legislation. The accession of Sweden and Austria, whose environmental standards are generally higher than in the EC, might induce a 'greening' of the Council's attitudes.

Interest Groups and Non-Governmental Organisations (NGOs)
EU sectoral trade associations and environmental NGOs are often invited by the Commission to express their views at a very early stage of the drafting of its proposals. The Brussels-based European Environmental Bureau (EEB) groups together 120 national environmental organisations.

IV. POLICY INSTRUMENTS AND ACTIONS

The general direction of environmental policy is laid out in *Environmental Action Programmes* (EAPs), prepared by the Commission and adopted by the Council. These contain general principles, objectives and criteria rather than any specific courses of action. So far, five programmes have been adopted (1973–6; 1977–81; 1982–6; 1987–92; currently running is the innovative fifth EAP, 1993–2000).

Environmental policy instruments and actions have been totally redefined by the fifth EAP, entitled 'Towards Sustainability'. The scope of activities was enlarged and new measures were introduced. Actions under the 5th EAP are inspired by the following principles:

— *Sustainable development.*

— *Integration of environmental objectives* in the other European policies (in particular, industry, energy, agriculture, transport and tourism).

— *Shared responsibility*, i.e., joint actions by the EC, Member States, regional and local authorities and citizens, as a way to bypass the difficult application of subsidiarity.

— Adoption of *market-based instruments* to encourage environmentally friendly choices.

The fifth EAP identifies the six main areas in which EC environmental action is needed:

(a)   the sustainable management of natural resources;
(b)   integrated pollution control and prevention of waste;
(c)   a reduction in the consumption of non-renewable energy;
(d)   improved transportation management and land planning;
(e)   environmental quality in urban areas;
(f)   improvements in public health and safety.

In order to conduct these activities, the EAP recommends the following policy instruments.

IV.1 Legislative Instruments

These use a classic regulatory approach to counter pollution.

Since the 1970s some 400 pieces of EU environmental legislation (especially directives) have been adopted in fields like water, waste, air quality, chemicals, noise, and nature conservation.

Even though the new prevention principle induced a proactive, rather than reactive, environmental policy, legislative instruments retain their usefulness. Legislative intervention is still needed to fix standards and impose prohibitions to ensure the functioning of the IM; to implement international obligations and guarantee a high level of environmental protection in general. A prime example is the 1996 directive on integrated pollution prevention and control (IPPC) which introduced a single permit system for air, water and ground emissions for industrial plants throughout the EC. The permit will indicate emission limit values based on the best available technology (BAT).

However, the very nature of environmental legislation itself has changed during recent years:

(a)   Constraining instruments have become rather rare, most probably as a result of the new emphasis on subsidiarity.

(b)   Voluntary schemes and financial support systems which leave a wide margin of manoeuvre in national implementation are ever more common.

(c)   The preparation of legislation includes extended consultation periods, with a greater emphasis on Green and White Papers.

IV.2 Market-based Instruments

These might be of an economic or fiscal nature, intended to encourage the use of more environmentally friendly processes and products, and are either 'soft' or 'hard'.

'Soft' instruments are merely intended to provide information to the general public to increase their environmental awareness, e.g., eco-audits and eco-labels. The Eco-audit Regulation of 1993 allows for voluntary participation of companies willing to establish an environmental policy and management scheme. In return the companies can advertise their involvement in the scheme.

'Hard' instruments, such as fiscal incentives or disincentives, aim at 'internalising' the environmental cost in the price of the product, e.g., the (failed) tax on CO_2 emissions and energy (see chapter 8).

Moreover state aids, subsidies, loans or tax discounts can be given by Member States to undertakings or consumers for 'environmental reasons'. Since they might constitute obstacles to the IM, they fall under the careful control of the Commission (see chapter 11).

'Environmental liability' would be the ultimate deterrent to environmental damage. Proposed by the fifth EAP, the Commission moved in this direction with a 1993 Green Paper which advocates a combination of a strict liability regime and a joint compensation fund financed by the polluters. A follow-up White Paper is expected in 1998.

IV.3 Horizontal Instruments

(a)   *Improvement of environmental data.* The CORINE programme of the 1980s attempted to improve environmental data comparability in Europe by standardising statistical criteria. The European Environment Agency (EEA) is now charged with providing reliable and comparative information on the state of the environment in all Member States — an essential basis for environmental decision-making.

(b)   *Scientific research* and technological development to enhance the prevention, reduction and mitigation of environmental impacts. The latter is one of the objectives of the fourth Framework research programme (1994–8).

(c)   *Public planning procedures* to identify, and eventually exclude, non-sustainable projects. Dir. 85/337/EEC (later amended) on environmental impact assessment (EIA) represents the most important legislative tool in this respect.

(d)   *Public information and education*, e.g., Dir. 90/313/EEC on freedom of access to information on the environment allows private parties to obtain environmental information from public authorities. Eco-labelling schemes, awareness campaigns, university courses and vocational training also exist.

IV.4 Financial Instruments

Environmental expenditure amounts to only 3% of the EC budget and is spread across four instruments:

(a)   *EC Structural Funds* (see chapter 13): used, *inter alia*, for environmental projects, e.g., the adaptation of new agricultural structures and development of rural areas. ENVIREG (launched in 1990) is a new fund to finance environmental investments, especially in coastal areas.

(b)   *LIFE (L'Instrument financier pour l'environnement)*: is more limited in scope. It aims to finance demonstration schemes and awareness campaigns in the field of pollution control and nature protection.

(c)   *Cohesion Fund*: used to finance environmental and transport infrastructure projects in the poorest Member States.

(d)   *European Investment Bank*: finances projects to further regional development and productivity as well as projects of common interest to several Member States, around 20% of which are environmental projects.

V. THE EXTERNAL DIMENSION OF ENVIRONMENTAL POLICY

Since the 1970s, the EU has become an important player in international environmental cooperation. It is involved in the work of the United Nations Environment Programme (UNEP), the United Nations Economic Commission for Europe (UN-ECE), the United Nations Conference on Environment and Development (UNCED), the Organisation for Economic Cooperation and Development (OECD) and the Council of Europe. Moreover, the EU is a contracting party to a number of international environmental conventions:

— Vienna Convention for the Protection of the Ozone Layer (1985).

— Montreal Protocol on Substances that Deplete the Ozone Layer (1987).

— Basle Convention on the Control of Transboundary Movements of Hazardous Wastes and their Disposal (1989).

— Convention on Biological Diversity (1992).

— United Nations Framework Convention on Climate Change and its recent update, the Kyoto Protocol (1997).

Environmental issues have also entered the EU's bilateral relations and regional arrangements:
— Title on the environment in the fourth Lomé Convention (1989).
— 1990 Nicosia Charter on the environment in the Mediterranean region.
— 10% of the funds provided by the PHARE programme are devoted to environmental projects in the CEECs.
— TACIS programme for the former Soviet Republics contains environmental aspects.

Legally, EC involvement in international environmental conventions is explicitly provided for in TEC Art. 130r.4. Indeed, one of the objectives of the European environmental policy is the promotion of 'measures at international level to deal with regional or worldwide environmental problems' (TEC Art. 130r.1). However, EC competence is shared with the Member States. Virtually all international environmental conventions to which the Community is party are mixed agreements to which the Member States are also signatories, and fall under TEC Art. 228 provisions (see chapter 10).

VI. HISTORICAL DEVELOPMENT

1957–72
The EEC devoted no specific attention to environmental issues. These were only dealt with in connection with the IM, e.g., the 1967 directive harmonising the classification, packaging and labelling of dangerous substances.

1972–86
The 1972 Declaration of the Paris Summit gave an extensive interpretation of the idea of 'economic expansion' as enshrined in TEC Art. 2: economic expansion had to result in an improvement in the quality of life, in particular by paying special attention to environmental protection. Additionally, the Summit launched the idea at establishing an Environmental Action Programme (EAP) in the course of 1973.

Three EAPs were launched between 1973 and 1987. The first (1973–6) defined the principles and objectives of EC environmental policy and described the actions to be undertaken to put them into practice. The second EAP (1977–81) simply followed up the first one, but the third EAP (1982–6) indicated priorities for action and introduced new concepts such as the principle of integration and the need for a preventive approach to environmental matters.

In parallel with the Action Programmes a quite intensive legislative activity in the environmental field developed. The lack of a specific legal basis in the Treaty was overcome by using more general provisions (e.g., TEC Arts. 100

and 235; see II). TEC Art. 100 was used when differences in national environmental legislation had a detrimental effect on the IM. TEC Art. 235 could be used because of the Paris Summit's extensive interpretation of the objective of 'economic expansion'. Indeed, environmental protection was now considered one of the objectives of the Treaty.

1987–92
The SEA provided a specific legal basis for EC environmental policy with a whole Title VII devoted to 'Environment'. At the same period, the fourth EAP (1987–92) was established.

1993 until the Entry into Force of the ToA
The TEU (in force since 1993) introduced several 'environmental' amendments in response to the changes in the international context. Already in 1987 the Brundtland report, *Our Common Future*, had created the idea of sustainable development as a means to reconcile environmental protection and economic growth. This concept was taken up by the 1992 UN Conference on the Environment, in Rio de Janeiro, where several international conventions were signed. Therefore, it is not surprising that the TEU refers, in its objectives in TEC Art. 2, to the respect of the environment. It also explicitly mentions environment policy in TEC Art. 3.k) and the idea of sustainability in TEC Arts. 2 and 130u.1 as well as in TEU Art. B.

Meanwhile, the fifth EAP 'Towards Sustainability' (1993–2000) was issued. It identified new principles and instruments to enhance environmental protection at the European level (see IV).

From the Entry into Force of ToA
The Amsterdam Treaty, signed in June 1997, will probably enter into force in late 1998, after ratification by all Member States. It can be considered as the starting point of the fifth phase of the historical development of European environmental policy despite the limited changes it has introduced in this field (see VII).

VII. RECENT DEVELOPMENTS

VII.1 Identifying the Reasons for the Limited Progress So Far

The EAP identified most of the elements to make the progress work. What is lacking is the political will (Commission progress report on the implementation of the fifth EAP, 1996)

In particular, the Commission:

— stressed the need for a better integration of environmental considerations into other policies, such as agriculture, transport, energy, industry and tourism;
— insisted on the need to broaden the range of environmental policy instruments, following the guidelines of the 5th EAP;
— argued for better cooperation ·with the implementing authorities together with an increased use of awareness-raising actions;
— underlined the need for enhanced international cooperation, particularly with CEECs in view of the future enlargement, by giving them access to LIFE funding.

VII.2 A Partial Remedy: the Treaty of Amsterdam

Environmental policy was one of the few TEC policy areas to be comprehensively reviewed at the Inter-Governmental Conference of 1996–7 which produced the ToA. Even though QMV and the co-decision procedure were not extended, and an environmental 'integration clause' was not included into other chapters (agriculture, transport) — as the EP had suggested — some of the Commission's concerns have been taken up:

— The concept of *sustainable development* has been inserted into the Preamble to the TEU and the objectives of the Union (ToA/TEU Art. 2). The EC's tasks (ToA/TEC Art. 2) now include sustainable development, a high level of protection and improvement of the quality of the environment.
— *Environmental protection must be integrated* into the definition and implementation of the Community policies and activities with a view to promoting sustainable development (new ToA/TEC Art. 6).
— The new ToA/TEC Art. 95 contains technical and procedural changes which in fact foster a 'greener' policy formulation for harmonisation measures and strengthen the Commission's hand regarding the derogation regime.
— A new protocol to the Treaty on *animal welfare*. Animal welfare aspects now enter the formulation and implementation of other EC policies while respecting religious rights, cultural traditions and regional heritage of the Member States.

The impact of these changes will have to be evaluated in the future, once the ToA is in force. In any case, it is only through secondary law that greater progress in environmental policy can be expected, provided the Commission continues actively to promote 'green' legislation.

The ToA's revisions are summarised below:

Current Provisions	Provisions after Amsterdam
Preamble TEU, 7th indent	Preamble ToA/TEU, 8th indent — reference to sustainable development
TEU Art. B (Objectives of the Union)	ToA/TEU Art. 2 — reference to sustainable development
TEC Art. 2 (Tasks of the Community)	ToA/TEC Art. 2 — reference to sustainable development and high level of protection and improvement of the quality of the environment
TEC Art. 3.k (Activities of the Community)	ToA/TEC Art. 3.1 — unchanged
—	ToA/TEC Art. 6 — new integration clause
TEC Art. 100a (Approximation of laws)	ToA/TEC Art. 95 — new paragraphs 3 to 8
TEC Art. 130r (Environment principles)	ToA/TEC Art. 174 — unchanged
TEC Art. 130s (Environment procedures)	ToA/TEC Art. 175 — unchanged
TEC Art. 130t (Environment opt-ups)	ToA/TEC Art. 176 — unchanged

VIII. FURTHER READING

CORCELLE, Guy and JOHNSON, Stanley: *The Environmental Policy of the European Communities*, London, Kluwer Law International, 1995.

JANS, Jan: *European Environmental Law*, London, Kluwer Law International, 1995.

KISS, Alexander: *Droit international de l'environnement*, Paris, Pedone, 1989.

KRÄMER, Ludwig: *EEC Treaty and Environmental Protection*, London, Sweet and Maxwell, 1990.

SANDS, Philippe: *Principles of International Environmental Law*, Manchester, Manchester University Press, 1994.

SBRAGIA, Alberta: 'Environmental policy: 'push-pull' of policy-making' in WALLACE, Helen and WALLACE, William (eds): *Policy Making in the European Union*, Oxford, OUP, 1996, pp. 235–55.

STIBBE SIMONT MONAHAN DUHOT: *Environment and Europe*, Deventer, Kluwer Law and Taxation Publishers, 1994

Websites

DG XI (Environment, Nuclear Safety and Civil Protection)	http://europa.eu.int/comm/dg11/dg11home.html
European Environmental Agency	http://www.eea.dk

16   CONSUMER POLICY

Gabriel Glöckler

I. RATIONALE

The development of consumer policy should be seen as a flanking policy to the establishment of the Internal Market (IM). By stressing the benefit to all consumers of greater choice and diversity in the IM, the Community attempted to give a 'human face' to the process of economic integration, which was otherwise rather biased in favour of producers. Whilst producer interests are forcefully represented by well-endowed lobby groups, consumers are atomised market participants without a proper capacity to put pressure on producers to improve quality and safety of products at competitive prices.

As harmonisation within the IM proceeded, another, more functional, rationale for consumer policy was established by the Court of Justice. When the 1979 *Cassis de Dijon* ruling instituted the principle of mutual recognition (see chapter 6), it guaranteed the free movement of goods under the condition that certain minimum requirements were respected throughout the Community — including one on consumer protection. Thus, in order to avoid restrictions to the free movement of goods on grounds of consumer protection, some form of common consumer protection standards had to be agreed upon.

II. LEGAL BASIS, PRINCIPLES, OBJECTIVES

II.1 Legal Basis

Single European Act
— implicit recognition of EC activity in the field of consumer protection;
— TEC Art. 100a.3 requires Commission to base its legislative proposals for the Single Market programme on the premise of attaining, *inter alia*, a high level of consumer protection.

Treaty on European Union
Establishes a legal basis for EC activity regarding consumer protection:
— Title XI *Consumer Protection*: contains a single TEC Art. 129a: contribution of EC to attainment of high level of consumer protection;
— revision of TEC Art. 3 — activities of the EC include 'a contribution to the strengthening of consumer protection'.

II.2 Principles

Five fundamental rights were established in 1975. The use of the word 'right' reveals the acceptance by the Council that consumer interests transcend a purely economic focus:

(a) *Right to safety and health*: goods and services should not present any danger if used under normal conditions. If a product or service is found to be dangerous, a proper procedure should provide for its withdrawal from the market.

(b) *Right to redress* and to get remedies in case of damages incurred because of goods or services.

(c) *Right to protection of economic interests*: the buyer must be protected against certain selling practices, especially regarding loans, credits, contract clauses, after-sales service.

(d) *Right to information and education*: the consumer must be informed of the characteristics of products and services and regarding their safe use.

(e) *Right to representation*: consumers must be represented in the EC policy cycle in order to make their views known.

EC consumer policy is geared towards guaranteeing these rights, *inter alia*, by:
— ensuring that the interests of consumers are taken into consideration in the development of other EU policies (principle of *integration and horizontal implementation*);

— improving consumer information to provide transparency of the market and the fostering of consumer confidence;
— improving the safety of consumer products and services circulating in the IM;
— involving consumers' organisations in the EC policy process.

'Subsidiary'
The principle of *subsidiarity* means that EC action is to complement, rather than replace, national regulations on consumer protection.
— In practice, common norms are agreed at EC level, but allowance is made for stricter national norms, provided they do not present non-tariff barriers;
— subsidiarity is a powerful argument to oppose EC initiatives in the field: after the 1992 Edinburgh European Council, the Commission decided to revise and soften several proposals (on comparative advertising; on the liability of service suppliers).

> On balance, *subsidiarity has limited the scope of the policy*, excluding or restricting measures which are not directly linked with the achievement of the IM.

'Opt-up'
Member States are allowed to maintain more stringent national consumer protection standards. Sanctioned on grounds of public safety, 'the protection of health and life of humans, animals or plants' (TEC Art. 36), these measures may even amount to intra-EU trade restrictions (import bans). The recent BSE scare and the resulting import ban on British beef provides a vivid example.

III. LINKAGES WITH OTHER POLICY AREAS

Consumer policy is primarily conducted indirectly, which is to say through other policy activities (e.g., Common Agricultural Policy, competition, IM harmonisation), as the principle of integration and horizontal implementation requires. Since consumer issues are pervasive in economic integration — consumers represent, after all, the demand side of the common market — the objectives of consumer protection have entered the EC agenda in many policy areas.

Internal Market regulation; competition policy; liberalisation:
— under the leitmotif of greater consumer choice and lower prices, gradual opening up to competition of the monopolised utilities and telecommunications sectors (i.e., guaranteeing competition is the best consumer policy);

— liberalisation and competition within framework of tough consumer protection guidelines (e.g., consumer information, price and billing transparency);

— numerous initiatives for consumer-related regulation on EC level, e.g., on banking, insurance and financial services, postal services, electronic commerce.

Common Commercial Policy (CCP):
— Protectionist ambitions can be couched in terms of consumer protection requirements; for example, the EU import ban on hormone-treated meat from the US and Canada has been condemned by WTO (1997) as an illegal barrier to trade.

EMU:
— consumer issues are high political priorities in allaying fears of the European public: the advantages of the single currency are stressed, e.g., Commission attempts to push for a consumer-friendly change-over scenario (so far with limited success);

— technical issues such as design and metal content of euro coins.

Common Agricultural Policy (CAP) and public health and food safety policy:
— CAP policy regime aims at ensuring 'reasonable prices for consumers' and prohibition of 'discrimination between producers or consumers within the Community';

— more recently, food safety has become top priority (e.g., BSE, labelling of genetically altered foodstuffs). ·

Environmental policy:
Environmental standard-setting closely connected to consumer protection e.g., air or drinking and bathing water quality, car exhaust emissions.

IV. KEY ACTORS

European Commission:
Consumer Policy Service (CPS) detached from DG XI in 1989 and established as an independent service headed by a Director-General; in 1995, CPS became a fully fledged DG XXIV.

European Parliament:
Legislative involvement, consumer protection measures are dealt with through the co-decision procedure (TEC Art. 189b); active role of parliamentary

Committee on Environment, Health, Consumer Protection, especially regarding the financing of consumer activities.

Council:
Takes decisions with QMV under TEC Art. 129a, irregular meetings specifically to discuss consumer issues.

European Court of Justice:
Important role in guaranteeing access to justice; case law provides interpretation and guidance to consumer policy.

Consumers' organisations at EU and national level:
The Commission involves consumer representative groups, joined in the *Consumer Committee* (previously Consumer Consultative Council), which is the main channel of representation:
— Consumer Committee solely responsible to the Commission; prepares opinions to be addressed to the Commission;
— established in 1973 and reformed many times, at present composed of representatives from the five European consumer organisations:

BEUC	Bureau Européen des Unions de Consommateurs
COFACE	Comité des Organisations Familiales Auprès des Communautés Européennes
ETUC	European Trade Unions Confederation
EUROCOOP	European Confederation of Consumer Cooperatives
IEIC	Institut Européen Interrégional de la Consommation

as well as national consumer organisations (15 seats).
    In addition, a *European Consumer Forum* was created in 1994 to serve as a platform of dialogue between industry and consumer groups.

V. POLICY INSTRUMENTS

V.1 Instruments

The general direction of consumer policy is laid out in Consumer Policy Programmes prepared by the Commission and adopted by the Council. These .contain rather general principles, objectives and criteria and do not bring about any specific courses of action. So far, four programmes have been adopted (1975, preliminary programme stating the basic consumer rights; follow-up programmes for 1981–6, 1990–3, and 1993–5).

More specific actions, founded in the legal basis for consumer policy, are relatively rare. Generally, most consumer-related initiatives at EC level are taken indirectly through activities in other policy areas (see III).

(a) *General harmonisation measures* aiming to achieve IM (TEC Art. 100a): indirect consumer policy, IM harmonisation remains prime objective.

(b) *Specific action* to protect health, safety and economic interests of consumers and to provide adequate information to consumers. This is intended as support and supplement to Member States' policies, but so far only one programme has been adopted, destined for the poorest consumers. However, the definition of 'specific action' is very vague. (Does that include regulations? Are general and horizontal actions excluded?)

V.2 Financing

The budget of consumer policy reached some 20 million ECU in 1996 (around 0.01% of the EC budget). Every year, the Council attempts to cut back funds, but the EP regularly reinstates the consumer budget in the course of the budget procedure.

VI. HISTORICAL DEVELOPMENT

The 1957 Rome Treaty envisaged a common market, which was to benefit all European consumers (quasi-automatically) by providing them with diversity and quality; hence there was no explicit legal basis for activity on consumer protection.

In 1962, the Commission established a *contact committee* comprising representatives of trade unions and consumer organisations, to be consulted mainly on CAP. At the 1972 Paris Summit, environmental policy and consumer protection were launched, aiming at providing a new impetus to integration and giving a 'human face' to the EC (see chapter 15). The Commission was asked to prepare a policy project and set up a *Consumer Policy Service*; at the same time, the contact committee was upgraded to become the Consumer Consultative Committee.

Following a Council resolution, the Commission set up the first *Programme for Consumer Protection and Information* (1975) stating consumers' rights, for the first time (see II). In order to implement the principles, the Commission presented numerous proposals but these took a long time to get approval in the Council (in some cases more than 10 years). The main focus of the legislation passed during the first years was safety and health, whilst sensitive issues (e.g., the protection of economic interests of consumers) never really got on the agenda. Economic stagnation in the late 1970s did not even allow for the completion of the programme. The second programme (1981) went further — requiring consumer interest to be taken into account in the development of common policies. But the non-binding and declaratory character of the programmes (stating principles for action without adequate enforcement mechanisms) meant that consumer policy since 1975 had to rely on 'soft law' — and in case of policy clashes, powerful economic interests frequently held the upper hand.

A new start came in 1985 with the *Commission Communication on a New Impetus for Consumer Protection Policy*, which implicitly recognised the relative insufficiency of action so far. It linked the future development of consumer policy to the benefits from completing the IM ('1992 Programme') and aimed at reshaping EC consumer policy to follow the 'New Approach' for harmonisation (see chapter 6). Rather than explicitly stipulating consumer protection standards for individual products in a cumbersome case-by-case method, the Commission proposed directives guaranteeing minimum levels of protection for a whole product range. Through this 'New Approach' to harmonisation, consumer policy was to find a place in the legislative initiatives of the 1992 Programme.

The *Single European Act* (1986) did not — despite the EP's pressure — include specific provisions on consumer policy. The Treaty did stipulate that proposals relating to IM legislation have to aim at high levels of consumer protection. It was an implicit recognition of EC action in the field but clearly subordinated consumer protection to the completion of the IM. In the run-up to '1992', legislation notably included directives on safety standards for toys, safety requirements for building materials and design requirements for personal protection equipment. New health controls and labelling requirements were also applied to food and agricultural products. In 1990, an ECJ ruling (*GB-INNO* v *Confédération du Commerce Luxembourgeoise*) held that the right to information of the consumers was a fundamental right — even though it was not provided for explicitly by the Treaty.

Institutionally, the 1975 Consumer Policy Service had become fully fledged DG XXIV by 1995; over the same time, the involvement of consumer organisations in EC policy-making was developed (1989 saw the enlargement of the Consumers' Consultative Committee to include national consumer organisations). The renamed Council's remit was enlarged to all measures which might have an impact on consumers.

> *Assessing the progress of consumer policy until 1991* (Huyse)
> The relative weakness of consumer policy at EC level with its declaratory character and lack of substantive output can be put down to economic and structural factors:
>
> – general lack of political will to pursue further integration, and consequently little willingness to take on common norms on consumer protection;
> – 'regulatory competition' whereby a number of Member States had established their own consumer protection standards during the 1960s and 70s and were reluctant to accept EC re-regulation;
> – absence of a legal basis;
> – lack of clout of European consumer organisations to push forward EC consumer policy;
> – inadequacy of Commission's 'total harmonisation' (prior to the 'New Approach').

The progress in consumer protection achieved through other EC legislation, mainly IM harmonisation, was to be consolidated by the Commission's 1990 *Three-Year Action Plan*. It focused on strengthening consumer representation, information, safety and transactions. The Plan also introduced the *subsidiarity principle* by stating that: 'practical consumer policy must be effectively managed by the Member States. ... It would be unrealistic to undertake such tasks continuously at Community level'.

The 1991 *Treaty on European Union* not only enshrined the subsidiarity principle but also stipulated, for the first time, a legal basis for consumer policy. In contrast to pre-Maastricht, the new title liberated consumer policy from its linkage with IM legislation. The TEU thus gave a new impetus to consumer policy at EC level; in the past few years a wide-ranging array of consumer protection measures have been adopted including rules on consumer credit, unfair consumer contracts (1993) and consumer rights in distance selling (1997).

Issues currently under discussion relate, *inter alia*, to proposals for EU-wide rules on injunctions for the protection of consumers' interests and a consumer-friendly regulation of the financial services sector. In the follow-up to the 1997 Green Paper, *Convergence of the Telecommunications, Media and Information Technology Sectors, and the Implications for Regulation*, a whole raft of initiatives has sprung up, many of them with a crucial consumer dimension, such as electronic commerce or payment cards (see chapter 18).

Yet despite the formal inclusion of consumer protection into the Treaty, a difficult tension persists between the airy rhetoric of safeguarding consumer interests and actual political outcomes where producers' pressure groups exert substantial, and often decisive, influence.

VII. FUTURE PROSPECTS

VII.1 Facing new challenges

In an attempt to adapt consumer policy to the current challenges the Commission set out (in 1995) its *Priorities for Consumer Policy: 1996–98*:
— new area of activity: protecting consumers' interest regarding essential public utility services; an aim which is potentially in conflict with projected deregulation in these sectors;
— updating of policy objectives to account for the rise of the information society;
— focus on Eastern enlargement. Aims at providing assistance to CEECs to help develop their own policies in favour of consumers.

As the 1995 communication showed, the Commission intends to tackle head-on the new issues of the information society and regulate the liberalised industries (telecommunications, postal services, water and gas providers, etc.) in a consumer-friendly way. Furthermore, the complexities arising from the introduction of the single currency will provide ample opportunity for a forceful expression of consumer interests in the process.

VII.2 Amsterdam and the Consolidation of the Treaties

Current TEC provisions	*Provisions after Amsterdam*
Title XI 'Consumer Protection Art. 129a (Consumer Protection)	Title XIV 'Consumer Protection' Art. 153 unchanged, apart from the insertion of Art. 153.1-2. Art. 153.1 adds a general provision that the EC is to promote the interests of the consumers and ensure a high level of consumer protection (by way of promoting consumers' rights to information, education and to organise themselves). Art. 153.2 includes the 'principle of integration and horizontal implementation'.

In conclusion, consumer policy is set to remain a peripheral, yet for symbolic reasons important, policy area, not least because the European integration process as a whole increasingly needs to justify itself in the eyes of EU publics. Emphasising the benefit to the consumer of further market integration, liberalisation, deregulation and re-regulation at EU level could help to generate a more positive connotation of 'Brussels' in the perception of Europeans. Finally, consumer policy at European level contributes to a levelling out of the still significant North–South gap in consumer awareness and information.

VIII. FURTHER READING

WEATHERILL, Stephen: *EC Consumer Law and Policy*, London, Longman, 1997.
REICH, Norbert and WOODROFFE, Geoffrey (eds): *European Consumer Policy after Maastricht*, Dordrecht, Kluwer Academic Publishers, 1994.
HUYSE, Luc et al.: 'La politique européenne des consommateurs,' *Courrier Hebdomadaire*, No. 1357, Brussels, CRISP, 1992.

Periodicals

Journal of Consumer Policy
Consumer Policy Review

Websites

DG XXIV (Consumer Policy and Consumer Health Protection)	http://europa.eu.int/en/comm/spc/spc.html
BEUC (Bureau Européen des Unions de Consommateurs)	http://www.beuc.org/

17 SOCIAL AND EMPLOYMENT POLICY

Gioia Scappucci

I. DEFINITION AND RATIONALE

At the European level 'social policy' has a restricted meaning, merely referring to *actions to improve working conditions and living standards for workers*. EC action is to *complement rather than replace Member States' social policies*. Until the Treaty of Amsterdam (ToA), 'employment' has never been considered as a 'policy' in itself: it has been regarded as an issue falling within the broader scope of the 'social field'.

The need to give the economic integration process a 'human face' led to a strengthening of the idea of 'Social Europe'. Not only would an EC social policy counterbalance the perceived bias of the Internal Market (IM) project towards producer interests, but it would also facilitate the free movement of workers.

II. OBJECTIVES, LEGAL BASIS AND INSTRUMENTS

II.1 Objectives

The Preamble of the Treaty of Rome stressed that the Member States were 'resolved to ensure the economic and social progress of their countries' by constantly improving the living and working conditions of their peoples. TEC Art. 2 indicated 'an accelerated raising of the standard of living' as an objective of the Community. To pursue it, TEC Art. 3.i provided that the activities of the Community should include 'the establishment of a European Social Fund in order to improve employment opportunities for workers and to contribute to the raising of their standard of living'. The Preamble of the SEA broadened the objective of social policy by referring to the aim of 'promoting social justice'.

The TEU combined the objective of promoting 'social progress' with the strengthening of 'social cohesion' (TEU Art. B). Correspondingly, it inserted in the TEC a new Art. 2 which highlighted that 'The Community shall have as its task ... to promote ... a high level of employment and of social protection, the raising of the standard of living and quality of life, and economic and social cohesion and solidarity among Member States'. To achieve this, a new TEC Art. 3.i pointed at 'a policy in the social sphere comprising a European Social Fund' and TEC Art. 3.j stressed the 'the strengthening of economic and social cohesion' (see chapter 13).

II.2 Legal Basis and Instruments

II.2.1 The Original Treaty Provisions

TEC Title III 'Social Policy', Chapter 1, 'Social Provisions'

— TEC Art. 117 stipulates the need to promote improved working conditions and an improved standard of living for workers, so as to simultaneously harmonise these while maintaining their improvement.
— TEC Art. 118 requires the Commission to promote close cooperation between the Member States in the social field, particularly in matters relating to:
- employment;
- social security;
- labour law and working conditions;
- vocational training;
- prevention of occupational accidents and diseases, occupational hygiene;
- the right of association, and collective bargaining between employers and workers
— TEC Art. 119 guarantees the application of the principle of equal pay for men and women for equal work.

— TEC Art. 120 relates to equivalence between paid holiday schemes in the Member States.

— TEC Art. 121 foresees that the Council may assign tasks to the Commission to implement common measures adopted to guarantee free movement of workers, e.g., social security of migrant workers (see chapter 6).

— TEC Art. 122 provides for a Commission report on social matters.

TEC Title III, Chapter 2, 'The European Social Fund' (ESF)

— TEC Art. 123 sets out the objectives of the ESF: improving employment opportunities, *inter alia*, by increasing workers' geographical and occupational mobility.

— TEC Arts. 124–7 regulate the administration of the ESF (i.e., by the Commission, Member States and social partners) as well as the establishment of its tasks and the conditions for its working.

— TEC Art. 128 relates to general principles of a common vocational training policy.

With the exception of TEC Art. 119, the original treaty provisions were *very weak*. They conferred no legislative competence on the Community and did not produce any direct effect for individuals. The nature of these provisions (except for TEC Art. 119) was essentially 'aspirational': no specific obligation was imposed. This choice mirrored the belief that social progress would indirectly flow from the improved economic conditions which would result from the IM (see V).

Given the absence of a specific legal basis to ensure social progress, the Commission could also base its proposals on TEC Art. 235, which permits actions necessary to attain an EC objective when the Treaty has not provided the Community with the necessary powers. If a link with the IM was feasible, the Commission could also propose initiatives using TEC Art. 100 (harmonisation) as a legal basis.

II.2.2 The Single European Act
The SEA added two new provisions:

— TEC Art. 118b: A rather weak provision in line with the 'aspirational character' of the original provisions, which allows the Commission to encourage social dialogue at EC level. The article does not say how the Commission may achieve such an objective, nor what aims such a dialogue should pursue.

— TEC Art. 118a provides, for the first time, a *legal basis* for the adoption of Directives to improve, especially in the working environment, the health and safety of workers. EC harmonisation is to provide minimum requirements for health and safety of workers.

According to O'Keeffe, TEC Art. 118a 'marks a definite policy decision. Instead of aiming at an optimal social policy, setting high level standards throughout the Community, the SEA testifies to the realisation that this might be an unrealistic goal. Thus the less controversial path of gradual implementation of minimum requirements aims only at setting minimum thresholds in terms of health and safety'.

Examples of legislation adopted under TEC Art. 118a:

— Dir. 89/391 on parental leave.

— Dir. 92/85 on pregnant and breast-feeding workers.

— Dir. 93/104, the so-called 'working-time directive' on the reduction of working hours to 48 hours per week.

— Dir. 91/383 on the protection of the health and safety of fixed-term or temporary workers.

Since TEC Art. 118a.3 allows Member States to maintain or introduce more stringent measures for the protection of working conditions, debates on the costs of social policy and the potential for social dumping in the IM have flourished after the entry into force of the SEA.

As O' Keeffe explains, TEC Art. 118a also 'illustrates the tensions inherent in a Community with different levels of prosperity and therefore different levels of ability on the part of the Member States to pay for an optimal system of worker protection'.

When the scope of the measures went beyond TEC Art. 118a, the Commission continued to use TEC Arts. 100 and 235. It also tried to use TEC Art. 100a (harmonisation; see chapter 6) even though it was limited by TEC Art. 100a para. 2, which explicitly forbids its application to the approximation of provisions relating to the free movement of persons as well as those relating to the rights and interests of employed persons.

II.2.3 The Treaty on European Union

Treaty provisions
While the substance of the provisions remained unchanged, renumbering was agreed upon, leading to a new TEC Title VIII 'Social policy, education, vocational training and youth' consisting of:

(a)   Social provisions (TEC Arts. 117–22).

(b)   The European Social Fund (TEC Arts. 123–5, former TEC Arts. 126–7 were deleted).

(c)   Education, vocational training and youth (new TEC Arts. 126–7).

Other new provisions of a social nature were included in the new titles on culture (TEC Title IX), public health (TEC Title X), consumer protection (TEC Title XI) and economic and social cohesion (TEC Title XIV).

TEU Protocol No. 14 on Social Policy

Agreed by all Member States (12 at the time, 15 since 1995), *the Protocol on Social Policy* authorises all willing Member States (i.e., all except the UK) to pursue a broader social policy, the substance of which was set out in the *Agreement on Social Policy* annexed to the Protocol itself. Both the Protocol and the Agreement are to be 'without prejudice to the provisions of this Treaty, particularly those relating to social policy which constitute an integral part of the *acquis communautaire*'.

The *Protocol* authorises the signatories of the Agreement to use the institutions, procedures and mechanisms of the Treaty to give it effect (Art. 1). The relations with the UK are regulated in Art. 2, which stresses the UK's exclusion from Council deliberations on Commission proposals based on the Social Protocol and Agreement. It consequently clarifies that voting modalities applying to these decisions have to be calculated excluding the weight of the UK.

The *Agreement* on Social Policy underlines the wish of its signatories to implement the 1989 Social Charter (see V) on the basis of the *acquis communautaire*. The following articles give the Member States competence to go beyond the scope of the Treaty provisions.

Art. 1 sets out the expanded objectives of Social Policy: 'promotion of employment, improved living and working conditions, proper social protection, dialogue between management and labour, the development of human resources with a view to lasting high employment and the combating of exclusion'. But EC action is limited by an emphasis on national practices and the pressures of maintaining competitiveness.

Art. 2 states that improvement of the working environment to protect workers' health and security; working conditions; information and consultation of workers; equal job opportunities for both sexes and remedying social exclusion are areas in which EC action (Directives with minimum requirements) is to complement Member States' activities.

The Council may take measures in the areas of social security and social protection of workers, protection of workers where their employment contract is terminated, representation and collective defence of interests of workers and employers, conditions of employment of third-country nationals, financial contributions for promotion of employment and job creation. Member States are allowed to maintain or introduce more stringent protective measures.

Implementation of Directives may be entrusted to the social partners at their request. Great importance is attached to collective bargaining at Community level. The social partners are granted a substantial role in the formulation and implementation of legislation (see IV).

Pay, the right of association, the right to strike and the right to impose lock-outs are excluded from EC competence.

Art. 3 describes the Commission's role in encouraging *social dialogue* and Art. 4 highlights the consequences of a positive outcome of social dialogue (see III and IV).

The Council has only adopted one directive so far on the basis of the Social Agreement, namely the Works Council Directive of September 1994.

III. DECISION-MAKING

III.1 Treaty provisions (TEC, binding all Member States)

— For measures under TEC Art. 118a, cooperation with consultation of the Economic and Social Committee (ECOSOC).
— If measures are taken under TEC Art. 235 and TEC Art. 100, the Council acts unanimously, on a proposal of the Commission, after having consulted the EP.
— TEC Art. 100a requires co-decision with consultation of ECOSOC.

III.2 Social Agreement (binding 14 Member States, not the UK)

— *Cooperation procedure and QMV in the Council* for the vast majority of issues.
— *Unanimity* in the Council with EP consultation for measures concerning social security and social protection of workers, protection of workers where their employment contract is terminated, representation and collective defence of interests of workers and employers, and employment conditions of third-country nationals.
— *If social dialogue is successful* the agreement concluded at Community level may be implemented:
  • in accordance with the procedures and practices specific to management and labour and the Member States;
  • by a decision taken by the Council by QMV (unless the agreement in question covers areas where the Council votes by unanimity). The Council acts on the basis of a Commission proposal. The EP is not involved in the procedure.

IV. KEY ACTORS

The ECJ, a crucial activist role
Its case law has given social policy provisions a more substantive content. By extensively interpreting the notion of 'health and safety of workers', it recognised the legality of regulations adopted on the basis of TEC Art. 118a which might have otherwise fallen outside the scope of its application. Its interpretation of TEC Art. 119 has given the Council the impetus to adopt a series of measures to guarantee equal treatment. The ECJ's rulings have also had a significant impact on the Member States requiring, at times, national reforms (e.g., *Barber* case, C-262/88).

The Commission, an ambitious actor
The Commission, through DG V (Employment, Industrial Relations and Social Affairs), launches reflection and suggestions through the adoption of Social Action Plans, communications, Green and White Papers, and legislative proposals. It also has an important role in encouraging consultation of the social partners as well as in promoting social dialogue at Community level. The Commission heightens its profile through involvement in international organisations such as the International Labour Organisation (ILO).

The Council, a reluctant actor
The Council's reluctance to act in the social field reflects not only the Member States' attachment to their national social policies but also the diverging views on the scope of EC intervention in labour relations. The Council adopts Directives or measures necessary to realise the social objectives set by the Treaty.

The EP, a weak actor seeking to strengthen its role
The EP is briefed and consulted on issues where the Council votes by unanimity. If measures are adopted on the basis of the Social Agreement, it is involved through the cooperation procedure. It is not involved at all in 'social dialogue'.

Social partners: potentially significant actors
Labour and management are represented at the Community level by the European Trade Union Confederation (ETUC), the European Confederation of Industries (UNICE) and the European Centre for Public Enterprises (CEEP).
    According to Social Agreement provisions (Arts. 3 and 4), labour and management:

—should be consulted by the Commission on the contents of its envisaged proposals before their submission;
—may ask the Commission to initiate a 'social dialogue' process;
—may, as a result of 'EC social dialogue', conclude contractual relations (including agreements);
—if the 'social dialogue' outcome is an agreement, may implement it according to the procedures and practices specific to management and labour.

ECOSOC
Consisting of representatives of the various categories of economic and social activity, it plays an advisory role. It is generally consulted on matters relating to social policy and may issue an opinion on its own initiative when considered appropriate (TEC Art. 198).

Member States
Member States are responsible for the correct implementation of Directives, even when the implementation of these is entrusted to the social partners.

V. HISTORICAL DEVELOPMENT

Until the 1970s, in line with the Member States' experience of fast economic expansion and increasing wealth of their populations, it was assumed that the social dimension of European integration would flow indirectly from the establishment of the common market. In the 1960s, the EC's main preoccupation was to harmonise common health and safety standards.

During the 1970s, as economic shocks and rising unemployment hit the Member States, the EC attempted to tackle unemployment, but the Treaty did not provide the means to meet such an ambitious goal. Only the ESF supported some work and education programmes. The Commission's first Social Action Programme (1974) led to the development of programmes for the promotion of vocational training and worker adaptation. 1975 saw the establishment of the European Foundation for the Improvement of the Living and Working Conditions in Dublin.

At the beginning of the 1980s, Member States realised that the 'trickle-down' effects of market integration did not materialise and the economic integration had to be accompanied by action in the social field. In 1981, the Commission defined the 'European Social Space' as an area within which social legislation should be harmonised, *inter alia*, through:

(a)   intensification of social dialogue;
(b)   heightening of cooperation and consultation on social protection;

(c)   pursuit of employment as the cornerstone of EC policy.

In the mid 1980s, following the adoption of the Adonnino report, *A People's Europe* (1985) and the Cecchini report, *The Costs of Non Europe* (see chapter 6), the Commission set up a working group to examine the social dimension of the IM. The economic project of the '1992 programme' had to be coupled with social action, leading to a proper legal basis for social policy in the SEA (see II). In 1985, Commission President Delors launched the 'Val Duchesse dialogue' between the social partners encouraging them to conclude framework agreements.

The airy commitment to a Social Europe demanded substantive action. However, setting out social rights was not possible within the EC framework, given the UK's opposition. The other Member States circumvented British intransigence by adopting the *1989 Social Charter*. It proclaimed a whole set of social rights for the European citizens by highlighting the social needs in particular of the young, the old, the handicapped and the unemployed. The Charter has no legally binding character but it can be referred to by the ECJ while interpreting EC legislation.

In 1989, the Commission produced a Social Action Programme suggesting measures to implement the Social Charter. In doing so, it faced the problem that many areas covered by the Charter had no corresponding legal basis in the Treaty (see II). If the measures could not fall within the scope of TEC Art. 118a, the Commission tried to base its proposals on TEC Arts. 100, 100a and 235. Inevitably, conflicts arose with the Council, since the choice of the legal basis determined whether the Council should vote by QMV or by unanimity (see III).

The need to provide the Community with broader competences to implement the 1989 Social Charter was discussed during the 1991 IGC. No consensus was possible with the UK on including new social policy provisions in the body of the TEU. Nevertheless a compromise was reached: all 12 Member States signed a Social Protocol under which the 11 Member States wishing 'to continue along the path laid down in the 1989 Social Charter' adopted an Agreement to that end.

The Social Protocol and the Social Agreement introduced a *twin-track social policy*, i.e., the possibility of expanding EC social policy but also the risk of endangering the IM by creating competitive imbalances and the possibility for social dumping. In order to lower the chance of these risks, the Commission strategically continued to base its proposals on Treaty provisions. Only when the support of the UK was not forthcoming, was the Social Agreement used as a legal basis.

In 1994, the Commission produced a White Paper explaining its approach to social policy after the entry into force of the TEU. It identified a number of key principles and objectives for social policy: these particularly emphasised the employment dimension of social policy. It reiterated that the Community should concentrate on the identification of common goals in the social domain and not aim for total harmonisation. This reflected a growing recognition of Member States' divergent conceptions of the scope and usefulness of government action in the social field. Thus, in the 1995–7 Social Action Programme the Commission:

— highlighted the wide diversity of opinions among the Member States on further developments of social policy;

— suggested a wide variety of initiatives aimed at fighting unemployment and stimulating training and education;

— stressed the need to build a European labour market and to encourage high labour standards.

However, the wider context of globalisation and a widespread perception of the supremacy of the Anglo-Saxon model of capitalism, have altered the goalposts of social policy at EC level and generated an extensive debate about the nature and viability of a 'European Social Model'.

VI. RECENT DEVELOPMENTS

Labour's victory in the British elections in May 1997, combined with the challenge of bringing Europe closer to the citizens, led to the inclusion of the Social Agreement in the body of the Treaty. At the same time, the pressure of public opinion pushed the Member States to add specific provisions on employment in the Treaty.

VI.1 Amsterdam and Social Policy

The ToA incorporates the Social Agreement into the TEC and its scope is slightly broadened. But even so, social policy objectives have to be pursued by the Community and the Member States — as before. 'Best practice' and information exchange between the Member States have gained prominence as means to tackle social problems.

A significant change concerns the explicit reference, in ToA/TEC Art. 136, to respect for fundamental social rights — such as those enshrined in the 1989 Social Charter — which will bind all Member States (including the UK which did not sign the original Social Charter).

Whilst the policy objectives remain unchanged, the instruments have been expanded with:

— a new legal basis to adopt measures to combat social exclusion (ToA/TEC Art. 137.2);

— a broader legal basis on equal opportunities (ToA/TEC Art. 141): the treaty now espouses the principle of equal pay 'for equal work or work of equal value' and allows Member States to maintain 'positive discrimination' measures.

The social dialogue provisions of the Social Agreement were incorporated into the Treaty with no change (ToA/TEC Arts. 138–40).

The ToA makes the co-decision procedure and QMV in the Council the general rule for areas which were previously under the cooperation procedure as well as for new areas (combating social exclusion and equal opportunities).

The Commission's annual report to the EP will have to include a separate chapter on social developments within the Community (ToA/TEC Art. 145). The Commission will also have to draw up a report each year on progress in achieving social policy objectives. The EP may invite the Commission to draw up reports on particular problems concerning the social situation (ToA/TEC Art. 143).

The integration of the Social Agreement in the Treaty

Current TEC provisions	Social Agreement	Provisions after Amsterdam
Art. 117	Art. 1 (objectives)	Art. 136
Arts. 118 and 118a	Art. 2 (means)	Art. 137 — broadened
Art. 118b	Art. 3 (social dialogue)	Art. 138
	Art. 4 (social dialogue)	Art. 139
	Art. 5 (cooperation)	Art. 140
Art. 119 (equal pay)	Art. 6 (equal opportunities)	Art. 141 — broadened
Art. 120 (paid holidays)		Art. 142 — unchanged
	Art. 7 (Commission social policy report)	Art. 143 — unchanged
Art. 121 (implementation of the free movement of workers)		Art. 144 — unchanged
Art. 122 (Commission annual report)		Art. 145 — modified
Art. 123 (social fund)		Art. 146 — unchanged
Art. 124		Art. 147 — unchanged
Art. 125		Art. 148 — co-decision replaces cooperation

VI.2 The New Social Action Programme, 1998–2000

In April 1998, on the initiative of Commissioner P. Flynn, the Commission adopted a Communication containing its Social Action Programme for 1998–2000. By putting employment at the heart of social policy, the programme integrates the conclusions of the Amsterdam European Council (June 1997) and the Luxembourg 'Jobs Summit' (November 1997, see VI.4). It also announces several Commission proposals, e.g., an updated approach to social protection, social integration and racial discrimination.

VI.3 Amsterdam and Employment

In the middle of the 1990s, the EU's 18 million unemployed not only exerted domestic pressure on Member States' governments but threaten to undermine the legitimacy of the integration process as a whole. Despite a universal recognition of the severity of the unemployment problem, there is little agreement about the ways to rectify it. The Member States have very different conceptions of what state intervention can and/or should do to reduce unemployment. During the 1996 IGC the Nordic Member States (with a long tradition of state-supported employment programmes) as well as some traditionally more interventionist Member States (France, Italy) pushed for concrete EC action in this field. The UK, on the other hand, sought to 'export' to the EU level its doctrine of flexible labour markets as a cure to unemployment; and Germany and Spain were wary about an EC competence on employment. The resulting employment provisions in the ToA reflect a difficult compromise between the various national views and are thus very weak.

Objectives
The objective of promoting 'a high level of employment' (ToA/TEU Art. 2 and ToA/TEC Art. 2) was coupled with the need to promote 'coordination between employment policies of the Member States with a view to enhancing their effectiveness by developing a coordinated strategy for employment' (ToA/TEC Art. 3.1.i).

Legal basis
After the title dedicated to Economic and Monetary Policy, the ToA adds a new title dealing specifically with employment: ToA/TEC Title VIII 'Employment'.

The promotion of employment is considered as a 'matter of common concern' (ToA/TEC Art. 126.2) but Member States maintain exclusive competence:

> *Member States and the Community shall ... work towards developing a coordinated strategy for employment and particularly for promoting a skilled, trained and adaptable workforce and labour markets responsive to economic change (ToA/TEC Art. 125)*

Such a coordinated strategy has to be consistent with EMU provisions (ToA/TEC Art. 126.1). At the same time, the employment objective should be integrated in the formulation of other EC policies (ToA/TEC Art. 127.2). Institutionally, cooperation between Member States is to be facilitated by an advisory Employment Committee (ToA/TEC Art. 130).

Instruments

The EC wants to achieve coordination of national employment policies on the basis of *common guidelines*. EC guidelines for Member States' economic policies are drawn up by the European Council — after advisory input from the EP, ECOSOC, the Committee of the Regions and the Employment Committee. Compliance with these guidelines is checked annually through Commission reports. Similar to the EMU surveillance measures (see chapter 19), the Council can give recommendations to Member States not respecting the common guidelines (ToA/TEC Art. 128). Yet Member States could not agree to set employment targets similar to the EMU convergence criteria.

Similar to social policy, 'best practice' and information exchange are advocated as policy instruments, together with incentive measures designed to encourage cooperation between Member States (ToA/TEC Art. 129.1) without ever leading to a harmonisation of the laws and regulations of the Member States (explicitly stipulated in ToA/TEC Art. 129.2).

VI.4 The 'Jobs Summit', 20/21 November 1997

Rather than waiting for the entry into force of the ToA, the 1997 Amsterdam Summit agreed to implement the Employment Title immediately . On the basis of this agreement, a Commission Communication (October 1997), 'Proposal for guidelines for Member States employment policies', provided a framework for discussion for an extraordinary European Council ('Jobs Summit'), Luxembourg, 20/21 November 1997.

In terms of substantive — rather than declaratory or symbolic — results, the Summit agreed upon *Employment Guidelines for 1998*. Taking up the suggestions of the Commission, four main lines of action for the Member States to follow were put forward in the Presidency's conclusions:

(a)   improving employability;
(b)   developing entrepreneurship;
(c)   encouraging adaptability in businesses and their employees;
(d)   strengthening the policies for equal opportunities.

The stated objective of these measures is 'to arrive at a significant increase in the employment rate in Europe on a lasting basis' (Presidency conclusions, point 22).

In longer-term vision, as the success of EMU convergence has already proved, EC employment policy aims at creating 'for employment, as for economic policy, the same resolve to converge towards jointly set, verifiable, regularly updated targets' (Presidency conclusions, point 3).

Clearly, the rhetoric and symbolic value of a European Council exclusively devoted to employment is considerable, but the practical effect on Member States' employment policies remains to be seen.

VII. FURTHER READING

FALKNER, Gerda: 'The Maastricht Protocol on Social Policy: theory and practice', *Journal of European Social Policy*, vol. 6, 1996, pp. 1–16.

LIEBFRIED, Stephen and PIERSON, Paul: 'Social policy', in WALLACE, Helen and WALLACE, William (eds), *Policy-Making in the European Union*, Oxford, OUP, 1996, pp. 185–207.

LODGE, Juliet: 'The social dimension and European Union', in TELÒ, Mario (ed.), *Quelle Union Sociale européenne?*, Brussels, Editions de l Université de Bruxelles, 1994, pp. 63–76.

O'KEEFFE, David: 'The uneasy progress of European social policy', *Columbia Journal of European Law*, March 1996.

OUAZAN, Jean-Marc: 'La dimension sociale de la construction européenne: étapes, perspectives et réalités', *Revue des Affaires Européennes*, vol. 3, 1995, pp. 53–70.

SINTES, Giles.: La politique sociale de l'Union européenne, Brussels, PIE, 1996.

For an analysis of the changes introduced by the Treaty of Amsterdam see EP Report, DOC–EN/DV/332/332457,15 July 1997, pp. 10–14.

Websites

DG V (Employment, Industrial Relations and Social Affairs)	http://europa.eu.int/en/comm/dg05/home.htm
Information on the Jobs Summit	http://europa.eu.int/en/comm/dg05/elm/summit

18 THE INFORMATION SOCIETY AND TELECOMMUNICATIONS POLICY

Simon Usherwood

I. RATIONALE

The rapid pace of technological change since the 1970s has presented new challenges to the EU. Massive increases in processing power and communication volume potential have had profound effects both on the economy and society, in a way not seen since the Industrial Revolution.

Information is becoming the material which holds together the new, service-sector-based economy: it is impossible to operate effectively or competitively without it. In short, there is a move from the industrial society to the information society (IS), a term which covers all of the diverse elements which contribute to this shift, such as the Internet, audio-visual (AV) policy and information technology (IT). As control of information flows becomes as important as the information itself, the informational industries — comprising both service provision (telecommunications) and content industries (media and AV) — have become a vital growth sector.

But it has also created new problems. As an effectively 'new' part of the economy, *old regulatory procedures are often unable to plan for future developments*, with the IS's inherent tendency to cross borders in ever more complex physical and commercial webs. This provides a prime motivation for the EU to try to develop an IS policy, since it is better placed to deal with such trans-border, indeed global, issues. By creating EU standards, the Union can *better spread the benefits of the IS to all of its regions.*

At a more concrete level, the IS is seen as a means to push forward the *completion of the Internal Market (IM).* Telecommunications has long been an obstacle to this, with deeply entrenched national monopolies, which Member States have long been loath to open up to competition. However, this has been turned around in the past 10 years, and now the EU is starting to see the benefits of a fully liberalised market.

II. LEGAL BASIS, PRINCIPLES, OBJECTIVES

II.1 Legal Basis

Neither IS nor telecommunications policy has a specific legal base. This is understandable, as the former is a very recent development (essentially since the early 1990s) and the latter is treated as merely another section of the IM. Consequently, legislation tends to be based on articles such as TEC Art. 100a (IM harmonisation) and TEC Arts. 57 and 66 (right of establishment and services).

AV policy has more legal scope, utilising IM provisions for free movement of goods (TEC Arts. 9, 12, 30 and 31) and workers, right of establishment and services (TEC Arts. 48–66).

Also of relevance are the provisions for research and development (TEC Arts. 130f–o), for TENs (TEC Arts. 129b–d) and for competition (TEC Arts. 85–6).

II.2 Principles

In terms of principles, the key document has been the 1994 report of the High-level Group on the Information Society, *Europe and the Global Information Society,* the so-called Bangemann report (after its chairman). Here the broad lines of the Union's approach to the IS were laid out. They can be summarised as follows:
— Market forces as a driver of the IS.
— Universal service (in terms of interconnection and interoperability of networks) as a key requirement.
— Financing of the IS to come primarily from the private sector.
— Protection and promotion of cultural and linguistic diversity.
— Protection of personal privacy.

—Cooperation with other, lesser developed areas, especially the Central and Eastern European Countries (CEECs).
—Need to inform both economic operators and the general public of the opportunities which the IS can bring.

A quick glance at these principles suggests that there may be some problems of compatibility, especially between the use of market forces and the commitment to universal service. This is not peculiar to IS — for instance, consider the long debate over natural gas liberalisation (see chapter 8) — but it is an issue which has exercised many minds in the past few years.

II.3 Objectives

While the objectives of IS and telecommunications policy have not been explicitly stated, there are three clear goals which stand out.

The increasing importance of the IS sector as a whole, and the telecommunications sector in particular, means that there is more potential for impeding the development of the IM. Therefore, a key goal of EU policy is to *introduce competition* to the industry, in order to more fully extend the benefits of a liberalised European market to economic operators and consumers.

At the same time, there are substantial gaps in the current regulatory system. Until now, regulation has been based on a sectoral approach (in telecommunications, media and IT), but this is now proving inadequate for new 'convergent' technologies (which combine various elements of these sectors). Consequently, the EU is striving to *cover these regulatory gaps* and, in developing regional standards, to *strengthen its position as a global actor*.

III. KEY ACTORS

Since IS is an essentially new legislative field, there are big opportunities for different actors to take a leadership role. The Commission has been most successful to date, being keen to take on new developments and lead by example. It also benefits from not being constrained by the traditional national telecommunications monopolies, which have guided many Member States in the Council.

Commission
DG XIII (Telecommunications) and DG III (Industry), both under Commissioner Bangemann, have the main responsibility for IS policy, along with DG X (Information, Communication, Culture and Audio-visual). DG IV (Competition) has been more active in the field of telecommunications regulation,

while DG I (CCP) has coordinated much of the external representation of both of these policies. While cooperation between DGs is widespread (e.g., the Green Paper on convergence of December 1997 was a joint effort by DGs XIII and X), there is still much confusion on the best way forward, given the differing preoccupations of the different actors. This reaches up to the level of the Commissioners themselves, where the strong personalities of Bangemann, Van Miert and Brittan are not always in agreement.

The Commission has also set up the Information Society Project Office (ISPO) as a separate office, to coordinate the dissemination of information both inside and outside the Commission.

Council
There are two Telecommunications Councils each year. Here, Member States try to promote their own national interests (e.g., France and media content quotas), while also limiting the Commission's accrual of power. This said, the latter's proactive approach to IS has encouraged some Member States into conceding that EU regulation is better than merely coordinating Member States' policies.

European Parliament
The EP plays a fairly strong role in IS, given its co-decision powers in TEC Art.100a, and it tries to promote the interests of the citizen and the consumer vis-à-vis economic operators. At the same time it favours the development of a European level policy.

Lobbies and interest groups
European-level lobby groups are relatively underdeveloped, but this is compensated for by the strong networks which national operators, especially the larger telecommunications companies, have developed. They often provide prepared materials to the Commission which, given its time and manpower constraints, makes much use of such materials, in conjunction with the reports which it outsources to private consultancies.

IV. POLICY INSTRUMENTS

IV.1 Telecommunications Liberalisation

The key objective of telecommunications liberalisation has been achieved in stages since 1988. The two primary directives were Dir. 88/301/EEC of 1988 on competition for terminal equipment and Dir. 90/388/EEC of 1990 on competition in markets and value-added services. This latter directive was amended in 1996 by Dir. 96/19/EC to implement full competition in telecommunications (i.e., basic voice telephony), with the deadline of 1 January 1998 for Member State liberalisation (with extensions for Greece, Portugal and Spain of up to five years).

Liberalisation does not mean that regulation ends, but rather that it is shifted from the Member State to the European level, covering:

— Market entry conditions (common framework for licensing).

— Maintenance of public interests (universal service, data protection and privacy).

— Interconnection and interoperability (via Open Network Provision (ONP)) and fair allocation of resources (see V).

— Standardisation of technical standards for mobile communications (GSM), satellite broadcasting and integrated services digital network (ISDN).

— Procurement rules.

The focus is clearly on the regulatory framework, rather than content, and the Union works on the basis of minimal regulation, setting minimum standards which Member States can then apply to their domestic operators.

The February 1997 WTO/GATS Agreement on Basic Telecommunications is also in line with the liberalisation project, providing for limited liberalisation of voice telephony, data transmission and mobile services by 71 states.

IV.2 Information Society

With the development of new, interactive technologies several problems arise. Unlike print publishing, materials sent over the Internet can be exactly reproduced with great ease, raising questions of *copyright and intellectual property rights*. In response to this, the Commission is currently proposing to harmonise Member States' provisions with a draft Directive on copyright in the IS, while simultaneously encouraging international developments, of which the World Intellectual Property Organisation (WIPO) Treaty on Copyright of December 1996 is the most important.

With the huge volumes of data being transmitted across networks, users need to be sure that their material has not been tampered with or altered. Thus *digital signatures* and *data encryption* are of vital importance to the Internet's development. These two subjects were covered by a Communication of 1997 (COM(97)503 final), which proposed common legal requirements for Member States' certification authorities and legal recognition of digital signatures by 2000, as well as the avoidance of disproportionate restrictions on encryption products (see VI).

Data protection is another issue of concern, given both the large databases which many public and private bodies hold and the increasing ease of movement across national borders to states with lower levels of protection. Dir. 96/9/EC of 1996 provides for the legal protection of databases, while Dir. 95/46/EC of 1995, on the protection of individuals with respect to data processing, harmonises Member States' rules in this field in order to ensure a lower chance of abuse of such data. This latter Directive, which comes into effect in October 1998, will make illegal the transfer of data to third countries which do not have an adequate level of data protection.

The final area of regulation in the IS has been the *protection of minors and regulation of harmful content*. Since the Internet is highly difficult to regulate, much public concern has been raised about the availability of pornographic and slanderous material. While legislation is still to come (probably in 1998), the large number of Commission, EP and Council documents on the topic indicate a strong will to create effective instruments to protect against, and deal with, such material.

IV.3 Audio-Visual Policy

Here policy instruments fall under the free movement of services (TEC Art. 59). The main legislative tool has been the so-called Television without Frontiers Directive (Dir. 89/552/EEC), which coordinates Member States' regulation of television broadcasting, most notably on the matter of content. This states that a 'majority' of airtime should be given to 'European programmes where practicable' (see V). The directive was modified somewhat in 1997, but still leaves the primary responsibility for content and regulation in Member States' hands.

Beyond this, legislation has covered areas such as copyright issues in satellite and cable retransmission and the legal protection of conditional access services.

IV.4 Research and Development

The major R&D programme for IS policy is ESPRIT. This was started in the early 1980s, to develop IT technologies, but it was only after the 1994 Action Plan (see V) that it took its current form. Its main areas of funding (approximately 2 billion ECU in 1994–8) were in computing, software and applied technologies, working both through R&D projects and transfer activities to improve the adoption of these new technologies.

RACE, created in 1988, works with telecommunications technologies and processes to create a Union-wide integrated broadband communications system. Further smaller programmes exist for telematics and for advanced communication technologies.

Under the Fifth Framework Programme, some 3,363 million ECU (33.5% of the total) is designated for projects under the title of 'Creating a user-friendly Information Society' (see chapter 12).

IV.5 Trans-European Networks

The TEN-Telecom programme forms an important part of the wider TEN infrastructure development project and it is anticipated that substantial funds will be needed (possibly 400 billion ECU to 2015). However, unlike transport TENs, TEN-Telecom has been limited to the development of ISDN, rather than dealing with networks per se. In the next financial perspectives (2000–6) the Commission wants to extend this to cover the development of broadband networks (especially using satellite and mobile networks) and of new multimedia applications. Despite the stated political will to use TENs to combat unemployment, progress has been somewhat limited to date in comparison to other TEN networks, given the more dispersed nature of the projects (see chapter 9).

IV.6 Competition Policy

DG IV has made extensive use of the instruments available to it under TEC Arts. 85 and 86 in an effort to break up old monopolistic situations and provide a level playing field in new areas (see chapter 11). This has meant a somewhat lopsided approach to ensuring competition, hitting monopolies very hard, while simultaneously giving new companies much more leeway, so that they can properly establish themselves.

IV.7 External Representation

Given the high level of activity within the EU, it is not surprising that it has tried to export its work to other parts of the world. The EU has been very proactive in fora such as the Ministerial Conference on the Information Society of the G7, the WTO/GATS, the International Telecommunications Union (ITU), the OECD and so on. Bilateral relations with the US are also of key importance, given the latter's leading role in the development of most aspects of the IS (see VI).

In CEECs, the Union has tried to help states to integrate into the European IS, by implementing legislation on information and communication technologies and identifying regional weaknesses in networks and service provision. This has been achieved primarily through the use of PHARE funding, although the CEECs may shortly be allowed to participate in TEN-Telecom projects.

V. HISTORICAL DEVELOPMENT

In 1957, when the Treaty of Rome was signed, the IS did not even exist as an idea and Member States' telecommunications companies were considered to be 'natural monopolies', which is to say that they had to have complete control of the telecommunications network in order to provide a useful and universal service. In any case, the technology of the time did not really permit anything more advanced than simple voice telephony. As such, it is not surprising that the treaty contained no provisions for telecommunications, and indeed under TEC Art. 90 Member States had the opportunity of limiting the application of competition rules in these 'services of general economic interest'.

However, with the development of silicon technology in the 1970s computing power started to become faster, cheaper and more widely available. There was increased interest at the European level in supporting such a growth sector, which fitted into a general refocusing of EC R&D funds at the time (see chapter 12). The result of this was the European Strategic Programme for R&D in Information Technology (ESPRIT), which was created in 1984 to develop the new technologies.

At the same time, the traditional image of telecommunications companies as natural monopolies was being attacked. In the UK, the Conservative government began to privatise British Telecom in 1984, as part of a wider programme of liberalisation and privatisation. While initial steps were small, the precedent had been set and when the SEA came into force in 1987, telecommunications liberalisation was one of the areas identified by the Commission as necessary for completion of the IM. The landmark document in this respect was the Green Paper of 1987, *Development of the Common Market for Telecommunications Services and Equipment*, which proposed both harmonisation of technical standards and liberalisation. The Member States adopted this programme and by 1988 had introduced legislation to liberalise the supply of telecommunications terminal equipment.

In a parallel development, the Community was making its first steps into the AV field. During the late 1980s there was much protracted debate on the introduction of a directive concerning the coordination of Member States' television broadcasting, in particular trans-border services. For some Member States, notably France, this coordination was seen as opening up broadcasting to unlimited foreign imports, especially from the US. This was not acceptable to French public opinion at the time and consequently the French government pushed to include rules on quotas on foreign programmes, giving them no more than 40% of airtime. This clashed with other Member States, who felt that the French were overreacting and that in any case quotas were not the best way forward, particularly in an environment of deregulation. In a compromise, it was agreed that 'a majority' of airtime would go to domestic production, 'where practicable'. This formula allowed each Member States to apply the directive with a large degree of flexibility.

By the late 1980s and early 1990s it was becoming clear that the effects of the technological revolution were going to be immense. Economic models of organisation were being radically redefined to integrate the new informational technologies, with knock-on effects on society and on the regulatory environment. Consequently, the 1990s were to see a veritable explosion of discussion documents and legislative proposals, alongside the ongoing telecommunications liberalisation programme, which was opening up value-added services and data communications from 1990 onwards. Open Network Provision, which allowed other operators access to existing networks, and which helped to prepare the telecommunications market for competition was introduced as a framework directive in 1990, and was extended to leased lines in 1992. A specific R&D programme for telecommunications technologies (RACE) was begun in 1988. The White Paper, *Growth, Competitiveness and Employment*, of 1993 also provided a boost to the sector's development, identifying it as a key to future economic growth (see chapter 12).

1994 was to see the report of the High-level Group on the Information Society, set up under the chairmanship of Commissioner Martin Bangemann to report back to the European Council on the future paths of development for the Information Society (IS), as it was now called (in contrast to the US term 'Information Superhighways' which focuses primarily on infrastructure). This report argued for the creation of an IS which would boost the economy while simultaneously ensuring that all social groups were also included in its development: this humane vision of the IS set the tone for subsequent legislation. 1994 also saw the start of the development of legislation in the field of mobile telecommunications, one of the most successful fields of EC activity. Through the creation of harmonised standards, and in particular the pan-European GSM operating standard, the EC can now fairly be described as the global leader in this field.

From 1995–6 the pace of telecommunications liberalisation picked up, with first satellite services and equipment and then telecommunications using television or alternative networks and mobile networks falling under the liberalised regime. At this point agreement was also reached on the extension of Open Network Provision to voice telephony, the most visible and most coveted telecommunications service, with a 1996 directive establishing a deadline of 1 January 1998 for its introduction.

In the past few years we have witnessed the extension of regulation into associated areas, such as copyright, harmful content, data protection and encryption (see IV). This has been driven in part by the realisation that the new technologies are creating new problems for old legislation, and in part because the EC wants to remove as many obstacles as possible in the path of the development of the IS. Electronic commerce is a classic example in this instance, since it requires a climate of certainty and trust between vendor and purchaser. This has meant that commercial codes have to be amended, digital signatures have to gain force of law and encryption products have to be able to prevent abuse of data. All of these potential problem areas were recognised by the Commission in its 1997 'European Initiative in Electronic Commerce', which has set in motion the creation of a suitable environment for future development.

Most recently, the Commission began a new phase of action with the publication in December 1997 of its Green Paper on convergence (see VI). This confidently promises to take the IS, telecommunications, AV and IT policy into the next century.

VI. RECENT DEVELOPMENTS

VI.1 Green Paper on Convergence

In December 1997, the Commission published its Green Paper, *Convergence of the Telecommunications, Media and Information Technology Sectors, and the Implications for Regulation* (COM(97)623 final). This represents the most important proposal for action since the 1987 Green Paper and the 1994 Bangemann report (see V). It outlines the increasing crossover, or convergence, between the various sectors at the levels of technology, industrial alliances and mergers, and services. It then considers the existing and potential barriers to technological and market developments before proposing some principles and options for future regulation:

1997 Green Paper on Convergence

Principles for future regulation of convergent sectors:

— Limit regulation to minimum necessary to achieve clear objectives.
— Regulation should be responsive to users' needs.
— Need for clear and predictable framework.
— Need for full participation in a convergent environment.
— Key role for independent and effective regulators.

Options for future regulation:

— Build on current structures — continue with current vertical regulation of each sector.
— Develop a separate regulatory model for 'new activities', alongside existing telecommunications and broadcasting regulation — carve out new services.
— New regulatory model for all existing and future services — use of horizontal principles.

The Commission would seem to be pushing for the third option, albeit to be phased in on a gradual basis, since this would circumvent the problems of coverage and scope definition of the other options. The consultation period for this Green Paper should eventually lead to a Convergence Action Plan by the end of 1998.

VI.2 Telecommunications Liberalisation

On 1 January 1998, the final phase of telecommunication liberalisation began, with the introduction of competition into voice telephony, the most basic telecommunications service. This marked the end of the 10-year process which had come out of the 1987 Green Paper, and promises to increase choice and lower prices for the consumer. That this will happen has been shown by the experience of those Member States which liberalised early, notably the UK. There, the former monopoly British Telecom has radically reduced international and long-distance prices by over two-thirds in response to increased competition, marking a move away from the cross-subsidisation of before (see V).

VI.3 Electronic Commerce

The Internet has created new opportunities for business, and all main actors are keen to encourage the development of this electronic commerce. This includes provisions for digital signatures, encryption and data protection (see IV), but there have also been moves to coordinate regulation of this sector further. In 1997, US President Bill Clinton outlined such a framework, stressing the principle of self-regulation, and this was followed up in December of that year by a 'Joint EU–US Statement on Electronic Commerce', which laid out some principles of cooperation. However, Commissioner Bangemann's proposal of February 1998 encouraged a more active role for regulators. It suggested a global charter, to coordinate legal and technical elements so as to reduce the amount of conflicting national regulation, which might slow electronic commerce's development. This does not sit very comfortably with the US's position, and during 1998 there are likely to be further consultations between the two bodies.

VI.4 Internet Domain Names

In 1997 and 1998 the question of the Internet domain name system (DNS; which attributes addresses on the Internet, such as *europa.eu.int* or *www.coleurop.be*) became a bone of contention between the EU and the US, as demand for addresses grew and the physical limits of the system were approached. The current system, whereby DNS allocation was contracted out to a private US firm, Network Solutions Inc., was due for review in February 1998. This system was somewhat chaotic and US-centric, leading the International Ad Hoc Committee (IAHC), a composite body of various international bodies such as the ITU and WIPO, to set up a review process. This process produced a Memorandum of Understanding on generic Top-Level Domains (gTLD-MoU; such as the *.com* or *.org* at the end of the address), which the EU strongly supported, given its internationalisation of DNS through the Council of Registrars (CORE). The US, however, had different ideas and its own review process led to a proposal which largely ignored the gTLD-MoU and concentrated on preserving US control of DNS.

This prompted a sharp response from the Commission, which produced a communication in December 1997, and the Council, which sent a reply to the US administration in February 1998. Both institutions called for the US to limit its efforts to control the Internet to those areas clearly inside its jurisdiction, but whether this will be enough to convince the US remains to be seen.

VII. FUTURE PROSPECTS

The EU has established itself as a key actor in the IS and telecommunications regulation, both at a European and a global level. It now faces the challenge of mediating global solutions with its own preferences and requirements. To this end, we can consider to what extent there is agreement between the EU and the other major actors on the future development of the IS, in all its constituent parts.

Generally speaking, there is broad agreement between the EU, the US and Japan on the majority of IS issues (see Vittet-Philippe 1997). The need for a coordinated approach with a clear legal environment and consistent principles is widely understood and accepted, even if some of those principles (such as minimal regulation) mean different things to different people.

At a more particular level, there has been recent convergence of views in several fields. The WIPO Copyright Treaty has largely resolved the intellectual property rights question, while the WTO/GATS Agreement on Basic Telecommunications has started to develop general guidelines on telecommunications liberalisation. There have also been developments in the field of commercial codes in electronic commerce and a steady convergence of opinions on data protection towards a mixed system of market solutions and international regulation.

However, many issues are either unclear or even points of conflict. The US 1997 proposal that the Internet should be a tariff-free zone has not been comprehensively addressed by the EU to date, but it is not clear whether this means it is against the idea. Conversely, it is the US which is playing a cautious role in the field of global interoperability, fearing that early standardisation would embed outdated technologies and preclude market solutions. But in both of these cases it would appear that some kind of agreement is possible.

Agreement may well be more difficult in the fields of security and privacy, however. For several states, both inside and outside the EU (including the US), the development of strong encryption technologies poses a threat to national security (e.g., criminals would be able to enjoy secure communications). But such encryption is essential for the development of electronic commerce, which is universally seen as a key driver of the IS. Whether a trade-off between these two important interests is possible remains to be seen. This also holds true for the conflict between freedom of expression and regulation of harmful content, which has characterised US and EU policies respectively.

In short, the next 10 years will see substantial developments in the regulation of the IS, quite possibly based on a mixed system of horizontal (e.g., on competition or harmful content) and vertical (e.g., for each sector such as telecommunications or AV) rules. The effects of the IS revolution are still to be fully felt.

VIII. FURTHER READING

Given the relatively recent development of the sector, most academic literature is to be found in journals (and on the Internet) rather than in books. Fortunately, the two most recent key documents, the Green Paper on convergence and the Bangemann report, are both interesting and readable. The Dumort and Dryden book provides a useful introduction to the technological and economic aspects of the IS, while the ITU report gives an overview of recent developments.

DUMORT, Alain, and DRYDEN, John: *The Economics of the Information Society*, Luxembourg, OECD/EU, 1997.

EUROPEAN COMMISSION, *Green Paper on the Convergence of the Telecommunications, Media and Information Technology Sectors, and the Implications for Regulation*, December 1997, available at website: http://www.ispo.cec.be/convergencegp/greenp.html.

HIGH-LEVEL GROUP ON THE INFORMATION SOCIETY, *Europe and the Global Information Society: Recommendations to the European Council*, May 1994, available at website: http://www.ispo.cec.be/infosoc/backg/bangeman.html.

INTERNATIONAL TELECOMMUNICATIONS UNION, *World Telecommunications Development Report*, Geneva, ITU, 1997.

VITTET-PHILIPPE, *Towards a Common Framework for Global Electronic Commerce: A Comparative Analysis of US, EU and Japanese E-Commerce Policies*, European Commission, DG XIII, 1997.

Websites

DG XIII (Telecommunications)	http://europa.eu.int/en/comm/dg13/13home.htm
DG X (Information, Communication, Culture, Audiovisual)	http://europa.eu.int/en/comm/dg10/dg10.html
Information Society Project Office	http://www.ispo.cec.be
World Intellectual Property Organisation	http://www.wipo.org
International Telecommunications Union	http://www.itu.int
gTLD-MoU	http://www.gtld-mou.org

19 ECONOMIC AND MONETARY UNION

Gabriel Glöckler

I. RATIONALE

I.1 'One Market, One Money' — EMU as Completion of the Internal Market

The benefits of having a common currency increase with the degree of openness of an economy. Given the high degree of interpenetration of European economies in the IM, a single currency would crown and logically complement the IM by eliminating exchange rate risk as a non-tariff barrier to trade (NTB). Only a common monetary policy can guarantee equal monetary conditions in all parts of the IM and thus create a 'level playing field'. Yet passing from IM to EMU requires primarily a political motivation as opposed to solely economic considerations.

I.2 Economic Cost-Benefit Analysis

The benefits from sharing a common currency derive from:
    (a)   elimination of transaction costs (savings of up to 0.5% of EU GDP);
    (b)   greater macroeconomic stability and thus lower risk premiums on investment;
    (c)   price transparency, greater competition with positive impacts on competitiveness, growth and, eventually, employment.

The costs derive mainly from the loss of several policy instruments:

(a)   the exchange rate as macroeconomic adjustment instrument;

(b)   the ECB's 'one-fits-all' monetary policy cannot respond to specific national conditions;

(c)   policy conflicts between Member States over budgetary measures.

Theoretical underpinnings — Theory of Optimal Currency Areas
(see De Grauwe)

Definition: a group of countries form an optimal currency area (OCA) if and when the benefits of having a common currency outweigh the costs of abolishing their exchange rate as adjustment tool.

The determining factor for this cost-benefit analysis is the ability to respond to *asymmetric shocks* (e.g., demand or supply shocks that only hit a particular region of the OCA). The likelihood of asymmetric shocks diminishes and alternative adjustment mechanisms exist if the countries:

(a)   are open economies;

(b)   have diversified and yet similar industrial structures;

(c)   have flexible prices and wages;

(d)   exhibit a high mobility of labour and capital;

(e)   establish some form of fiscal transfer system between themselves ('fiscal federalism')

I.3 Political Considerations

There are various interpretations for the political motivations behind the bold step of pursuing EMU:

(a)   *Neo-functionalist* approach: as with the IM, economic integration will inevitably lead the way to closer political integration ('Money is just the start'). Monetary integration, as a very advanced form of economic integration, requires a high degree of policy coordination, sooner or later approaching some form of 'political union'.

(b)   *Federalist* vision: EU with its own currency and supranational ECB acquires another set of state-like attributes.

(c)   *Realist* interpretation: latest attempt to create EMU was a response to particular political circumstances: German unification and perceived danger (especially in France) of German economic domination within the EC. 'Communitarising' the DM would counterbalance Germany's economic weight and regain monetary policy autonomy at EC level.

(d)   *Domestic politics*: EMU installs in inflation-prone Member States a strict monetary regime of price stability; EMU's budgetary discipline provides governments with powerful arguments against domestic resistance to push through structural reforms (e.g., modernisation of welfare systems and labour markets).

II. LEGAL BASIS, PRINCIPLES, OBJECTIVES

II.1 Legal Basis

Economic Policy
TEC Title VI (Economic and Monetary Policy) Chapter 1:
— TEC Art. 103.2 stipulates formulation of broad guidelines on economic policy.
— TEC Art. 103.3 and 4: multilateral surveillance mechanisms.
— TEC Art. 104b: so-called 'no bail-out' clause stating that the EC is not liable for Member States' debts.
— TEC Art. 104c sets out the 'excessive deficit procedure'.
— TEC Art. 109e.2 provides basis for convergence programmes.

Monetary Policy
TEC Title VI, Chapter 2:
— TEC Art. 105: objectives (price stability) and tasks of ESCB.
— TEC Art. 105a: ECB's exclusive right to authorise issuing of banknotes.
— TEC Art. 109: external monetary policy and exchange rate policy.

Institutional Provisions
TEC Title VI, Chapter 3:
— TEC Art. 109a–d refer to the establishment of the ECB and the Economic and Financial Committee.

Transitional Provisions
TEC Title VI, Chapter 4:
— TEC Art. 109e sets out provisions on stage 2 of EMU.
— TEC Art. 109f concerns the European Monetary Institute.
— TEC Art. 109j sets out convergence criteria (specified in Protocol 6) and the procedure for the selection of those Member States to enter stage 3 (May 1998).
— TEC Art. 109k classifies 'outs' of the first wave as 'Member States with a derogation'.

II.2 The Maastricht Blueprint.

II.2.1 Parallel Approach to EMU
The Maastricht EMU blueprint makes a structural distinction between *Economic Union* and *Monetary Union*.

Economic Union is not a very well-defined concept and is related primarily to the EC. It includes:

(a)   a single market;

(b)   a common competition policy;

(c)   common policies aiming at structural change and regional development;

(d)   a degree of macroeconomic policy coordination, especially binding budgetary rules.

The TEU foresees only economic policy coordination and not a common macroeconomic policy — using existing institutions (such as the ECOFIN Council).

Monetary Union comprises:

(a)   irrevocably fixed exchange rates or a single currency;

(b)   full convertibility of currencies;

(d)   a complete liberalisation of capital movements;

(d)   a centralised monetary policy.

The TEU supranationalises monetary policy-making, and creates new institutions (ESCB).

II.2.2 Three-stage Structure
A legally binding and clearly mapped-out plan leads up to full EMU and a single currency in 1999:

Stage 1: strengthening economic and monetary policy coordination within existing institutional framework, aiming at the complete removal of obstacles to capital markets integration (1 July 1990 to 31 December 1993).

Stage 2: transitional stage to prepare the institutional monetary framework for stage 3, including establishment of the EMI and giving independence to national central banks (1 January 1994 to 31 December 1998).

Stage 3: to begin with the irrevocable fixing of exchange rates and the transfer of necessary powers to Community institutions (1 January 1999); the national currencies are to be replaced by a single European currency (by 1 July 2002).

Philosophies behind the EMU design

'Great Leap Forward' School: convergence criteria make little economic sense, more rapid convergence process will automatically come about within a monetary union; see example of German monetary union of 1 July 1990. Early institutionalisation of common monetary policy in ECB to kick off convergence development ('Locomotive Strategy'); close to French idea of EMU',

Convergence School: full EMU to 'crown' the success of a prolonged and sustainable convergence process; beyond fulfilment of (nominal) convergence criteria, real convergence of economic and social structures between economies needed; establishment of ECB only in advanced stage of convergence ('Coronation Strategy'); close to German conception of EMU.

The Maastricht blueprint represents a compromise between these philosophies: largely following German conception (convergence required *prior* to EMU, strict convergence criteria, late full institutionalisation in ECB); yet — on France's demand — with strict timetable attached to accelerate convergence progress (the 1999 deadline), and early (in Stage 2) establishment of European Monetary Institute (EMI).

As yardsticks to measure the convergence progress, the treaty stipulated *convergence criteria* (TEC Art. 109j, Protocol 6) relating to:

(a)   price stability;

(b)   public finances (national debt maximum 60% of GDP; maximum 3% budget deficit);

(c)   exchange rate stability: ('within normal fluctuation margins of the ERM for two years')

(d)   stability being reflected by long-term interest rates.

II.2.3 Multi-speed Model

The convergence criteria classify Member States in terms of their 'ability' to proceed to stage 3, with the possibility to qualify in several waves:

— elaborate procedures apply in first phase when countries failing the criteria are considered as 'Member States with a derogation';

— further classification in terms of 'willingness': Denmark and UK reserved the right to 'opt out' of stage 3: institutionally, they maintain a similar status to 'Member States with derogation'; an 'opt-out' is an explicit provision for a

Member State to choose not to participate in a common institutional arrangements for reasons other than economic (see chapter 4).

III. KEY ACTORS

European Council
Sets macroeconomic policy guidelines.

Special case (May 1998): Council in composition of Heads of States and Governments decided on selection of countries to participate in stage 3 of EMU.

Economics and Finance Ministers Council (ECOFIN)
Adopts legislative instruments, drafts policy guidelines and coordinates macroeconomic policies.

Commission
DG II (Economic and Financial Affairs), DG XV (Internal Market and Financial Services) and DG XXI (Customs and Indirect Taxation). The Commissioner primarily responsible for EMU is Y.-T. de Silguy (France). The Commission:
— proposes legislation and policy initiatives;
— proposes macroeconomic policy guidelines and recommendations under 'excessive deficit procedure' (see IV);
— monitors Member States' economic policies;
— participates in the G7 meetings.

European Parliament
Debates economic policies and issues reports and recommendations.
— Assent procedure for a decision to give the European Central Bank (ECB) a role in the supervision of credit institutions and for any amendments in the statutes of the ECB and the European System of Central Banks (ESCB).

European Monetary Institute
Precursor of European Central Bank, with technical preparatory tasks for stage 3 (see IV).

European Central Bank
To be set up 1 July 1998.
— true bank and independent EC 'agency' for the pursuit of a common monetary policy (for tasks and roles, see IV);

—Governing Council consists of members of Executive Board of ECB (six members) and Central Bank Governors of Member States.

The ECB is the central authority and supervising institution of the network of Member States' national central banks, the *European System of Central Banks*.

IV. POLICY INSTRUMENTS

IV.1 Economic Policy

IV.1.1 Multilateral Surveillance: Economic Policy Guidelines
Member States are required to regard their economic policies 'as a matter of common concern' and coordinate them within the Council; policy framework established by European Council.

Policy process:

(a)   The Commission recommends a set of guidelines for the Member States' economic policies.

(b)   On the basis of the Commission recommendation, ECOFIN Council adopts draft to be presented to Heads of State.

(c)   European Council conclusions set guidelines for recommendations to be adopted by ECOFIN.

Aided by Commission reports, ECOFIN monitors developments in each Member State for consistency with the EU guidelines. If national policies risk jeopardising the proper function of EMU, the Council can single out the Member State for a communication recommending policies. If there are no subsequent adjustments of that particular national policy, the Council can exert further pressure by publicising the recommendation. That way 'peer pressure' induces policy coherence within the EC.

IV.1.2 Multilateral Surveillance: Excessive Deficit Procedure
Under the 'excessive deficit' procedure ECOFIN monitors a country's total outstanding public debt (target 60% of GDP) and its budget deficit (target 3% of GDP).

There is a lengthy process if a country is found to be failing on the criteria:

(i)   ECOFIN has to decide by QMV on existence of 'excessive deficit';

(ii)   ECOFIN issues a private recommendation to the Member State (if there is no response from the Member State in question, this is done again publicly);

(iii)   ECOFIN gives notice to the Member State in question, and can, as a last resort, apply sanctions (e.g., invite the EIB to reconsider lending to that

Member State; require the Member State to make a deposit with the EC until the deficit is rectified).

The decision-making procedure is cumbersome, mostly requiring a two-thirds majority, excluding the Member State concerned.

IV.1.3 Convergence Criteria
—TEU convergence criteria provide a measure for the assessment of convergence process by Commission and the European Monetary Institute.
— Brought about 'peer pressure' in European Council and testing of Member States' commitments by the financial markets; appears to be the most effective and immediate control mechanism.

IV.1.4 Convergence Programmes
Voluntary programmes presented to ECOFIN, on initiative and in responsibility of Member States; all Member States have adopted such programmes.

IV.1.5 'Stability and Growth Pact' (Amsterdam 1997)
Further institutionalises budgetary surveillance (see VI).

IV.1.6 'Euro-11' Council — 'Gouvernement Économique' for the Euro-area
French response to predominantly German-inspired design of EMU:
—Proposals to set up a political counterweight to the independent ECB, a formal 'Stability and Growth Council' or 'gouvernement économique' with guiding powers over ECB.
—Compromise solution: informal meetings of euro-area ministers prior to regular ECOFIN meetings (Euro-11 forum), without real teeth.

IV.2 Monetary Policy

IV.2.1 Financial Integration and Removal of Capital Controls
Mainly concerned with ensuring free movement of capital (see chapter 6); attempts to harmonise tax rate at EU level have not amounted to much, but EMU provides new incentives.

IV.2.2 Operations of the European Monetary Institute (EMI)
The EMI was the main structure for a joint approach to monetary policy in the run-up to EMU with the following tasks:
(a)   Coordination and stimulus to cooperation between national central banks of Member States in conduct of monetary and exchange rate policies.

(b)   Design, harmonisation, realisation of rules, procedures and infrastructures necessary for:

   (i)   the establishment of the ESCB,
   (ii)   the creation of single currency and,
   (iii)   the conduct of single monetary policy;

(The EMI has thus set up, *inter alia*, an intra-EMU payments system — TARGET; laid down guidelines for banking supervision in euro-area; and devised joint intervention mechanisms for euro vis-à-vis third currencies).

(c)   Operational and technical function in connection with EMS and management of national central banks' reserves.

(d)   Ensure smooth transition of works to the ECB.

Frankfurt was the seat of the EMI; President (since 1997) Wim Duisenberg (Netherlands), chairs Council of governors of the Member States' central banks.

IV.2.3 Post-1999: Independent Monetary Policy of the ECB

Most striking feature of ECB is its *independence* and the absence of a higher *political* authority (there is no 'EU government'):

(a)   Primary objective of ECB is maintenance of price stability (TEC Art. 105).

(b)   Also wider objectives: 'Without prejudice to the objective of price stability, the ESCB shall support the general economic policies in the Community as laid down in Article 2' (TEC Art. 105).

(c)   Further roles and tasks: control over money supply and interest rates; consultation to ECOFIN; supervision of credit institutions; exclusive issuing of banknotes.

(d)   Exchange rate policy:

   (i)   independently steered by ECB for a floating euro against third currencies, with general orientations from ECOFIN,

   (ii)   unanimous decision of ECOFIN required for entering into fixed exchange rate systems with third currencies.

(e)   External representation (G-7, International Monetary Fund) yet to be decided.

V. HISTORICAL DEVELOPMENT

EMU should be seen as a long-term objective of the EC. A first proposal for EMU dates back to 1962, but it was only at the *1969 Hague Summit* that the Heads of State took up the idea. Interest in EC monetary agreement had been revived by:

(a) externally, the imminent collapse of the Bretton Woods system;

(b) internally, the importance of monetary aspects to the functioning of the IM and CAP (problem of agro-monetary arrangements — see chapter 7).

At the Hague, Member States commited to full EMU; and commissioned the *1970 Werner Report* which foresaw a three-phase plan, culminating in EMU by 1980.

Internationally, monetary conditions worsened, and Member States sought a remedy by establishing the *1971 'snake'*, an arrangement for approximating the exchange rates of member currencies one to another while holding their value jointly to the dollar. The *1972 Smithsonian Agreement* established a system in which signatories' currencies fluctuated within a ±2.25% band around their central parity against the US$. Since the prescribed bands were too large for EC Member States (and contrary to the Werner Report), a stricter monetary arrangement (*'snake in the tunnel'*) was agreed upon in which EC currencies fluctuated around the US$ within ±2.25% band, but within tighter bands (±1.125%) between one another. This unstable system collapsed in 1973, the US$ floated freely — the snake lost its tunnel. The subsequent oil crisis and world recession increased speculative pressures, bringing great difficulties for weaker currencies to maintain parities. In 1977, of the nine EC Member States, only Germany, Benelux and Denmark were still members. *Within Europe, the DM had emerged as the hardest currency in the system and effectively replaced the dollar as the anchor currency by the late 1970s.*

1978 proposal for a European Monetary System (approved by the Bremen European Council) in response to failure of the snake; on initiative from Commission President, Roy Jenkins, put into action by Helmut Schmidt and Giscard d'Estaing.

1979: European Monetary System (EMS)
Rationale

— avoidance of the excessive exchange rate fluctuations that occur under a free float regime;
— accelerating inflation (and its impact on employment and growth) induced Member States to accept German philosophy of giving priority to stable prices;
— unreliable and disappointing US monetary leadership;
— Benelux and Denmark favoured cooperation because they were part of the DM zone;
— France sought a more symmetrical form of cooperation, less biased towards DM;
— Italy and Ireland were prepared to participate (on condition of side-payments);
— Britain alone opted to remain outside the exchange rate mechanism of the EMS.

The aim of the EMS was to create a *zone of monetary stability* by means of a relatively flexible mechanism (allowing for the wider fluctuation of currencies). Its main elements are:

The European Currency Unit (ECU)

— the ECU = 'weighted basket' of EC currencies; ECU was to become the benchmark of the EMS against which all the variations are measured;
— Establishment of European Monetary Cooperation Fund (EMCF) a Committee of Central Bank Governors which supervised the entire system;
— since the ECU represented average performance of EC economies, the EMS with the ECU at its centre would be less asymmetric than (US$-dominated) Bretton Woods or (DM-dominated) 'snake'.

The Exchange Rate Mechanism (ERM)

— system of *fixed but adjustable exchange rates*;
— central parity for each participating currency defined *in ECU*;
— from these central rates, the bilateral exchange rate grid is derived;
— original fluctuation margins ±2.25% (during certain periods, Italy, Spain and Portugal had wider margins of ±6%);
— if bilateral rate reaches the margin of fluctuation band, obligation to intervene for both central banks to maintain the exchange rate within the range;
— creation of 'divergence indicator' when a currency approaches 75% of its fluctuation band, this is an indication for a 'presumption to act' (not an obligation) to rectify the situation.

1979–83: diverging economic policies in Member States (Keynesian expansion in France, monetarist consolidation in Germany) resulting in frequent realignments.

1983–87: radical change in France's economic policies (1983: U-turn to '*rigueur* and '*franc fort*); also in other Member States slow convergence on prudent fiscal and monetary policy, resulting in convergent inflation rates and less frequent realignments — but increasing asymmetry in the system (DM replaced ECU as anchor currency).

1987–92: '*hard EMS' — no realignments*, facilitated by economic growth and more effective intervention mechanism, maintaining quasi-fixed parities was increasingly politically motivated ('quasi-monetary union').

1992–93: Crises and Collapse of the System

Mounting speculative attacks in 1992–93 put EMS under strain; recession and unemployment brought to the fore the still diverging economic fundamentals of the Member States. Origins of the crisis:

(a)   German unification increased inflationary pressures on the German economy; the Bundesbank pursued restrictive monetary policies of high interest rates.

(b)   At the same time, most Member States wanted to overcome the European recession of the early 1990s by setting interest rates low.

(c)   There was *de facto* policy setting in the EMS by the Bundesbank but using its own national objectives, which constrained non-German Member States — either they had to follow Germany or drop out of the system.

(d)   Markets viewed the system as unsustainable and speculated against it (capital flight out of French Franc and sterling and into DM).

The 1992 ejection of sterling and lira from the ERM and subsequent devaluations of peseta and escudo 1992–3 led to the *virtual collapse of the EMS* Diverging economic fundamentals and a waning political will to retain a symmetrical system of binding obligations led the Member States to opt for an extension of fluctuation bands to meaningless ± 15%.

VI. RECENT DEVELOPMENTS

VI.1 Interpretation of Criteria and Discussion on Postponement.

While the economic rationale of convergence criteria is doubtful (only nominal criteria, producing 'self-fulfilling prophecies') the political intentions of criteria as exclusion mechanism to limit first-wave membership to 'core Europe' (i.e., France, Germany, Benelux, Austria, Denmark representing an OCA) are certainly discernable. The original treaty stipulations of the criteria are relatively ambiguous, inducing discussion about:

— flexible interpretation of criteria, allowing for wide membership, but risking a 'soft' euro;

— strict interpretation, limiting membership, with increased chances for 'hard' euro.

Since countries essential to the project (Germany, France) found it difficult to squeeze below the threshold of the criteria, there was widespread *discussion on delay* which would have:

— allowed governments to progress further with the consolidation of public finances;

— brought about a greater degree of real convergence of EU economies;

— given more time to sell EMU to publics;

— given governments more time to make their labour markets more flexible and restructure their economies to cope with the strains of a single currency.

But a delay would have also:

— violated the legally binding 1999 deadline (TEU);

— led to potential relaxation of fiscal austerity and worsened the economic climate for later fulfilment of criteria;

— possibly induced currency speculation and even undermined the IM in the face of 'competitive devaluations';

— brought the danger of indefinite postponement.

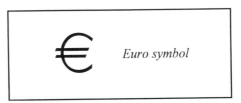

Euro symbol

At the Madrid Summit (1995), the Member States agreed to call the new currency the 'euro'. It will be a currency in its own right and is to be exchanged against the ECU at par.

VI.2 The 'Stability and Growth Pact' (Amsterdam 1997)

Enshrines fiscal discipline beyond the 1999 deadline; intended to enhance credibility of euro and affirm the 'no bail-out' clause (TEC Art. 104b). Explicit objective is to '*deter excessive general government deficits*' and, if they occur, to '*further their prompt correction*' by application of semi-automatic sanctions and fines. It consists of:

(a)   Regulation on the strengthening of surveillance of Member States' budgetary positions and coordination of economic policies (to enter into force on 1 July 1998): defines the procedures for presentation of Member States' stability programmes and convergence programmes (before 1 March 1999 with annual updates) and assessment mechanisms for these programmes.

(b)   Regulation for a more clarified and rapid 'excessive deficit procedure' (to enter into force 1 January 1999):

(i)   specifies the sanctions to be applied to Member States with excessive deficits, application arrangements, etc.;

(ii)   stipulates volume of non-interest-bearing deposits, their conversion into fines and the timetable for corrections.

VI.3 Provisions for an 'EMS 2' (Amsterdam 1997)

New exchange rate mechanism, centred around the euro as its anchor currency, which takes into account the lessons of 1992–3:

— came into force after announcement of first-wave membership in May 1998;

— intended to *institutionalise relationship between EMU-'ins' and 'pre-ins'*, avoid competitive devaluations of 'pre-ins', and prepare 'pre-ins' for eventual joining of EMU;

— based on central rates in terms of euro with standard fluctuation band of ±15%;

— voluntary for EMU-'pre-ins', who nevertheless have to regard the exchange rate to the euro as 'matter of common concern'.

VI.4 Economic Recovery and Convergence

Since mid 1990s: actual convergence of Continental economies; convergence criteria induce policy changes in most Member States, demonstrating the firm resolution to be part of EMU:

— consolidation of public finances: budget discipline, austerity packages, privatisations;

— slow but steady structural reforms of inflated social security and pension systems;

— independence granted to central banks.

Efforts so far are rewarded by:

— converging inflation rates on low levels;

— converging interest rates towards German levels;

— relatively stable exchange rates; re-entry of Italian lira and first-time entry of Finnish markka and Greek drachma into ERM; (exception: volatility of Sterling);

— relative synchronisation of economic cycles between Continental economies;

— good growth prospects and slightly decreasing unemployment for EU economy as a whole;

— according to data presented by the Member States in March 1998, 14 Member States fulfil the Maastricht criteria, only Greece would not qualify; but continued discussion over sustainability of convergence (many Member States used one-off measures, e.g., privatisation revenues and accounting tricks to squeeze public deficit below the Maastricht threshold in the reference year 1997).

	Public deficit (as % of GDP)		Government debt (as % of GDP)	Entry into Stage 3?
Austria	2.5		66.1	✔
Belgium	2.1		122.2	✔
Denmark	− 0.7	(surplus)	64.1	✗
Finland	0.9		55.8	✔
France	3.0		58.0	✔
Germany	2.7		61.3	✔
Greece	4.0		108.7	✗
Ireland	− 0.9	(surplus)	67.0	✔
Italy	2.7		121.6	✔
Luxembourg	− 1.7	(surplus)	6.7	✔
Netherlands	1.4		72.1	✔
Portugal	2.5		62.0	✔
Spain	2.6		68.3	✔
Sweden	0.4		76.6	✗
United Kingdom	1.9		53.4	✗
TEU limits	3.0		60.0	

Source: Agence Europe 28/02/98

VI.5 Decision on First-wave Participants in Stage 3 (May 1998)

In May 1998, the Council, meeting as Heads of State and Governments, decided by QMV:
— on the basis of economic data of 1997;
— on recommendation from the Commission (suggesting 11 Member States to proceed to stage 3);
— after a report from the EMI (approving these 11 Member States to introduce the euro).
that *Germany, France, Italy, Belgium, the Netherlands, Luxembourg, Austria, Ireland, Finland, Spain and Portugal* fulfil the criteria and are willing to proceed to Stage 3. At the same time, ECOFIN announced fixed bilateral conversion rates between the currencies of these 11 Member States, in an attempt to discourage speculation in the transition period until January 1999.

After a protracted discussion, Wim Duisenberg (Netherlands) was named President of the ECB and the other members of the ECB's Executive Board were nominated. Thus, *a large EMU — comprising 11 Member States — will start on 1 January 1999.*

VII. FUTURE PROSPECTS

VII.1 The Changeover to the Euro (Decided at Madrid 1995)

Timing	Actions to be taken	Responsibility
As soon as possible after the decision on participating Member States	(a) Appointment of Executive Board of the ECB (b) Set the day for the introduction of Euro banknotes and coins (c) Start production of Euro banknotes (d) Start production of Euro coins	participating MS ECB; Council (participating MS) ESCB Council and Member States
Up to 1 January 1999	Final preparation of the ECB/ESCB (a) Adoption of secondary legislation, including: key for capital subscription; collection of statistical information; minimum reserves; consultation of ECB; fines and penalties on undertakings (b) Rendering the ECB/ESCB operational (setting up the ECB; adoption of regulatory framework; testing monetary policy framework; etc.)	Council ECB/ESCB
1 January 1999	Irrevocable fixing of conversion rates and entry into force of legislation related to the introduction of the Euro (legal status, continuity of contracts, rounding)	Council at unanimity of participating Member States
From 1 January 1999	(a) Definition and execution of the single monetary policy in Euro (b) Conduct of foreign exchange operations in the Euro (c) Operation of TARGET payment system (d) Issue new public debt in Euro	ESCB ESCB ESCB Member States
1 January 1999 to 1 January 2002 at the latest	(a) Exchange at par value of currencies with irrevocably fixed conversion rates (b) Monitor changeover developments in the banking and finance industry (c) Assist the whole of the economy in an orderly changeover	ESCB ESCB and public authorities in Member States and EC
1 January 2002 at the latest	(a) Start circulation of the Euro banknotes and withdrawal of national banknotes (b) Start circulation of the Euro coins and withdrawal of national coins	ESCB participating Member States
1 July 2002 at the latest	(a) Complete changeover in the public administration (b) Cancel the legal tender status of national banknotes and coins	Council; Member States; ESCB

VII.2 Consolidation of the Treaties (Amsterdam 1997).

Current TEC Provisions	Provisions after Amsterdam
Art. 102a (Economic policy as contribution to EC objectives)	Art. 98
Art. 103 (Coordination of economic policy)	Art. 99
Art. 103a ('Severe difficulties' procedure)	Art. 100
Art. 104 (Prohibition of overdraft facilities)	Art. 101
Art. 104a (Prohibition of privileged access)	Art. 102
Art. 104b (Non-liability for Member State debt)	Art. 103
Art. 104c (Excessive deficit procedure)	Art. 104
Art. 105 (ESCB objectives and tasks)	Art. 105
Art. 105a (ECB right to issue banknotes)	Art. 106
Art. 106 (ESCB composition)	Art. 107
Art. 107 (ECB and national central bank independence)	Art. 108
Art. 108 (Compliance of national central banks with EC provisions)	Art. 109
Art. 108a (ECB instruments)	Art. 110
Art. 109 (External monetary policy and exchange rate policy)	Art. 111
Art. 109a (ECB Governing Council)	Art. 112
Art. 109b (ECB–EC institutions relations)	Art. 113
Art. 109c (Monetary Committee)	Art. 114
Art. 109d (Council/Member State right to make recommendations)	Art. 115
Art. 109e (Stage 2 of EMU)	Art. 116
Art. 109f (EMI)	Art. 117
Art. 109g (ECU basket to be unchanged)	Art. 118
Art. 109h (Balance of payments procedure)	Art. 119
Art. 109i (Exceptional balance of payments procedure)	Art. 120
Art. 109j (Convergence criteria)	Art. 121
Art. 109k (Rights of 'outs')	Art. 122
Art. 109l (Stage 3 of EMU)	Art. 123
Art. 109m (Exchange rate policy competence)	Art. 124

VIII. FURTHER READING

CURRIE, David: *The Pros and Cons of EMU*, London, Economist Intelligence Unit, 1997.
CURRIE, David: *Will the Euro Work? The Ins and Outs of EMU*, London, Economist Intelligence Unit, 1998.
DE GRAUWE, Peter: *The Economics of Monetary Integration*, Oxford, OUP, 1997.

EMERSON, Michael, GROS, Daniel et al.: *One Market, One Money: An Evaluation of the Potential Benefits and Costs of Forming an Economic and Monetary Union*, Oxford, OUP, 1992.

EUROPEAN COMMISSION: *Report on Economic and Monetary Union in the EC 'One Market, One Money'*, Luxembourg, EUR-OP, 1989.

EUROPEAN COMMISSION: *The Euro: Explanatory Notes*, DG II, Brussels, 1998, available at website: http://europa.eu.int/euro/default.asp?lang = en.

MINKKINEN, Petri and PATOMÄKI, Heikki (eds): *The Politics of Economic and Monetary Union*, Dordrecht, Kluwer Academic Publishers, 1997.

PELKMANS, Jacques: *European Integration: Methods and Economic Analysis*, Harlow, Longman, 1997 (esp. pp. 289–306).

TSOUKALIS, Loukas: *Economic and Monetary Union: What is at Stake* (forthcoming).

Websites

DGII (Economic and Financial Affairs)	http://europa.eu.int/en/comm/dg02/dg2home.htm
European Commission server on the euro	http:// europa.eu.int/euro/
EMI/ECB	http://www.ecb.int/
Association for the Monetary Union of Europe (AMUE)	http://amue.lf.net/.

PART IV

THE SECOND PILLAR

20   COMMON FOREIGN AND SECURITY POLICY

Julian Vassallo

I RATIONALE

The underlying reason for the EU adopting a Common Foreign and Security Policy is to give the Union a voice in international relations equal to its economic weight.

An effective Common Foreign and Security Policy (CFSP) should be seen as a natural means for the Member States (MS) to further their national interests as well as those of the Union.

In effect the CFSP is different things to different Member States. It provides smaller countries who would otherwise have an insignificant role on the world stage the opportunity to increase their clout. From the outset France saw foreign policy cooperation at a European level as a means of arresting its decline in foreign policy prowess. Britain, which has suffered a similar fate, has instead looked to the US to prop up its international relevance and been less keen on foreign policy *concertation* with the Continentals.

Germany, still hesitant to act assertively on the international stage, uses Europe as an acceptable context in which to exert influence. On entering the European Community in 1986 Spain and Portugal soon learnt that their agendas, even if sometimes different from those of the original Member States, are best pursued with their European partners.

Ireland sought to reconcile its neutral stance with participation in the European foreign policy cooperation by avoiding military aspects of security whenever possible. By the time they were joined by Austria, Finland and Sweden the concept of neutrality had lost much of its significance. It is (NATO member) Denmark's sovereignty concerns, rather than neutrality, which lies at the heart of its lack of enthusiasm for greater foreign policy cooperation.

II. LEGAL BASIS, PRINCIPLES AND OBJECTIVES

II.1 Legal Basis

Titles I and V (Arts. J.1 to J.11) of the TEU.

The Common Foreign and Security Policy constitutes the 'Second Pillar' of the EU structure as set out in the Maastricht Treaty (see chapter 2). Thus it operates outside usual Community rules, including those on decision-making and the roles of the different institutions.

II.2 Objectives

TEU Art. B sets the overall objective of the CFSP as the assertion of the Union's 'identity on the international scene'.

The individual objectives of the CFSP are set out in TEU Art. J.1:

— 'to safeguard the common values, fundamental interests and independence of the Union.

— to strengthen the security of the Union and its Member States in all ways;

— to preserve peace and strengthen international security, in accordance with the principles of the United Nations Charter as well as the principles of the Helsinki Final Act and the objectives of the Paris Charter;

— to promote international cooperation;

— to develop and consolidate democracy and the rule of law, and respect for human rights and fundamental freedoms'.

The TEU also provides the basis for the elaboration of a common defence policy and goes so far as to provide for the possibility of the Union eventually framing a common defence.

The common foreign and security policy shall include all questions related to the security of the Union, including the eventual framing of a common defence policy, which might in time lead to a common defence (TEU Art. J.4.1)

Nevertheless the different concerns of particular Member States, in particular the neutrals, Denmark and the UK, make significant progress in this area unlikely in the medium term.

The Treaty of Amsterdam (ToA) provides for slight modifications to the list of objectives by adding the notion of the integrity of the Union, in accordance with the principles of the United Nations and, on the demand of Greece, respect for the principles related to the external borders of the Union.

II.3 Principles

TEU Art. J.1.4 lays down the *good faith* principle, which obliges the Member States to commit themselves to the objectives of the policy. They must support the Union's external and security policy actively and unreservedly, and refrain from any action which is contrary to the interests of the Union or likely to impair its effectiveness as a cohesive force in international relations.

TEU Art. C requires that there be a principle of *consistency* between the 1st Community pillar and the 2nd CFSP Pillar (see chapter 3). The obligation to ensure the respect of this principle lies with the Council and the Commission. The respect of this principle has been the source of tensions between the two pillars and the two institutions.

III. KEY ACTORS

European Council
Foreign policy cooperation remains a largely inter-governmental affair. The informal proceedings of the European Council are often dominated by discussions on how the EU should respond to global events. The impetus for CFSP measures often comes from such meetings. The European Council also provides the general political guidelines for CFSP and plays a central role in the definition of Joint Actions (See IV).

Council of Ministers
This is the main forum of cooperation and the centre of decision-making. The Council has three functions:
— to define the principles and guidelines of the CFSP;
— to ensure unity, consistency and efficiency of the Union's activities;
— to decide by unanimity on measures to be taken to implement the policy.

COREPER and the Political Committee
The COREPER prepares the more technical work of the Council.

The Political Committee is composed of the directors of political affairs in the national foreign affairs ministries. It is involved in the more political aspects of the preparation of the work of the Council, producing policy recommendations and opinions on its own initiative or following a request from the Council. It seeks to develop a common analysis of the international situation and provides a forum for consultation and *concertation*.

The Working Groups
The several geographical and thematic Working Groups support the work of COREPER by providing background information.

The Secretariat-General
Assists the Presidency in the preparation and the implementation of CFSP.

The European Correspondents Group
Organises the mutual information flow between the Member States on the basis of COREU. (See IV)

The Presidency
The Presidency is responsible for the external representation and the implementation of CFSP matters. It is aided in its work by the Commission.

The Troika
The Member State holding the Presidency, together with the Member State holding the Presidency immediately previously and the Member State about to hold the Presidency make up the Troika. The aim of the Troika is to ensure some continuity in the external representation of the EU while allowing the Presidency the opportunity to rely on the two other Member States for support. The rotation order of the Presidency was set in a manner which ensures that the Troika will always include one of the larger Member States (see IV).

The Commission
The Commission is 'fully associated' with the CFSP and, together with the Council, must oversee the coherence between the action of the Union and the activities undertaken in the EC framework, in particular in the fields of security, economics and development. In addition,
— the Commission enjoys a non-exclusive right of initiative in the second pillar as opposed to its exclusive right of initiative in regular Community areas.
— together with the Presidency, the Commission is involved in the implementation of external activities and in the external representation of the Union.
— the activities of the Commission in the area of CFSP are carried out by the various external relations services and coordinated by DG 1A.

The European Parliament
The EP is consulted by the Presidency on the main aspects and basic choices of CFSP and is kept regularly informed of developments by the Presidency and the Commission.

The EP's Security, Foreign Affairs and Defence Policy Committee holds a special colloquium four times a year with the Presidency. In between these meetings the Committee's bureau meets with the Chairman of the Political Committee (i.e., the Political Director of the Ministry of Foreign Affairs of the Member States holding the Presidency)

The European Court of Justice
The Court has no jurisdiction over decisions taken under Title V.

The Treaty of Amsterdam provides for some alterations to the roles of different institutions and creates completely new actors (See IV).

IV. POLICY INSTRUMENTS AND DECISION-MAKING PROCEDURES

IV.1 Systematic Cooperation

IV.1.1 Information and Concertation *on Matters of General Interest*
This is done through exchanges of view in the different CFSP meetings, informal meetings (known as Gymnich Meetings) as well as through the telex network linking the different capitals (COREU) (TEU Art. J.2.1).

IV.1.2 Concertation *in the external representations*
This includes cooperation between Member States' embassies in third countries and their permanent representations in international organisations through the exchange of information, the elaboration of common reports and the provision of diplomatic and consular protection for citizens of non-represented Member States (TEU Art. J.6).

IV.1.3 Cooperation in International Organisations in which not all the Member States are represented
Those Member States who are actually members keep the others informed on topics of common interest.

IV.1.4 Activities in the UN Security Council
In the execution of their functions Member States which are members of the Security Council should ensure the defence of the positions and the interests of

the Union, without prejudice to their responsibilities under the UN Charter (TEU Art. J.5).

IV.2 Common Positions (TEU Art. J.2)

Common positions are defined and adopted by the Council acting by unanimity. Member States are obliged to ensure that their national foreign policies conform to all common positions.

Amongst the more politically important common positions one may point to the broad framework approaches for the EU's relations with Rwanda, Ukraine and Burundi. Nevertheless many common positions are of a purely technical nature.

IV.3 Joint Actions (TEU Art. J.3)

Joint actions oblige Member States to act in a particular manner in order to support a common position. The more salient joint actions include those relating to the convoying of humanitarian aid in Bosnia-Herzegovina, the administration of the town of Mostar in the former Yugoslavia (with policing supplied by the Western European Union (WEU)), the preparation of the Conference on the Nuclear Non-Proliferation Treaty and the sending of observers to parliamentary elections in Russia, South Africa and the Middle East.

The 1994 Stability Pact for Central Europe, aimed at fostering good neighbourliness together with democratic and human rights principles, was also based on a joint action. Responsibility for following up the implementation of the Stability Pact has since been passed on to the Organisation for Security and Cooperation in Europe (OSCE) (1995).

IV.3.1 Procedure for the Adoption of Joint Actions (TEU Art. J.3)
Joint actions are adopted through a unanimous Council decision. They are generally adopted on the basis of broad guidelines and the general strategy on the issue set out by the European Council.

In its role of defining the broad guidelines for the adoption of joint actions the European Council is responsible for the determination of areas of '*essential interest*'. The 1992 Lisbon European Council determined the following geographical areas of Common Interest:
   (a)   Eastern Europe;
   (b)   the Maghreb;
   (c)   the Middle-East; and
   (d)   the states of the former Soviet Union.

IV.3.2 Content of Joint Actions

Using unanimity the Council decides the scope, objective, duration, means, procedures and conditions for implementation of a joint action. There is a possibility to define by unanimity the matters on which decisions may later be taken by qualified majority voting (QMV).

In the conduct of their foreign policies Member States are committed to and obliged to follow a joint action that they have adopted (TEU Art. J.3.4). Nevertheless this disposition is subject to the safeguard clause of TEU Art. J.3.6, which reads as follows:

> *In cases of imperative need arising from changes in the situation and failing a Council decision, Member States may take the necessary measures as a matter of urgency having regard to the general objectives of the joint action. The Member States concerned shall inform the Council immediately of any such measures.*

IV.4 CFSP and the Treaty of Amsterdam

The Treaty of Amsterdam provides for measures aimed at strengthening the decision-making procedure through the introduction of new instruments and voting modalities. The decision-making capacity of the Council is strengthened in different ways.

IV.4.1 New Instruments and Voting Modalities introduced in the Treaty of Amsterdam

A new instrument: common strategies (ToA/TEU Art. 13)
Common strategies define the objectives of the Union and the means to achieve these objectives. They are adopted by the European Council on the recommendation of the Council of Ministers in areas where the Member States have important interests in common.

A hierarchy of instruments
Once a common strategy is adopted, the Council can adopt joint actions and common positions to implement the strategy by QMV. In the absence of a common strategy, the Council of Ministers must operate through unanimity. However, the measures necessary to implement these common positions and joint actions are adopted by QMV. QMV will not apply to decisions having military or defence implications. The Council will act by simple majority for procedural questions (ToA/TEU Art. 23).

The five instruments of the CFSP that will be applicable when the Amsterdam Treaty comes into effect are listed in ToA/TEU Art. 12 as follows:
— principles and general guidelines;
— common strategies;
— joint actions;
— common positions;
— systematic cooperation between Member States.

According to ToA/TEU Art. 13 the European Council is to define the principles and general guidelines for the CFSP including those with defence implications, on the basis of which the Council must take the decisions necessary for defining and implementing the CFSP.

A precise definition of each instrument avoiding confusion in their use
Common strategies (ToA/TEU Art. 13) are implemented in areas where the Member States have important interests in common and will define the objectives, duration and means to be adopted.

Joint actions (ToA/TEU Art. 14) shall address specific situations where operational action by the Union is deemed to be required. They lay down the objectives, scope, means, duration and the conditions for implementation. The Council may ask the Commission to submit appropriate proposals to ensure the implementation of a joint action.

Common positions (ToA/TEU Art. 15) shall define the approach of the Union to a particular matter of a geographical or thematic nature.

Much will depend on the willingness of Member States to establish common strategies. The Member States will be very careful in doing so since they know that they would be opening up the possibility for being outvoted by QMV at a later stage. It will probably also be difficult to establish a common strategy before a crisis emerges. When such a crisis does emerge it is unlikely that the European Council will be well placed to provide a rapid response.

Constructive abstention (ToA/TEU Art 23.1)
If a decision has to be taken by unanimity, the abstention of one or more Member States will not prevent the adoption of that decision. Such Member States may also submit a formal declaration during a vote to ensure that they are not obliged to apply the decision, but they will accept that the decision is binding on the Union. If the number of Member States making such a declaration reaches one third of the weighted votes in the Council (see chapter 3), the decision is not adopted. A country that obtains such an 'opt-out' is nevertheless bound to refrain from any action likely to conflict with or impede Union action based on that decision.

Important and stated reasons of national policy (ToA/TEU Art. 23.2)
If a decision has to be taken with QMV, the matter will not be put to a vote if a Member State declares that for 'important and stated reasons' of national policy it intends to oppose the adoption of such a decision. In that case, the Council may, acting by QMV, refer the matter to the European Council for a decision by unanimity.

IV.4.2 New Structures to Assist the Council in the Preparation of Decisions and Representation of the Union

Representation of the Union
The system of the Troika is replaced by a new formula where the Presidency represents the Union in the sphere of the CFSP and is assisted by the Secretary General of the Council in his new function of High Representative for CFSP (see below). The Commission is fully associated with the task of representation of the Union and the Presidency may be assisted by the Member State which will exercise the next presidency (ToA/TEU Art. 18).

Policy planning and early warning unit
A declaration attached to the Treaty of Amsterdam establishes a policy planning and early warning unit in the Council Secretariat, under the responsibility of its Secretary General. This unit will consist of personnel from the General Secretariat, the Member States, the Commission and the WEU. Its duties include monitoring and analysing developments in areas relevant to the CFSP, the provision of timely assessments and early warning of important events or crisis, and assisting the formulation of policies by the Council. The unit's reports would contain analyses, recommendations and proposed strategies for CFSP. The Member States and the Commission may make suggestions to the unit for possible activities and must provide the unit with all relevant information, including confidential information.

The High Representative for CFSP (ToA/TEU Art. 26)
The Secretary General of the Council will fulfil the new function of High Representative for CFSP. ToA/TEU Art. 26 sets out the duties of the High Representative. He will assist the Council in matters falling within the scope of the CFSP, in particular by helping to formulate, prepare and implement policy decisions and, when appropriate, conduct political dialogue with third parties on behalf of the Council and at the request of the Presidency.

He is to be nominated by the Council by unanimity and assisted by a Deputy Secretary General who will assume the Secretary General's traditional tasks of overlooking the management of the General Secretariat of the Council.

Special representative (ToA/TEU Art. 18)

ToA/TEU Art. 18.5 allows the Council to appoint, whenever it deems necessary, a special representative with a mandate to act on particular policy issues. Moratinos, as EU envoy to the Middle East, would fit this description.

IV.4.3 New Capacity to Conclude International Agreements under CFSP (ToA/TEU Art. 24)

The Union receives the capacity to conclude international agreements in the sphere of CFSP. The Council decides with unanimity to authorise the Presidency, possibly assisted by the Commission, to start negotiations with other states and international organisations. On the basis of a recommendation of the Presidency, it is up to the Council, acting unanimously, to conclude agreements, which will not be binding for Member States which declare in the Council that they need to comply with their own institutional requirements, although they will be binding on the other Member States.

V. THE WESTERN EUROPEAN UNION AS A TOOL OF THE COMMON FOREIGN AND SECURITY POLICY

The TEU gives the WEU a very particular role in the process of European integration by designating it as the defence arm of the European Union. The CFSP was defined to include all aspects of security, but nevertheless it does not deal with defence issues itself. It was therefore given the power to request the WEU, should it so wish, to 'elaborate and implement decisions and actions of the Union which have defence implications' (TEU Art. J.4.2).

Although the WEU and the EU may be seen as natural partners, in the past the EC was confronted with many obstacles in cooperating with this defence organisation, including:

— Problems with Ireland as a neutral country.

— Problems with Denmark, which always perceived the EC as a predominantly economic organisation with no role in defence matters.

— The age-old debate on whether a European or an Atlantic NATO-led defence approach was best.

Nevertheless the WEU was awoken from dormancy with the Rome Declaration of 1984 and given a new *raison d'être* in the TEU.

Since then several practical measures have been taken in order to facilitate cooperation between the two organisations including:

— The transfer of the seat of the WEU to Brussels bringing it physically close to both the EU and NATO (1993).

—The synchronisation of EU and WEU meetings, working methods and presidencies through a declaration annexed to the TEU.

A major step was taken with the adoption of the WEU Petersberg Declaration of June 1992 which outlined:
(a)   The readiness of WEU members to implement measures on a case-by-case basis for conflict prevention and crisis management, including peace-keeping activities;
(b)   the regulation of WEU enlargement with its different levels of association:
● full membership for EU Member States;
● observer status for EU Member States unwilling to join the WEU;
● associate membership for other European NATO states.

Two years later the Kirchberg Declaration of May 1994 provided for the creation of another level of association:
● associate partnerships for nine (later 10) Central and Eastern European countries.
In January of the same year the joint NATO-WEU Ministerial decision supporting the creation of a European Security and Defence Identity (ESDI) and the strengthening of the European pillar of the Alliance through the WEU as the defence component of the European Union marked a renewed impetus for Europe to take on more responsibility for its own military security. Europe's operational capability also increased through the NATO offer to put its collective assets at the disposal of the WEU for operations implementing CFSP measures (after consultations in the North Atlantic Council).

The same meeting endorsed the concept of Combined Joint Task Forces (CJTF) providing separable but not separate military capabilities that could be employed by NATO or the WEU, in situations affecting European security in which NATO itself is not involved. Although all use of NATO resources is subject to a possible US veto, it does give the EU the possibility of reacting to security threats in Europe without necessarily having the US on board.

V.1 The Treaty of Amsterdam and the Reinforced EU–WEU Relationship

The Treaty of Amsterdam contains significant provisions on the future direction of EU–WEU cooperation including the following.

V.1.1 The Defence Dimension and the WEU (ToA/TEU Art. 17)
Paragraph 1 of the new article specifies the role of the WEU in the progressive framing of a common defence policy already mentioned in the TEU. It also

reiterates the possibility of the creation of a common defence, should the European Council so decide. In that case it will recommend to the Member States the adoption of such a decision in accordance with their constitutional requirements.

Whether or not the ToA proves to be a simple stepping stone for the integration of the WEU into the EU it is clear that the relationship between the two organisations has been strengthened. While the wording of the TEU speaks of the Union 'requesting' the WEU to carry out specific tasks, the ToA refers to the Union 'availing itself' of the WEU in a manner which suggests a more integrated WEU than was previously the case.

Paragraph 2 deals specifically with the WEU, which is recognised (as in the TEU) as an integral part of the development of the Union and provides the EU access to an operational defence capability. The WEU is to support the Union in the framing of defence aspects of the CFSP. The Union accordingly undertakes to foster institutional relations with the WEU, which may ultimately lead to the integration of the WEU into the Union, should the European Council so decide.

Paragraph 3 states that the Union will avail itself of the WEU to draw up and implement European Council decisions and actions with defence implications.

V.1.2 The Incorporation of the (WEU) Petersberg Tasks

The so-called Petersberg tasks (humanitarian and rescue tasks, peacekeeping missions and tasks of combat forces in crisis management) have been included in the TEU (ToA/TEU Art. 17.2). The Treaty allows the EU to use the WEU to elaborate and implement actions related to the Petersberg tasks (ToA/TEU 17.3). In such a case all Member States (including those not members of the WEU) shall be entitled to participate fully in such tasks

V.1.3 Armament Cooperation (ToA/TEU Art. 17)

This article states that the Member States may support the progressive framing of a common defence policy by means of cooperation in the field of armaments. Efforts by some Member States to include armaments in the Internal Market (IM) through the ToA were not successful.

VI. HISTORICAL DEVELOPMENT

In the aftermath of the Second World War two different logics were followed in the process of putting into place some form of cooperation in the area of foreign and security policy in Europe:

   (a)   in a first phase, the creation of political or defence communities;

(b)   in a second phase, the step-by-step pragmatic approach in the form of a slowly but steadily developing European Political Cooperation (EPC).

VI.1 The Creation of Political and Defence Communities

VI.1.1 From the EDC to the Fouchet Plans: a History of Failed Attempts:
After 1945, the French faced the dilemma of how to contain Germany while rearming it. The answer it came up with was the Pleven Plan and the proposal for the setting up of the European Defence Community (EDC, 1952; see chapter 2). This was followed by plans for a European Political Community (1953). These plans ultimately failed when the French Parliament refused to ratify the EDC Treaty in August of 1954. Ultimately the solution to the German question came through the Atlantic Alliance.

VI.1.2 The Fouchet Plans and 'l'Europe des États'
In 1959 De Gaulle proposed the creation of European Political Cooperation which would involve cooperation on common foreign policy and in the field of defence. This was done in parallel to the work of a Committee chaired by Fouchet — the French Ambassador to Denmark whose draft Treaty for a 'Union of States' was published in November 1961.

Nevertheless concerns of exactly what form the cooperation would take, together with the Benelux fear of a Franco-German *directoire* and the rebuff of their efforts to involve the UK, meant that both proposals were met with scepticism. Also, the unclear relationship that would exist between the proposed EPC and the Atlantic Alliance made agreement even more difficult to attain.

Ultimately both proposals were rejected in the negative atmosphere that followed the French veto of the accession of the United Kingdom. When De Gaulle finally left office in 1969 it was possible for the Hague Summit of December of that year to both put the first enlargement on track and finally to approve a modest but nevertheless quite real *European Political Cooperation (EPC)*.

VI.2 The Building of EPC: A Pragmatic Approach

The history of EPC is characterised by a progression of improvements, often occurring as a response to the failure of the existing procedures and tools to cope effectively with a given situation.

.   The birth certificate of EPC came with the *Luxembourg/Davignon Report* of October 1970, which suggested that the first concrete steps towards political union should be made in the field of foreign policy. Common positions were introduced at this time.

The *Copenhagen Report* of July 1973 stepped up the sharing of information between the Member States with the establishment of the COREU telex network. It also increased the frequency of EPC meetings on all levels, elaborated the role of the Presidency and formalised the position of the working groups.

The European Council, which would play an ever-greater role in the external policy of the EC, was institutionalised at the *Paris Summit of 1974*.

The *Tindemanns Report of 1975*, which aimed at a substantial strengthening of EPC, turned out to be ill-timed and led nowhere.

The *London Report of 1980* ushered in important new tools for EPC in the shape of sanctions and trade and aid instruments, thus giving the policy more teeth while marking the first major step in the rapprochement between EPC and pure EC matters. The report also provided for the strengthened role of the Presidency, the full association of the Commission with EPC and the confirmation of the role of the Troika Secretariat.

The *Stuttgart Solemn Declaration* of June 1983 followed up the *1981 Genscher-Colombo Report* and defined the scope of EPC, including the economic and political aspects of security and established explicit, though cautious, bridges with the Community institutions.

Another watershed decision for EPC came with the *1987 Single European Act*, which finally gave EPC a Treaty basis and provided for the long-awaited formal setting up of the EPC Secretariat. The political aspects of security become part of the EPC ambit at this time. The possibility of closer cooperation with NATO or the WEU was also specifically envisaged in the Treaty.

An Evaluation of the EPC System

Positive elements:

— Direct links between Member States' diplomatic corps were strengthened.
— One could witness the development of a natural reflex towards consultation in foreign affairs.
— The output included some successes.

Negative elements:

— Reactive system, not able to respond to crisis situations.
— Based on the political will of the Member States, and thus victim of divergences between them.
— Declaratory policy, no commitment to common action.
— Separation between EC framework and EPC was artificial and not workable.

VI.3 From EPC to CFSP

The success of the EPC in dealing with the flow of international relations challenges was mixed. Amongst the successes one may point to the CSCE Conference and to a lesser extent the Code of Conduct on South Africa.

Nevertheless the clear failures in situations such as the imposition of martial law in Poland, the invasion of Afghanistan and the collapse of Community solidarity in dealing with the Falklands crisis exposed the weaknesses of EPC.

The memories of these failures, together with the new challenges which came with the revolutions of 1989 and the Gulf War and the Yugoslav crisis, laid the groundwork for the replacement of EPC with a stronger and more ambitious Common Foreign and Security Policy. The CFSP was introduced as Title V of the TEU.

VI.4 The Financing of CFSP under the Treaty of Amsterdam

The financing of the CFSP has led to some serious problems in the past, especially in the relation between the Council and the EP. The problem was tackled in ToA/TEU Art. 28 which specifies that:

(a) provisions of Title V which entail administrative expenditure for the institutions will be charged on the Communities budget (as non-compulsory expenditure).

(b) the same is to apply to operational expenditure, except for expenditure arising from operations with military or defence implications and cases where the Council, acting unanimously, decides otherwise.

With regard to the budgetary procedure, ToA/TEU Art. 28.4 states that the budgetary procedure of the EC Treaty will apply to expenditure charged to the Communities budget. Also, an inter-institutional agreement between the EP, the Council and the Commission on provisions regarding the financing of the CFSP was added to the Treaty, stipulating the following:

(a) CFSP expenditure is to be charged to the Communities budget as non-compulsory expenditure.

(b) On the basis of a preliminary draft budget drawn up by the Commission, the Council and the EP will reach an annual agreement on the amount of operational CFSP expenditure to be charged to the Communities budget and on the allocation of such expenditure.

(c) The total amount of operational expenditure will be entered in its entirety into one budget chapter.

(d) An ad hoc consultation procedure will be set up to reach an agreement between the EP and the Council on the amount of CFSP expenditure and on the distribution of this amount. The procedure will apply, at the request of one or

the other institution, in particular if either of them intends to depart from the
preliminary draft budget of the Commission.

(e)   The EP is consulted and informed under the following conditions:

(i)   The Presidency of the Council will consult the EP annually on the
main aspects and basic choices of the CFSP, including financial implications
for the budget. The Presidency must inform the EP regularly on the
development and the implementation of CFSP actions.

(ii)   When adopting decisions in the field of CFSP entailing expenditures, the Council must communicate an estimate of the costs to the EP.

(iii)   The Commission must inform the budgetary authority about the
execution of CFSP actions and the financial forecast for the rest of the year on
a quarterly basis.

VII. FUTURE PERSPECTIVES

The Treaty of Amsterdam is generally perceived as providing for only modest
changes to the Union. Nevertheless the changes which are set to take place in
the area of CFSP are numerous. Of course, that is not the same as saying that
they are substantial or that they are likely to revolutionise the policy.

TEU provisions have been split up, rearranged, sometimes modified, mixed
in with new provisions and then renumbered. The table below shows which
provisions came from where:

TEU provisions	Amsterdam provisions	New Amsterdam numbering
Art. J1.1 and 2	Art. J1 (CFSP objectives)	Art. 11
Art. J1.3	Art. J2 (CFSP instruments)	Art. 12
Much modified Art. J8	Art. J3 (Role of European Council)	Art. 13
Art. J3	Art. J4 (Joint actions)	Art. 14
Art. J2.2 and 3	Art. J5 (Common positions)	Art. 15
Art. J2.1	Art. J6 (Obligation to consult)	Art. 16
Art. J4	Art. J7 (CFSP scope)	Art. 17
Art. J5.1 and 3	Art. J8 (Role of Presidency)	Art. 18
Art. J5.4	Art. J9 (Cooperation within international organisations)	Art. 19
Art. J6	Art. J10 (Role of Member States and common missions)	Art. 20
Art. J7	Art. J11 (Role of EP)	Art. 21
Art. J8.3	Art. J12 (Right to refer matters)	Art. 22
—	Art. J13 (Voting modalities)	Art. 23
—	Art. J14 (Opening of negotiations)	Art. 24
Art. J8.5	Art. J15 (Role of Political Committee)	Art. 25
—	Art. J16 (High Representative for CFSP)	Art. 26
Art. J9	Art. J17 (Full association of Commission)	Art. 27
Art. J11	Art. J18 (CFSP financing)	Art. 28

The changes provide for some improvement in several of the mechanisms, procedures and tools of the policy. They also provide for the creation of new actors and the development of the role of others. Unfortunately, in predicting whether one can expect to see meaningful advances in CFSP, or not, as a result of the Amsterdam Treaty one must fall into that now vintage truism that no institutional changes will make any difference in this arena in the absence of that ever-elusive political will.

VIII. FURTHER READING

HILL, Christopher: 'The capability-expectations gap, or conceptualising Europe's international role' in BULMER, Simon and SCOTT, Andrew (eds): *Economic and Political Integration in Europe, Internal Dynamics and Global Context*, Oxford, Blackwell, 1995, pp. 103–130.
HOLLAND, Martin (ed.): *Common Foreign and Security Policy — the Record and Reforms*, London, Pinter, 1997.
MARTIN, Laurence and ROPER, John: *Towards a Common Defense Policy*, Paris, Institute of Security Studies of the WEU, 1995.

PAPPAS, Spyros and VANHOONACKER, Sophie (eds): *The European Union's Common Foreign and Security Policy — The Challenges of the Future*, Maastricht, European Institute of Public Administration, 1996.
REGELSBERGER, Elfriede et al.: *Foreign Policy of the European Union*, London, Reiner, 1997.

Periodicals:

CFSP Forum
European Foreign Affairs Review

Websites

'CFSP homepage'	http://europa.eu.int/pol/cfsp/en/cfsp.htm
Council of Ministers	http://ue.eu.int/pesc/default.asp?lang = en

PART   V

THE THIRD PILLAR

21 COOPERATION IN JUSTICE AND HOME AFFAIRS

Gioia Scappucci

I. DEFINITION AND RATIONALE

The expression 'Justice and Home Affairs' (JHA) covers specific areas which are regarded as 'areas of common interest' among the Member States. They are all *very sensitive areas* which are closely linked to the sovereignty of the Member States. TEU Art. K.1 provides:

> *For the purposes of achieving the objectives of the Union, in particular the free movement of persons, ... Member States shall regard the following areas as matters of common interest:*
> *1.   asylum policy;*
> *2.   rules governing the crossing by persons of the external borders of the Member States and the exercise of controls thereon;*
> *3.   immigration policy and policy regarding nationals of third countries ...;*
> *4.   combating drug addiction ...;*
> *5.   combating fraud on an international scale ...;*
> *6.   judicial cooperation in civil matters;*
> *7.   judicial cooperation in criminal matters;*
> *8.   customs cooperation;*
> *9.   police cooperation for the purposes of preventing and combating terrorism, unlawful drug trafficking and other serious forms of international*

crime, including if necessary certain aspects of customs cooperation, in connection with the organisation of a Union-wide system for exchanging information within a European Police Office (Europol).

Not surprisingly the Member States were initially very reluctant to cooperate in these areas. They were pushed to do so since the late 1980s for two main reasons:

(a)   The *completion of the internal market* (IM) and the consequent removal of controls at internal EC borders had to be *flanked by measures* guaranteeing secure control of the *external borders*. Measures to avoid drug traffickers, terrorists and criminals benefiting from the free movement of goods, persons, capital and services were also felt to be necessary.

(b)   Increasingly *important cross-border threats* posed by terrorism, international organised crime, money laundering and drug trafficking, as well as the renewed wave of migration from the South and the East.

II. LEGAL BASIS AND OBJECTIVES

The sensitivity of these areas is reflected in the difficulties encountered by the Member States when choosing where to place the measures when negotiating the TEU. Some Member States (primarily Germany, but also Belgium and the Netherlands) wanted to see JHA provisions wholly within the EC Treaty. Others (mainly the UK and Denmark) sought their inclusion exclusively in a separate pillar, allowing only for purely intergovernmental cooperation. The TEU reflects a compromise between these two main trends. There is *no uniform solution but rather a mixed model*: one of the two intergovernmental pillars created by the TEU contains the provisions on cooperation in the fields of JHA (TEU Title VI), even though some issues related to JHA are to be found in the Community pillar.

II.1 Legal Basis

II.1.1 JHA within the EC Treaty

TEC Art. 100c provides for the drawing up of a *list of third countries whose nationals require a visa for entry into the EC* and the adoption of measures relating to a *uniform visa format*. This legal basis does not give the Community a general 'visa policy' competence. It enables the Council to take measures only in the two specific cases mentioned above. These are seen as part of the IM project.

Reference to Community action towards the *prevention of drug dependence* is included in TEC Art. 129 dealing with public health. Incentive measures, excluding any harmonisation of the laws and regulations of the Member States, may be adopted under this legal basis, using the co-decision procedure.

II.1.2 TEU Title VI: The 'Third Pillar'

The Union shall set itself ... to develop close cooperation on justice and home affairs (TEU Art. B, 3rd indent).

TEU Title VI contains the 'Provisions on cooperation in the fields of justice and home affairs' (TEU Arts. K to K.9). The matters listed as areas of common interest in TEU Art. K.1 are not the different facets of a 'common policy' in JHA: the TEU provides only for 'cooperation' in those areas.

A mechanism to transfer most of the matters covered by a 'Third Pillar' legal basis to the Community legal basis (TEC Art. 100c) is provided for in TEU Art. K.9. This mechanism is commonly referred to as the *'passerelle clause'*. It cannot be used for judicial cooperation in criminal matters, customs cooperation and police cooperation to combat terrorism, unlawful drug trafficking and other forms of serious international crime (i.e., for TEU Arts. K.1.7–9).

THE 'THIRD PILLAR' — A MIXED MODEL	
Intergovernmental Elements	*Supranational Elements*
1. The *Council* is the highest *decision-making body* in both TEC Art. 100c and the Third Pillar.	1. The *uniform institutional structure* (TEU Art C) combined with a *single coordinating committee* (TEC Art. 100d) might act in favour of supra-nationality.
2. Only *Member States* have the right of initiative in the areas of judicial cooperation in criminal matters, customs and police cooperation (Europol).	2. The *Commission shares the right of initiative* in areas covered by TEU Art. K.1.1–6 and is to be 'fully associated' with the work in the areas referred to in TEU Title VI.
3. The *EP is merely informed* about what is being discussed and decided in the framework of the Third Pillar.	3. Expenditure for activities under TEU Title VI may, but do not have to, come from the EC budget (if so, the EP has a chance to express its opinion in these areas).
4. The predominant decision-making procedure in the Third Pillar is *unanimity*.	4. A propensity towards supranationalism is built into the *passerelle clause*.
5. The *ECJ* has practically *no jurisdiction*.	

II.2 Objectives

No specific objective is indicated in the TEU for JHA cooperation. TEU Art. K.1 merely describes the matters listed in TEU Art. K.1.1–9 as 'matters of common interest' and stresses that cooperation is needed for the purpose of achieving the general objectives of the Union (TEU Art. B) and in particular *the free movement of persons* (TEC Art. 3.c–d).

III. KEY ACTORS

Council
— Takes the decisions necessary to implement 'visa policy' under TEC Art. 100c.
— Adopts joint positions and joint actions (TEU Art. K.3.2.a and b).
— Draws up conventions which it recommends to the Member States for adoption (TEU Art. K.3.2.c).
— If necessary, adopts the measures implementing conventions (TEU Art. K.3.2.c).
— Decides on expenditure for JHA (TEU Art. K.8).
— May decide on the use of the *passerelle* procedure (TEU K.9).
— Addresses recommendations, declarations and statements to the Member States.

Commission
— TEC Art. 100c: *monopoly of initiative* but obliged to submit a proposal if a Member State requests the Council to take into consideration specific measures.
— TEU Art K.1.1–6: *shared right of initiative* with Member States for asylum, immigration, external borders, combating international fraud, etc.
— TEU Art. K.9: shared right of initiative with the Member States to propose the use of the *passerelle* procedure.
— TEU Arts K.1.7–9: *no right of initiative* for judicial cooperation in criminal matters, customs cooperation and police cooperation.
— TEU Art. K.4.2: should be *'fully associated with the work'* of the Third Pillar.
   Because of the sensitivity of the areas of cooperation, the Commission has adopted a pragmatic and cautious attitude in JHA.

European Parliament
Very weak role: only consultation (TEC Art. 100c and TEU Art. K.6). The procedure of consultation in the Third Pillar has no legal consequences (unlike

the consultation procedure in the Community pillar, see chapter 3). In practical terms it implies that the EP is simply informed of what is being or has been done.

There are, however, two ways in which the EP can become more intensively involved in the fields of JHA:

(a)   When the *passerelle* is used, TEC Art. 100c gives the EP a more formalised role.

(b)   Possibility of increasing its role through *budgetary aspects*. Administrative expenditure is always charged to the EC budget. TEU Art. K.8 allows the Council, acting unanimously, to charge operational expenditure in Title VI to the EC budget. 'Operational expenditure' falls under non-compulsory expenditure in the budget, giving the EP the 'last say' (See TEC Art. 203).

European Court of Justice
— Full jurisdiction for the 'visa policy' (TEC Art. 100c).
— *No jurisdiction* in the Third Pillar with the sole *exception* of TEU Art. K.3.2.c, which provides that conventions may give the ECJ jurisdiction to interpret their provisions and to rule on any disputes regarding their application.

Member States
— Enjoy an *exclusive right of initiative* in the areas referred to in TEU Art. K.1.7–9 and *share the right of initiative* in areas referred to in TEU Art. K.1.1–6.
— Adopt 'Third Pillar' conventions.

The central role of the Member States reflects the intergovernmental character of TEU Title VI.

National parliaments
Ratify the conventions drawn up in accordance with TEU Art. K.3.2.c. This endows national parliaments with great bargaining power since conventions may not enter into force until ratified by all Member States.

IV. DECISION-MAKING AND WORKING PROCEDURES

IV.1 Decision-making

IV.1.1 Predominance of unanimity
— Unanimity is required for the adoption of *joint actions, joint positions and conventions*.

— It is also required for the Council to decide to use the *passerelle* clause and to charge *JHA operational expenditure* to the EC budget.

Whilst safeguarding Member States' national interests, the unanimity rule has been blamed for limiting the efficiency and speed of decision-making.

IV.1.2 Exceptions to the Unanimity Rule
— TEU Art K.3.2.b and c: the Council may unanimously decide that *measures implementing a joint action* are to be adopted by a qualified majority and *measures implementing conventions* may be adopted within the Council by a majority of two thirds of the High Contracting Parties to the convention.
— QMV may be introduced through the use of the *passerelle* by transferring areas to TEC Art 100c.

IV.1.3 Qualified Majority Voting
QMV is used for adopting measures relating to a *uniform format for visas* as well as for measures establishing the *list of third countries* whose nationals must be in *possession of a visa* when crossing the external borders of the Member States (TEC Art. 100c).

IV.2 Working Procedures: Five-level Working Structure
The TEU gave an institutional framework to the multiplicity of fora previously dealing with JHA (see V). This certainly entailed an increased accountability and transparency of JHA working structures which, nonetheless, remain complex and cumbersome. Instead of the normal three-level working structure (see chapter 3), the JHA Council works with *two extra levels*: a 'Coordinating Committee' (under COREPER) and three steering groups (above the working groups).

IV.2.1 The 'K.4 Committee'
TEU Art. K.4 foresees the setting up of a *coordinating committee* consisting of senior officials responsible for JHA within the national ministries. This committee is entrusted with contributing to the preparation of the Council's discussions in the areas referred to in TEU Art. K.1 and TEC Art. 100c (i.e., in all JHA matters). It also has the right to give opinions to the Council on its own initiative.

The reason behind establishing such a committee was the necessity of incorporating and coordinating the multitude of intergovernmental fora. It was hoped that this would avoid the excessive overlapping and duplication of work that existed before the TEU and that it would also provide greater transparency and control over decision preparation.

Although the K.4 Committee prepares all decisions taken at the ministerial level, it remains formally subject to the central coordinating role of COREPER.

IV.2.2 The Steering Groups
Hierarchically between the K.4 Committee and normal working groups one finds the so-called 'steering group level'. There are three steering groups, all formalising pre-TEU bodies and bringing them under the same umbrella:
— *Steering Group I* deals with asylum and immigration (replaced Ad Hoc Group on Immigration).
— *Steering Group II* deals with police and customs cooperation (took over the competencies of TREVI, CELAD and MAG).
— *Steering Group III* deals with judicial cooperation in civil and criminal matters (substituted European Political Cooperation groups on these specific matters).

The Steering Groups' work is prepared by the normal working group level. Working groups consisting of national experts exist for: asylum, immigration, visas, external frontiers, false papers, terrorism, police cooperation, fight against organised crime, Europol, drugs, customs cooperation, extradition, criminal law, the Brussels Convention (private international law), transmission of acts and driving bans.

V. POLICY INSTRUMENTS

V.1 Visa Policy (TEC Art. 100c)

V.1.1 Uniform Format for Visas
Reg. 1683/95 of 29 May 1995 lays down a uniform format for visas on the basis of TEC Art. 100c by taking up the *Schengen visa sticker* (common security standards agreed upon in the Schengen framework; see VI).

V.1.2 Common List
Reg. 2317/95 of 25 September 1995 establishes a legally binding list of 101 countries and entities whose nationals must be in possession of a visa when crossing the external frontiers of the EU. The list may be modified by the Council using QMV.
— The Regulation only applies to three-month and transit visas.
— It does not prevent Member States from maintaining national lists.
— A 'grey area' exists for nationals of countries for which there was no consensus on whether a visa is needed.

V.2 Third Pillar (TEU Title VI)

V.2.1 Joint Positions

The Council may ... adopt joint positions and promote, using the appropriate form and procedures, any cooperation contributing to the pursuit of the objectives of the Union (TEU Art. K.3.2.a)

— No strict interpretation of the meaning and scope of a joint position.
— Unclear legal status: no consensus on whether it is legally binding or not.
— Confusion between joint positions and common positions (TEU Art. K.5).

V.2.2 Joint Actions

The Council may ... adopt joint action in so far as the objectives of the Union can be attained better by joint action than by the Member States acting individually (TEU Art. K.3.2.b)

— Application of the principle of subsidiarity (TEC Art. 3.2.b).
— No strict interpretation of the meaning and scope of a joint action.
— Unclear legal status: no consensus on whether it is legally binding or not.
— Confusion between joint actions in the framework of JHA and those in CFSP (see chapter 20).

V.2.3 Conventions

The Council may ... draw up conventions which it shall recommend to the Member States for adoption in accordance with their respective constitutional requirements (TEU Art. K.3.2.c)

— Conventions are standard instruments in public international law.
— They *may stipulate that the ECJ shall have jurisdiction* for the interpretation of their provisions and to rule on disputes regarding their application.
   Conventions, as an instrument of cooperation in JHA, contain inherent weaknesses:
— their drafting can be very slow, because of unanimity voting modalities;
— the ratification process by national parliaments can also take years: all signatories must have ratified the convention before it can enter into force.

V.2.4 Common Position

> *Within international organisations and at international conferences in which they take part, Member States shall defend the common positions adopted under the provisions of this Title (TEU Art. K.5)*

It is not clear what differentiates a common position from a joint position, apart from the fact that the former are adopted within international organisations and at international conferences.

V.2.5 Resolutions, Recommendations, Declarations and Conclusions

Resolutions, recommendations, declarations and conclusions are instruments that the TEU does not explicitly foresee for JHA. Nonetheless, their essentially political nature means that the Council very often prefers to use these *not legally binding instruments.*

VI. HISTORICAL DEVELOPMENT

Neither the Treaty of Rome nor the SEA contained any provision on matters of JHA. These, nonetheless, progressively became a concern with the need to deal with the removal of internal barriers and increasing cross-border threats (see I). Because of the sensitivity of the issues involved, the Member States initially tried to deal with the consequences of the removal of internal barriers outside of the EC framework.

VI.1 Piecemeal Problem-solving outside the EC Framework

From the mid 1970s to the mid 1980s a multitude of *groups started to discuss JHA in an uncoordinated way*, including:

— *TREVI* (1975): established to organise regular meetings of internal security ministers and high civil servants with the aim of keeping one another informed of the state of *terrorist activities* in each country.

— *Judicial Cooperation Group*: met within the framework of EPC to deal with both criminal and civil aspects of judicial cooperation. Its aim was that of strengthening judicial cooperation among the Member States.

— *Ad Hoc Immigration Group* (1986): a high-level group comprising advisers to national immigration ministers. Its aim was to take action to achieve free circulation within the EC through combating illegal immigration, controls at external borders, visa policy, passport cooperation, information exchange between immigration authorities, the right of asylum, etc.

In this first phase all JHA cooperation was intergovernmental, presenting the following characteristics:
— it was voluntary;
— there was no legal basis for it;
— the EC institutional framework and decision-making procedures were not used;
— there was neither judicial nor democratic control;
— there was a complete lack of transparency.

The experts and practitioners in the field of JHA liked this system because it broke down distrust and it created useful networks among the Member States.

VI.2 The Schengen Laboratory (1985 and 1990)

VI.2.1 Objectives and Instruments
After the entry into force of the SEA, the lack of consensus among the Member States on the interpretation of the scope of 'free movement of persons' within the IM, together with the success of the non-institutionalised cooperation in JHA, pushed France, Germany and the Benelux to sign an international agreement on the progressive abolition of controls at their common borders (the 'Schengen Agreement', June 1985). The declared aim of this agreement was *to make possible the crossing of internal borders throughout the so-called 'Schengenland'*, without any checks on persons. This was accompanied by the need to maintain the level of security which existed before the lifting of the border checks. To achieve this, *compensatory measures* were also identified. The agreement provided for short-term concrete measures to ease border control and longer-term initiatives, e.g., uniform conditions for the crossing of external borders, common visa policy, police and judicial cooperation, etc. For these, a 'Schengen Implementing Convention' was signed in June 1990. Another crucial compensatory measure was the *Schengen Information System* (SIS), a computerised information system containing reports on persons and objects for the purpose of enhancing a secure free movement of persons within Schengenland.

VI.2.2 Principles and Main Characteristics
The Schengen experiment was *intergovernmental*, like the JHA groups of the mid 1970s and 1980s. It therefore presented most of the characteristics seen above, including lack of judicial and democratic control and an entirely secret decision-making process.

However, compared to the JHA groups of the mid 1970s and 1980s there were two fundamental differences: it was based on a comprehensive legal instrument and it was explicitly foreseen that Schengen provisions would apply only in so far as they were compatible with Community law. Because of this pre-emption for Community law, the Schengen experiment has been regarded as a *'laboratory' for measures to be adopted in the EC/EU framework for the free movement of persons*. The Schengen provisions on asylum were replaced by the 'Dublin Convention' when the latter entered into force on 1 September 1997.

"Schengenland"

13 Member States		*2 Associated Members*
1985: five Member States: Germany	1992: Greece;	1996: Norway, Iceland
France, Benelux;	1995: Austria;	
1990: Italy;	1996: Denmark, Finland,	
1991: Spain, Portugal;	Sweden	

The Schengen Convention is implemented in nine of its Member States (all signatories except Greece and the Nordic countries).

VI.3 Paving the Way to the Creation of the Third Pillar (1986–92)

By the time the TEU was being negotiated, all the frameworks of JHA cooperation analysed above were working and producing results, enhancing trust and therefore facilitating cooperation.

(a)   *TREVI*: from 1986 onwards, it was used as an instrument in the ever more viable idea of free circulation. After 1991, one of the group's main task was the preparation of the groundwork for the establishment of Europol.

(b)   *Ad Hoc Immigration Group*: it was responsible for the drafting of:

(i)   the *Dublin Convention*, which sets out a procedure for deciding which Member State is responsible for examining an *application for asylum*;

(ii)   the *Convention on External Border Controls*, which deals with matters such as *control of people crossing external EC borders*, material requirements for these people (such as passports, visas etc.), rules on when to enter someone on a 'blacklist', etc.

(c)   *CELAD* (Comité Européen pour la Lutte Anti-Drogues, 1989): aimed at organising cooperation against drug-producing and transit countries, as well as combating the associated money exchanges and action in the health sector.

(d)   *GAM'92* (Groupe d'Assistance Mutuelle): working group composed of representatives of the *customs authorities* in the Member States and a *Commission* representative with the aim of elaborating measures to *hinder the smuggling of goods such as drugs, firearms and pornographic material*.

(e)   *The Group of Free Circulation Coordinators* (1988): high-ranking group created by the Rhodes European Council *to coordinate the activities of the plethora of groups dealing with JHA and free movement of persons within the IM.* This Group became the umbrella group coordinating the activities of all other JHA groups.

It was commonly felt that some of the areas covered by these groups were ready to be dealt with within the EC framework: the Third Pillar was born with all the peculiarities described above.

VII. RECENT DEVELOPMENTS

During the 1996 IGC, progress in JHA cooperation was seen as an ideal opportunity to 'increase citizens' confidence in the European Union'. Four possible scenarios were discussed:

(1)   Full integration of JHA into the Community Pillar (maximalist strategy).

(2)   Maintain status quo to grant the Third Pillar enough time to properly establish itself (minimalist strategy).

(3)   Reform the Third Pillar (role of institutions, decision-making processes, clarification of legal nature of acts, rationalisation of working structures, more specific policy objectives and resources, etc.).

(4)   Transfer some, but not all, areas of common interest to the First Pillar whilst improving the overall effectiveness of the Third Pillar.

The results achieved in Amsterdam were a mix of the third and fourth scenario. The main characteristics of the reform may be described as follows:

First, the *lack of objectives for JHA was remedied.* Among the general objectives of the EU, the ToA added:

> *to maintain and develop the Union as an area of freedom, security and justice, in which the free movement of persons is assured in conjunction with appropriate measures with respect to external border controls, asylum, immigration and the prevention and combating of crime (ToA/TEU Art. 2, 4th indent).*

The ToA also identified a variety of specific objectives for the different areas of JHA (see chapter 22). Nonetheless, none of the areas of cooperation in JHA has been transformed into a common policy.

Secondly, most 'Third Pillar areas of common interest' have been *transferred to the Community pillar.* A new Title was inserted in the TEC on 'Visas, asylum, immigration and other policies related to the free movement of persons' (ToA/TEC Part Three Title IV). Cooperation against fraud and other illegal activities affecting the financial interests of the Community was fully communitarised (ToA/TEC Art. 280). The *only areas remaining in the Third*

Pillar are police cooperation and judicial cooperation in criminal matters (ToA/TEU Title VI).

A Protocol on *integrating the Schengen* acquis *in the framework of the EU* is annexed to the ToA. The legal basis of the Schengen *acquis* will have to be decided by the Council. The decision will be taken by unanimity by all 15 Member States. If not, the Schengen *acquis* will have the Third Pillar as a legal basis. 'New Schengen measures' (i.e., measures which build on the Schengen *acquis*) will be taken on the basis of the division of the matters in the ToA.

Thirdly, *closer cooperation* will be possible for all JHA matters (see chapter 22). Precisely because of the high degree of flexibility in JHA, the integration of the Schengen Agreement, as well as the communitarisation of many areas previously in the Third Pillar, was finally agreed upon. Interestingly, the same degree of flexibility will not be granted to future Member States of the EU. The Protocol on *integrating the Schengen acquis in the framework of the EU* explicitly provides that

> *for the purposes of the negotiations for the admission of new Member States into the EU, the Schengen* acquis *and further measures taken by the institutions within its scope shall be regarded as an* acquis *which must be accepted in full by all candidates for admission.*

Fourthly, *cooperation with third countries and international organisations* is envisaged for the areas remaining in the Third Pillar. The Council may use the new CFSP provisions enabling it to negotiate and conclude agreements with third countries (see chapter 20). According to well-established ECJ case law, the Community will be in a position to enter agreements with third countries on the 'communitarised' areas of JHA, if these matters are covered by EC legislation.

Finally, *the ECJ has a role* to play in JHA (see chapter 22).

VIII. FURTHER READING

BIEBER, Roland and MONAR, Jörg (eds): *Justice and Home Affairs in the European Union*, EIP, Brussels, 1995.

CULLEN, David, MONAR, Jörg and MYERS, Philip (eds): *Cooperation in Justice and Home Affairs — An Evaluation of the Third Pillar in Practice*, EIP, Brussels, 1996.

MONAR, Jörg and MORGAN, Roger: *The Third Pillar of the EU*, EIP, Brussels, 1994.

For an overview of the Third Pillar see EP, Directorate-General for Research Working Papers, PE 166.222, December 1996.

22 AN AREA OF FREEDOM, SECURITY AND JUSTICE

Gioia Scappucci

In the Treaty of Amsterdam (ToA) the expression 'JHA' no longer exists: the areas of common interest it covered are part of a larger project, that of establishing an 'area of freedom, security and justice'.

> *The Union shall set itself . . . to maintain and develop the Union as an area of freedom, security and justice, in which the free movement of persons is assured in conjunction with appropriate measures with respect to external border controls, asylum, immigration and the prevention and combating of crime (ToA/TEU Art. 2, 4th indent)*

The way to establish and maintain this area is defined in the first article of ToA/TEC Part Three Title IV on 'Visas, asylum, immigration and other policies related to the free movement of persons':

> *In order to establish progressively an area of freedom, security and justice, the Council shall adopt:*
> *(a) . . . measures aimed at ensuring the free movement of persons . . . in conjunction with directly related flanking measures with respect to external border controls, asylum and immigration . . . and measures to prevent and combat crime . . .;*

(b)   other measures in the fields of asylum, immigration and safeguarding the rights of nationals of third countries ...;

(c)   measures in the field of judicial cooperation in civil matters ...;

(d)   appropriate measures to encourage and strengthen administrative cooperation ...;

(e)   measures in the field of police and judicial cooperation in criminal matters aimed at a high level of security by preventing and combating crime within the Union in accordance with the provisions of the TEU (ToA/TEC Art. 61)

The area of freedom, security and justice will result from measures taken in both the Community Pillar and the Third Pillar. This chapter will first look at the areas of JHA which have been communitarised. Then it will analyse the areas of JHA which remain in the intergovernmental pillar.

I. VISAS, ASYLUM, IMMIGRATION AND OTHER POLICIES RELATED TO THE FREE MOVEMENT OF PERSONS

I.1 Legal basis and objectives

ToA/TEC Part Three Title IV: simplifies past complexities by bringing all provisions on the free movement of persons into the Community Pillar.

I.1.1 ToA/TEC Art. 62: Border Controls and Visas

To *ensure the free movement of persons* (citizens of the Union and third-country nationals) in the territory of the EU, it is necessary:

(a)   to take appropriate measures to abolish controls on persons crossing the internal borders of the single market;

(b)   to agree on conditions under which nationals of third countries shall have the freedom to travel within the territory of the Member States for not more than three months;

(c)   to determine common standards and procedures to: carry out checks on persons; grant short-term visas (common list of countries whose nationals must be in possession of a visa and those who are exempt; procedure to issue a visa, etc.).

I.1.2 ToA/TEC Art. 63: Asylum, Refugees and Immigration

Instead of containing a comprehensive common policy objective, this article lists measures to be taken to tackle specific issues of asylum, refugees and immigration.

(a)   *Asylum*: agree criteria and mechanisms for determining which Member States is responsible for considering an application for asylum; adopt minimum standards with respect to the qualification of nationals of third countries as refugees and on the procedures to grant or withdraw the refugee status.

(b)   *Refugees and displaced persons*: adopt minimum standards for their temporary protection; ensure that there is 'burden sharing' among the Member States receiving refugees and displaced persons.

(c)   *Immigration*: establish the conditions of entry and residence (long-term visas, family reunion, repatriation) of legal and illegal immigrants.

I.1.3 ToA/TEC Art. 65: Judicial Cooperation in Civil Matters
The creation of a common European judicial area is not the objective, as judicial cooperation in civil matters is still seen in the light of the proper functioning of the IM, which requires Member States:

(a)   to improve and simplify the system for cross-border service of judicial and extrajudicial documents, the taking of evidence, and recognising and enforcing decisions in civil and commercial cases;

(b)   to promote the compatibility of the rules applicable in the Member States concerning the conflict of laws and jurisdiction;

(c)   to eliminate obstacles to the good functioning of civil proceedings.

It is important to highlight that ToA/TEC Art. 64 expressly underlines that the measures taken to implement the above provisions 'shall not affect the exercise of the responsibilities incumbent upon Member States with regard to the maintenance of law and order and the safeguarding of internal security'.

I.2 Key Actors and Decision-making Procedures

ToA/TEC Art. 67 defines the decision-making procedure by distinguishing two phases:

(a)   *Five-year transitional period: 'imported intergovernmentalism'*. The decision-making procedure foreseen introduces some of the characteristics of intergovernmentalism into the EC sphere: the Commission shares the right of initiative with the Member States; the Council takes decisions by unanimity; the EP shall only be consulted. (Derogations exist for visas.)

(b)   *After the period of 5 years*. The Council may (acting unanimously, after having consulted the EP) decide to use the co-decision procedure. If it fails to do so, the decision-making procedure does not fully correspond to the Community method: the Commission will have the monopoly of initiative but it will be obliged to examine any request made by a Member State (this is generally not the rule in the Community Pillar, see chapter 3); as a general rule the Council shall act by unanimity and the EP shall only be consulted.

The working structures are the Community Pillar working structures (see chapter 3): the Council works on three levels and the Commission will probably have to create a new DG to deal with visas, asylum, immigration and other policies related to the free movement of persons.

I.3 Instruments

All the instruments provided for in the Community Pillar, i.e., Regulations, Directives, Decisions, Recommendations, Opinions (TEC Art. 189), may be used to implement the provisions of ToA/TEC Part Three Title IV.

ToA/TEC Art. 66 also stresses the need for *cooperation between relevant departments of the administrations of the Member States* in the areas covered by ToA/TEC Part Three Title IV.

I.4 The Scope of ECJ Jurisdiction

Even though the provisions on visas, asylum, immigration and other policies related to the free movement of persons are part of the Community Pillar, and should therefore be subject to the ECJ's full jurisdiction (see chapter 5), ToA/TEC Art. 68 restricts the use of preliminary rulings to specific circumstances and conditions:

— within the Member States' judicial systems, only courts of last resort may (no obligation) refer to the ECJ for a preliminary ruling;

— the Council, the Commission or a Member State may also request the ECJ to give such a ruling;

— the ruling given by the ECJ in response to such requests does not apply to judgments of courts or tribunals of the Member States which have become *res judicata*;

— the ECJ has *no jurisdiction on any measure or decision relating to the maintenance of law and order and the safeguarding of internal security.*

These restrictions of the ECJ's scope of jurisdiction are dangerous: most likely they will endanger the uniformity of interpretation of JHA provisions, thus entailing an unfortunately differentiated protection of the rights of individuals.

I.5 Flexibility

The 'communitarisation' of asylum, immigration and other policies related to the free movement of persons was accepted only because the possibility for flexibility in these areas was also recognised. Indeed three Member States have already negotiated special arrangements concerning ToA/TEC Part Three Title

IV and the integration of the Schengen *acquis* into the EC/EU framework. Their situation is foreseen in protocols annexed to the ToA.

I.5.1 UK and Irish Protocol

— General rule of non involvement of the UK and Ireland in the adoption by the Council of measures under ToA/TEC Part Three Title IV.

— The possibility to be involved in the adoption of certain measures is foreseen in ToA/TEC Part Three Title IV. A 'participation declaration' shall therefore precede the Council's adoption of measures. This declaration cannot block the decision-making process: if it is not delivered after a reasonable period of time, the Council shall adopt the measures without the participation of the UK and Ireland.

— Great freedom is given to opt-in. Britain and Ireland may in fact do so 'at any time', even after the adoption of a measure by the Council. An 'accession mechanism' is foreseen. The possibility of a selective 'opt-in' extends to both measures belonging to the 'Schengen *acquis*' and measures building on it.

— The measures adopted without Britain and Ireland, as well as any ruling of the ECJ interpreting such measures or any provision contained in ToA/TEC Part Three Title IV, are neither binding nor applicable in the UK or Ireland.

— The UK and Ireland will not bear the financial consequences of the measures adopted under ToA/TEC Part Three Title IV if they are not involved in their adoption.

The Protocol creates the *potential for fragmentation of EC law* and a consequent danger of *differentiated protection of the individual's rights*.

I.5.2 Danish Protocol

— *Elements in common with the UK and Irish Protocol*

Non-participation in the adoption of measures under ToA/TEC Part Three Title IV and the consequent lack of financial or legally binding effect of the measures for Denmark.

— *Particularity of the Danish Protocol*

If Denmark wishes to *opt-in* and adopt measures taken under ToA/TEC Part Three Title IV, it has to waive application of the Protocol. Denmark can either take all engagements or none: it cannot select on a case-by-case basis, as can the UK and Ireland.

If the Council decides to build on the 'Schengen *acquis*', within six months Denmark shall decide whether it shall implement the decision in its national law. If it decides to do so, the decision shall create an obligation of international law, not of Community law.

II. POLICE AND JUDICIAL COOPERATION IN CRIMINAL MATTERS

II.1 Legal Basis and Objectives

ToA/TEU Title VI. It still is an intergovernmental pillar even though it includes some typically 'Community characteristics'. It is the legal basis for the areas of JHA which remain in the Third Pillar, i.e., police and judicial cooperation in criminal matters.

> *Without prejudice to the powers of the European Community, the Union's objective shall be to provide citizens with a high level of safety within an area of freedom, security and justice by developing common action among the Member States in the fields of police and judicial cooperation in criminal matters and by preventing and combating racism and xenophobia.*
>
> *That objective shall be achieved by preventing and combating crime, organised or otherwise, in particular terrorism, trafficking in persons and offences against children, illicit drug trafficking and illicit arms trafficking, corruption and fraud (ToA/TEU Art. 29)*

By highlighting a general objective for the Third Pillar which stresses its implications for the citizens ('higher level of safety') and by adding to the areas of concern of the Member States the prevention and combating of racism and xenophobia, the ToA tries to respond to the IGC's challenge of 'bringing Europe closer to the citizen'. Like ToA/TEC Part Three Title IV, ToA/TEU Title VI prefers to identify an array of specific means to achieve the general objective rather than indicating a comprehensive strategy for the cooperation envisaged.

II.1.1   ToA/TEU Art. 30: common action in the field of police cooperation.
This includes operational cooperation between police, customs and other specialised law enforcement services of the Member States in relation to the *prevention, detection and investigation of criminal offences*; exchange of relevant information especially through Europol; joint initiatives in training the police; the agreement on common evaluation techniques in relation to the detection of serious forms of international crime.

II.1.2   ToA/TEU Art. 31: common action on judicial cooperation in criminal matters.
This includes facilitating cooperation between ministries and judicial authorities; facilitating extradition; preventing conflicts of jurisdiction; progressively *establishing minimum rules relating to the constituent elements of criminal acts and penalties* in the fields of organised crime, terrorism, drug trafficking.

The establishment of a European judicial area is not explicitly foreseen. Furthermore, there are no specific objectives as regards combating drug trafficking. Finally, there is no mention of how the Member States should prevent and combat racism and xenophobia.

The Third Pillar contains a similar *safeguard clause* to that in the Title on visas, asylum, immigration and other policies related to free movement of persons. ToA/TEU Art. 33 expressly underlines that measures taken to implement Third Pillar provisions: 'shall not affect the exercise of the responsibilities incumbent upon Member States with regard to the maintenance of law and order and the safeguarding of internal security'.

II.2 Key Actors and Decision-making Procedures

The ToA introduced some 'Community' elements in the Third Pillar.

II.2.1 The roles of the Commission and the EP have been extended:
— The Commission has a *right of initiative in all areas*, even though it is shared.
— The EP has *to be consulted* (the Council may lay down a *time limit* for it to deliver its opinion) *on all measures* except common positions.

II.2.2 Simplification of the working structures:
— The Steering Groups have been eliminated. A multidisciplinary group (the so-called 'GMD') was officially set up during the Amsterdam European Council (June 1997) for organised crime. It will be the coordinating group for the working groups on extradition, mutual assistance, terrorism etc. A Horizontal Drugs Group (HDG) was also created to deal with the 'cross-pillar' issues concerning drugs.
— The role of the 'K.4 Committee' (which will probably change name since the article dealing with it is to be renumbered ToA/TEU Art. 36!) should no longer overlap too much with COREPER: it will be competent for the preparation of the Council's work only for police and judicial cooperation in criminal matters.

II.2.3 Europol's role has been potentially extended:

> The Council shall promote cooperation through Europol and shall in particular, within a period of five years after the date of the entry into force of the Treaty of Amsterdam:
> (a) enable Europol to facilitate and support the preparation, and to encourage the coordination and carrying out, of specific investigative

actions by the competent authorities of the Member States, including operational actions of joint teams comprising representatives of Europol in a support capacity;

(b)   adopt measures allowing Europol to ask the competent authorities of the Member States to conduct and coordinate their investigations in specific cases . . .;

(c)   promote liaison arrangements between prosecuting/investigating officials specialising in the fight against organised crime in close cooperation with Europol;

(d)   establish a research, documentation and statistical network on cross-border crime. (ToA/TEU Art. 30.2)

II.2.4 Voting modalities
The voting modality in the Third Pillar remains predominantly unanimity but cases of strengthened QMV (see chapter 3) are provided for the adoption of implementing measures for Decisions (see below).

II. 3 Instruments

ToA/TEU Art. 34.1 provides that Member States shall inform and consult one another within the Council with a view to coordinating their action. For this purpose *collaboration between relevant departments of the administrations of the Member States* is also needed.

The confusion over the use and nature of the Third Pillar instruments has been tackled. Significant clarifications are contained in ToA/TEU Art. 34.2.

— Joint actions are no longer foreseen. *Common positions* shall define the approach of the EU to a particular matter.

— *Framework Decisions* are new instruments to be used for the purpose of the approximation of the laws and regulations of Member States. Like First Pillar Directives (TEC Art. 189) Framework Decisions shall be binding as far as results are concerned, leaving the national authorities the choice of the form and the method to achieve the result. They will not have direct effect.

— *Decisions* may be adopted for any other purpose consistent with the objectives of ToA/TEU Title VI. These have the same characteristics as the Framework Decisions.

— Some of the inadequacies of the use of *Conventions* have been remedied: the ratification procedures by the national parliaments shall be fixed within specified time limits (to be decided by unanimity). Unless provided differently, they shall enter into force once adopted by at least half of the Member States.

II.4 Scope of ECJ Jurisdiction

An important achievement of the ToA is the recognition of a role for the ECJ in the Third Pillar. However, the scope of the ECJ's jurisdiction is limited: not all remedies may be used in the Third Pillar (see chapter 5). Those which can are subject to specific conditions set out in ToA/TEU Art. 35:

(a) There is much scope for the flexible use of *preliminary rulings* (ToA/TEU Art. 35.1–3):

— Member States have to make a declaration to accept the ECJ's jurisdiction to give preliminary rulings.

— Member States shall specify whether only courts or tribunals of last resort shall be able to request the ECJ to give a preliminary ruling on a question raised in a case pending before them, or whether any court or tribunal may do so. In any case, no obligation to do so shall exist as it is up to the national court or tribunal to consider whether a decision on the question is necessary to enable it to give a judgment.

— The preliminary ruling may be given only on the validity and interpretation of Framework Decisions, Decisions, Conventions and measures implementing them. No possibility of asking for a preliminary ruling on the interpretation of the provisions of the ToA/TEU Title VI shall be allowed. Assessing the validity of an act without the possibility of interpreting the treaty will be complicated.

(b) An action for *annulment* (on the grounds of lack of competence, infringement of essential procedural requirement, etc.; see chapter 5) may be started only by the Commission or a Member States and is possible only against Framework Decisions and Decisions (ToA/TEU Art. 35.6).

(c) If a dispute arises between Member States on the interpretation or application of Third Pillar measures and if a Member States refers such a dispute to the Council, the Council has six months to resolve the dispute, otherwise the ECJ shall have jurisdiction to rule on it (ToA/TEU Art. 35.7).

(d) There is no remedy against *failure to act*.

In any case, according ToA/TEU Art. 35.5, the *ECJ will have no jurisdiction to review the validity or proportionality of operations carried out by the police or other law enforcement services of the Member States with regard to the maintenance of law and order and the safeguarding of internal security*. Such a safeguard clause for provisions concerning police and judicial cooperation in criminal matters potentially restricts the scope of the ECJ, especially in areas where the need for protection of individual rights is particularly great.

II.5 Flexibility

Closer cooperation in the framework of the Third Pillar is explicitly allowed, provided that it is aimed at enabling the Union to develop more rapidly into an area of freedom, security and justice and that it respects the powers of the Community and the objectives of the Third Pillar.

The *mechanism to grant the authorisation* to establish closer cooperation is foreseen by ToA/TEU Art. 40.2 and works as follows:

— The request by Member States willing to cooperate more closely is made to the Council.

— After having invited the Commission to present its opinion and having forwarded the request to the EP for information, the Council decides on the request by strengthened QMV.

— If a member of the Council declares, for important and stated reasons of national policy, that it intends to oppose the granting of the authorisation, the Council shall not vote. It may, by strengthened QMV, refer the matter to the European Council for a decision (to be taken by unanimity).

Accession by other Member States to the closer cooperation is also regulated by a specific mechanism (ToA/TEU Art. 40.3, see chapter 4).

III. FURTHER READING

MONAR, Jörg: 'Schengen and flexibility in the Treaty of Amsterdam: opportunities and risks of differentiated integration in the EU Justice and Home Affairs', in DEN BOER, Monica (ed.): *Schengen, Judicial Cooperation and Policy Coordination*, Maastricht, EIPA, 1997, pp. 9–28.

BARRET, Gavin (ed.): *Justice Cooperation in the European Union — The Development of the Third Pillar*, Institute of European Affairs, Dublin, 1997.

EHLERMANN, Claus Dieter: *Differentiation, Flexibility, Closer Cooperation: the New Provisions of the Amsterdam Treaty*, Badia Fiesolana, European University Institute, 1998, pp. 17–28.

For an analysis of the changes introduced by the ToA see EP Report, DOC–EN/DV/332/332457, 15 July 1997, pp. 4–10.

Website

Commission information on the 'Area of Freedom, Security and Justice'	http://europa.eu.int/comm/sg/scadplus/leg/en/s22000.htm

PART   VI

TOWARDS A WIDER UNION

23   THE PROSPECT OF ENLARGEMENT

Julian Vassallo

I. RATIONALE

The enlargement of the European Union to Central and Eastern European Countries (CEECs) is seen as a historic opportunity. The Union's decision to enlarge to a set of countries which are far less developed in both economic and political terms was taken long before any serious analysis of the implications of such a move was made. The context of the end of the Cold War led European leaders to think in terms of 'how' and 'when' rather than 'if'.

Enlargement to include Cyprus is overshadowed by the prospect of bringing a sufficient number of former Communist bloc countries into the EU to force it to reinvent itself, or risk becoming unworkable. The consensus in favour of enlargement is matched with a common understanding that the decision-making process must be reformed before enlargement takes place (see chapter 3).

The rationale of enlargement is also based on security considerations and the Union's wish to project peace and security to its 'near abroad'. Enlargement also promises to increase the size of the Internal Market (IM) from 370 to 475 million consumers with a potential for new economic opportunities and the resultant increase in the EU's already hefty economic weight on the world stage.

II. LEGAL BASIS

TEU Art. O states:

> *Any European State may apply to become a member of the Union. It shall address its application to the Council, which shall act unanimously after consulting the Commission and after receiving the assent of the European Parliament, which shall act by an absolute majority of its component members.*
>
> *The conditions of admission and the adjustments to the Treaties on which the Union is founded which such admission entails shall be the subject of an agreement between the Member States and the applicant State. This agreement shall be submitted for ratification by all the Contracting States in accordance with their respective constitutional requirements.*

The Preamble to the TEU together with TEU Art. F.1, which makes reference to the democratic nature of the governments of the Member States, also have relevance to enlargement.

TEC Art. 3a.1 is relevant to enlargement in so far as it specifies that Member States' economic policies must be based on an open market economy and free competition.

III. KEY ACTORS

European Council
In its role as direction-giver of the EU, the European Council is the body that effectively sets the enlargement ball rolling. There is no doubt that the choice of applicants and the momentum of enlargement are issues of the highest import for all Member States. It is in this forum that the political impetus for enlargement is conceived and maintained. The choices of with whom, when, how and with what instruments to proceed with enlargement are taken at this level. The Commission's central role in the negotiation process, as outlined below, only comes into play on the basis of the European Council's initiative and under its terms.

De Gaulle's two vetoes of the United Kingdom's accession in the 1960s stand out as the only case where the national interest of a single Member States prevented the enlargement of the EC/EU. This time around, the seeds of potential disruption by Member States lie in two distinct areas: first, the likelihood of Greece vetoing enlargement if other Member States seek to disqualify divided Cyprus (see XI); second, the poorer 'cohesion countries'

(Spain, Portugal, Greece and to a lesser extent Ireland) who will see their export markets threatened while being forced to accept deep cuts in their cohesion and structural funds. Both problems threaten to take the enlargement process hostage if they are badly managed. It is in the European Council that such crises are likely to be resolved.

The Presidency

Technically the Presidency negotiates with the applicants on behalf of the Member States. In reality the Presidency acts more like a spokesman for the Union, often simply reiterating what has already been negotiated between the Commission and the applicants.

The Presidency may nevertheless use its position to bring particular issues to the forefront of the enlargment Agenda. The launch of the Austrian presidency, in July 1998, with a warning to the CEECs not to expect full migration rights on accession is one such example.

European Parliament (EP)

According to TEU Art. O the EP's only role in the enlargement process is to give or withhold its assent to the treaty of accession. The EP cannot be said to play a central role in the negotiation process. In spite of this, the sheer importance of enlargement coupled with the implications that it has for policies where the EP is an actor, means that it is in its interest to involve itself in the process. The EP scrutinises the Commission's performance in the negotiation process and pronounces itself thereon. It also monitors and reacts to the strategy for enlargement adopted by successive European Councils.

Traditionally the EP can be said to be pro-enlargement, with only a small minority of MEPs opposing the process. Nevertheless a third new movement can be detected in the EP. Although not openly opposed to the prospect of enlargement, this faction nevertheless declares itself unready to support a process that implies a reduction in funds allocated to, or economic dangers being levelled on, a particular constituency. One can expect this force to become larger and more vociferous as the exact 'price' of enlargement becomes apparent.

European Commission

Contrary to what is suggested in TEU Art. O it is the Commission rather than the Member States which is the main actor in the accession negotiations. Even if the final decision lies in the hands of the Member States, the central role of the Commission remains a reality throughout the process. When, as at present, the Commission is negotiating accession with several countries it does so in parallel although there is a different track of negotiations for each applicant.

Commission internal organisation for enlargement negotiations

The Correspondents Group. The Commission's organisational response to the prospect of enlargement negotiations starts with the appointment of a group of correspondents made up of one or two representatives of each Directorate-General (DG). These correspondents carry out most of the preparatory work for the enlargement negotiations before passing on this coordinating role to the Task Force for Enlargement around the time of the actual start of negotiations. At this point the group of correspondents becomes more of an information channel to the different DGs.

The Task Force for Enlargement. The Task Force for Enlargement is charged with screening the implementation of the *acquis* and for negotiating the issues for which immediate adjustment to the *acquis* is impossible for the applicant. The Task Force is involved in negotiations on three levels:

(a)   With the different DGs, in order to create a coherent position on the basis of often widely diverging interests.

(b)   With the applicants, with whom it tries to resolve as many of the outstanding issues as possible. It does so while chairing meetings between the EU and the applicant state during and after the screening process.

(c)   With the Council, to whom it presents its draft common positions (DCPs) for negotiation and approval.

The Task Force is set up under aegis of Commissioner Van Den Broek, who is responsible for enlargement. An Enlargement Task Force is a horizontal structure, covering all vertical DGs and enjoying a relatively high level of independence. In March 1998, Dutch–German national Van Den Pas was appointed head of the Enlargement Task Force.

Separate from the Enlargement Task Force is another Commission task force aimed at facilitating the enlargement process. GISELA (Groupe Interservice Élargissement) seeks to bring together the many divergent interests of different parts of the EU's administration with representatives from all DGs but also from the Secretariat General, the Legal Service, the Statistical Office, the Forward Planning Unit, the Task Force on Justice and Home Affairs, and Euratom.

The Negotiating Process
The process starts with the exploratory talks that take place in the preparatory stage before the actual start of negotiations. Even at this early stage negotiations may be said to have already started. At this time the Commission will be explaining the *acquis* to the applicant as well as the limits of what it is possible to achieve.

In the 1995 'EFTA Enlargement' the Commission was not granted an official negotiating mandate contrary to what is often the case when the Union negotiates with third countries. The Member States refuse to do so because the Commission is generally seen by the Member States as being too 'applicant friendly' in its dealings. However, it is likely that the sheer complexity and the number of applicant countries will militate in favour of the Council resorting to such a measure this time around. This will further increase the Commission's already substantial influence on the negotiation process. Any compromises that the Commission may negotiate on the basis of such a mandate would nevertheless be subject to Member States' approval.

In general the Commission's position can be described as a 'neutral broker' assuming an intermediary position between the applicant and the Member States. This is not to say that the Commission does not have interests of its own. The Commission should be perceived as the defender of the Treaties and the *acquis communautaire*. As such it ardently rejected any suggestions of permanent derogations to the *acquis* in the last negotiations. The Commission is not only keen on limiting all temporary derogations, and avoiding any permanent ones, but is just as keen to be seen to do so. Thus even when it accepted that a permanent derogation for Sweden in respect of snuff was unavoidable, it sought desperately to disguise it by offering an incomprehensible 25-year temporary derogation, renewable on the insistence of either party.

Nevertheless since the *acquis* is a relatively objective basis for the Commission's positions, the applicants continue to perceive the Commission as a neutral broker which strives to reconcile three often conflicting interests. First, the need for the *acquis* to be respected; second, the need to find ways for the applicant to adopt the *acquis* in a manner which is least prejudicial to its interests; and third, in finding these compromises, to ensure that no Member State turns out to be the effective 'loser' on too many occasions. The Commission negotiates these compromises in the form of draft common positions, which require the approval of the Member States. Thus it becomes apparent that the most arduous negotiations often take place within the two camps, rather than between them.

This is not to say that the negotiations between the EU and an applicant state will prove easy. While Cyprus has already adopted and implemented a large portion of the *acquis*, to demand full adherence from the CEEC applicants on entry is effectively to postpone enlargement to a date long beyond those presently being mooted. A greater accommodation of the applicant states could make the Commission's position more complex. In coming to draft common positions conflicts are likely to appear between the Member States which are more, or less, eager for enlargement on how far to push the applicants to adopt the *acquis* before accession. The cohesion countries, whose production base is more similar to the CEECs than the other Member States are the ones most likely to find themselves being demanding on the applicants.

Although the Commission may be perceived as the applicants' 'best friend', in presenting the limits of what is possible it sometimes presents a more restrictive picture to the applicants than the Member States themselves set out. In doing so the Commission may be seeking to keep some margin of manoeuvre. In finding out whether the Commission is really presenting the 'bottom line' on the issue or not the applicants will do well to rely on inside information gathered from sympathetic Member States — a tactic successfully used in the last enlargement negotiations.

Council of Ministers
In the past the key actor for the Council of Ministers was the Council Working Group on Enlargement, with Member States' Foreign Ministers in the General Affairs Council also meeting regularly with the applicants. The sheer number of countries with which negotiations have begun makes it impossible for these two actors to take on the whole burden without being completely overwhelmed by the process. Therefore it is likely that a new division of labour will be forthcoming possibly through a Commission negotiating mandate.

The Member States
Technically speaking, accession negotiations take place through an ongoing applicant–Member States intergovernmental conference, leading one to believe that the latter are the central players. However, in reality most of the negotiating work is delegated to the Commission. In the past it was only when politically highly sensitive issues were discussed, or when the deadline for concluding the negotiations approached, that solutions were sought in direct consultations between Member States and the applicant country.

IV. POLICY INSTRUMENTS

IV.1 Europe Agreements

The EC has concluded Europe Agreements with the ten CEECs that have applied for membership. These agreements are essentially Association Agreements, which were only linked to accession after their political reorientation at the Copenhagen European Council of 1994. The agreements define the strategies for ever-closer cooperation in almost all areas of public administration and economic structures. The PHARE programme is the financial arm of the Europe Agreements and defines the framework within which the transfer of funds takes place.

IV.2 The PHARE Programme

The philosophy behind PHARE is to bring the CEECs back into mainstream Europe with the prospect of joining the EU. The initial priorities for the programme were related to helping these countries in their transformation into democracies. As the new democratic structures took hold the programme also focused on supporting their ongoing economic transformation. Through non-commercial public and private enterprises in the associated countries PHARE channels funds and know-how, both in terms of policy advice and training, to initiatives in the following areas:
— the restructuring of state enterprises including agriculture;
— private sector development;
— institutional reform;
— legislation and public administration;
— reform of social services;
— development of energy, transport and telecommunications infrastructure;
— employment;
— education and health;
— environment;
— nuclear safety.
In the years 1989–95 the EU made 5.4 billion ECU available to the CEECs. As accession approaches funding will become more focused on direct investment in infrastructure projects.

IV.3 Commission White Paper on CEECs and the IM

In June 1995 the Commission published a White Paper, *Preparation of the Associated Countries of Central and Eastern Europe for Integration into the Internal Market of the Union* (COM(95)163 final; see chapter 6). The document, which was endorsed at the Cannes European Council of the same year, sets out a very detailed legislative programme for the CEECs to comply with the rules of, and ultimately join, the IM. It concentrates on the fundamental aspects of the vast IM legislation, in terms of the implementation of the four freedoms and competition rules. The document does not legally prejudge the accession negotiations themselves (the bulk of which also deal with the adoption of the rules of the IM) yet it does contribute to the creation of an irreversible legal framework for integration (Maresceau 1997).

V. HISTORICAL DEVELOPMENTS

The first of the pending applications for membership, from Turkey, was lodged only months after the Iberian enlargement of 1986. However, as the 1995 enlargement to Sweden, Austria and Finland shows, the progression of applications need not correspond to the order of accessions.

The Copenhagen Summit of June 1993 explicitly provided that the CEECs that so wished could join the Union so long as they satisfied a set of political and economic criteria (see VII). As soon as the revolutions of 1989–90 took place the Union's immediate reaction was to welcome these countries' overtures to Western Europe. The Copenhagen Summit confirmed that the EU was prepared to go all the way and eventually embrace these countries as full members of the Union.

The Essen Summit of December 1994 created a comprehensive pre-accession strategy for preparing the applicants for membership on the basis of four main points:

(a) implementation of the Europe Agreements;
(b) support by the EU for the transition process from PHARE;
(c) alignment of single market legislation;
(d) a 'structured dialogue' in preparation for membership between Ministers from the 15 Member States and those of all associated countries of Central and Eastern Europe, together with Cyprus and Malta.

At the Corfu Summit of Spring 1995 the Union established that accession negotiations with Cyprus and Malta were to begin six months after the conclusion of the 1996–7 Inter-Governmental Conference (IGC).

The Madrid European Council of December 1995 stipulated that within six months of the conclusion of the 1996–7 IGC all the procedural requirements for the launching of accession negotiations would be made, taking into consideration the conclusions of the same IGC. It also called on the Commission to hasten the conclusion on its opinions on all the Central and Eastern European applicants, prepare a composite paper on enlargement and draw up a communication on the financial framework for the Union beyond the year 1999. Agenda 2000, dealt with below, was the Commission's comprehensive response. It was published in July 1997.

The Luxembourg European Council of December 1997 adopted the proposal of the Commission to open accession negotiations with Poland, Hungary, the Czech Republic, Slovenia, Estonia and Cyprus. But the Summit conclusions differed from the Commission proposals in the manner in which they dealt with the other applicants. The 'screening process', which was originally only to include the 5 + 1 group, was extended to all applicants making the prospect of new countries joining the front-runners more of a real possibility. While the 'screening process' for the 5 + 1 group will be carried out by the Task Force for Enlargement, the remaining countries will participate in a slower process in the hands of DG 1A. In terms of financial aid, the strong emphasis in favour of the selected countries that the Commission proposed was replaced with a package that helps to reduce, rather than accentuate, the gap between the two groups. This was done out of fears that the combination of non-selection for early accession and reduced financial support could destabilise these countries and potentially steer them away from the EU.

The Accession Partnerships with the 10 CEEC applicants were approved on 30 March 1998. Accession negotiations were officially opened at the London European Conference of 12 March 1998 and actually began on 31 March 1998.

Applicant State	Date of application	Commission opinion	Status
Turkey	14 April 1987	Negative 20 December 1989	No accession negotiations envisaged
Cyprus	3 July 1990	Positive 30 June 1993	Accession negotiations in progress
Malta	17 July 1990	Positive 30 June 1993	Application in abeyance
Switzerland	20 May 1992	None	Application in abeyance
Hungary	31 March 1994	Positive 16 July 1997	Accession negotiations in progress
Poland	5 April 1994	Positive 16 July 1997	Accession negotiations in progress
Romania	22 June 1995	Positive 16 July 1997	Assessed as not yet fit to begin accession negotiations
Slovakia	27 June 1995	Positive 16 July 1997	Assessed as not yet fit to begin accession negotiations
Latvia	27 October 1995	Positive 16 July 1997	Assessed as not yet fit to begin accession negotiations
Estonia	28 November 1995	Positive 16 July 1997	Accession negotiations in progress
Lithuania	8 December 1995	Positive 16 July 1997	Assessed as not yet fit to begin accession negotiations
Bulgaria	14 December 1995	Positive 16 July 1997	Assessed as not yet fit to begin accession negotiations
Czech Republic	17 January 1996	Positive 16 July 1997	Accession negotiations in progress
Slovenia	10 June 1995	Positive 16 July 1997	Accession negotiations in progress

VI. AGENDA 2000

Agenda 2000 does not represent the approved plan of action of the Union for the years to come. It simply represents the Commission's view of how the Union should proceed. Some suggestions have been accepted by the Member States and implemented; others have already been rejected. Technically the document is simply a Communication of the Commission to the Council entitled *For a Stronger and Wider Union.*

Although the document deals with several interrelated aspects of the future of the Community, such as financial perspectives and agricultural reform, it is the part referring to the 'challenge of enlargement' that is of most interest for our purposes.

Agenda 2000 included the long-awaited Commission opinions on all the Central and Eastern European applicants made on the basis of the 1993 Copenhagen criteria for accession (see VII). The criteria related to democracy and the rule of law, on the one hand, and the requirements of a functioning market economy and the ability to cope with competitive pressures and market forces, on the other.

With the exception of Slovakia, all applicants passed the political tests of democracy and the rule of law. But none of the applicants satisfied the economic criteria and the Commission pointed out that economic restructuring had a long way to go in all applicant states. Despite this the Commission hand-picked the candidates which it judged to have made most progress and/or had the best prospects of making progress in these areas and recommended the launching of accession negotiations with those countries.

VII. THE COPENHAGEN CRITERIA

VII.1 The Political Criteria

These criteria deal with the existence and respect of the following three main issues:

(a)   democracy and the rule of law;

(b)   human rights;

(c)   respect for minorities.

The Commission's decision to fail only Slovakia outright does not imply that it did not perceive problems in other applicants. It is simply a recognition that the situation in Slovakia was markedly worse than in all other applicants due primarily to its constitutional set-up and its treatment of the Hungarian minority.

VII.2 The Economic Criteria

These criteria sought to ascertain 'the existence of a functioning market economy as well as the capacity to cope with competitive pressure and market forces within the Union'.

VII.2.1 Existence of a Functioning Market Economy
The tests for this criterion were set as the following:
— Equilibrium between supply and demand is established by the free interplay of market forces; prices, as well as trade, are liberalised.
— Significant barriers to market entry (establishment of new firms) and exit (bankruptcy) are absent.
— The legal system, including the regulation of property rights, is in place; laws and contracts can be enforced.
— Macroeconomic stability has been achieved including adequate price stability and sustainable public finances and external accounts.
— The financial sector is sufficiently well-developed to channel savings towards productive development.

Commission Conclusion on the first economic criterion
The Commission concluded that the Czech Republic, Estonia, Hungary, Poland and Slovenia were to be considered functioning market economies, even if in all these countries important features, such as capital markets, still need to mature and develop further.

It also concluded that the other countries have made important progress but are not expected to satisfy this criterion before the beginning of the 21st century. Their main concern at present should, according to the Commission, be to strengthen the implementation of their legal and institutional reforms and to avert the risk of further macroeconomic instability.

VII.2.2 Capacity to Withstand Competitive Pressure and Market Forces within the Union
Since the evaluation is a forward-looking one a key question was whether firms have the necessary capacity to adapt, and whether their environment supports further adaptation. The elements that were taken into account were thus:
— The existence of a functioning market economy, with a sufficient degree of macroeconomic stability for economic agents to make decisions in a climate of stability and predictability.
— A sufficient amount, at an appropriate cost, of human and physical capital, including infrastructure (energy supply, telecommunication, transport, etc.), education and research, and future developments in this field.

—The extent to which government policy and legislation influence competitiveness through trade policy, state aid, support for SMEs, etc.

—The degree and the pace of trade integration a country achieves within the Union before enlargement. This applies both to the volume, and to the nature, of goods already traded with Member States.

—The proportion of small firms, partly because small firms tend to benefit more from improved market access, and partly because a dominance of large firms could indicate a greater reluctance to adjust.

The analysis of the Commission led to the following conclusions:

(a)   Trade integration in most countries and foreign direct investment (FDI) in some countries have progressed substantially. However in some countries there has been a reversal from initial trade liberalisation, mainly for macroeconomic reasons.

(b)   The functioning of capital markets and competition rules is improving everywhere, but is generally still far from satisfactory.

(c)   The state of infrastructure remains poor.

(d)   Wage levels are still well below Union levels.

(e)   Privatisation has progressed at different rates and the process remains to be completed.

Commission conclusion on the second economic criterion

In terms of country-by-country analysis the Commission concluded that Hungary and Poland should satisfy this criterion in the medium term so long as they stay on their current course.

The Czech Republic, Slovakia and Slovenia should be in the same position so long as they strengthen their efforts and avoid policy reversals.

Estonia, having radically modernised and liberalised its economy comes close to the second group but its large external trade imbalance is worrying.

Latvia, Lithuania and Romania have made great strides recently but will require further consolidation of their efforts. Bulgaria is still shedding the legacy of its past but should be able to catch up with the others in the next decade.

Commission conclusion on the two economic criteria

On the basis of the two economic criteria together the Commission concluded that Hungary and Poland come closest to meeting both criteria, with the Czech Republic and Slovenia not far behind. Estonia has difficulty meeting the second criterion. Slovakia meets the second criterion but cannot be considered as a functioning market economy.

VII.3 Other Obligations of Membership

Together with the purely political and economic benchmarks which have to be satisfied, the Commission also analysed the applicants' potential ability to cope with several other demands that membership would place upon them. These include the effectiveness of the power structures of the country, together with the policy line adopted on several of the declared aims of the EU. These 'other obligations of membership' were placed under the following three headings:

VII.3.1 Aims of Political, Economic and Monetary Union

Given the relatively weak position in which applicant states generally find themselves, it is not usually possible for them to secure opt-outs on any policies or projects during accession negotiations. It is only once a country has entered the Union, and can threaten to withhold its approval of a new Treaty, that such an option would exist. Thus at the present stage the pursuit of membership involves the unconditional acceptance of all the approved plans for economic and monetary union together with a measure of political union.

In analysing the applicants' efforts in these areas, the Commission noted that these countries have already shown themselves committed to CFSP, generally taking up the invitation of the Union to associate themselves with CFSP measures and positions.

The Commission recognised that applicants are unlikely to be ready to join the euro on accession but insists that applicants will be obliged to take on the conditions of stage two of EMU, including Central Bank independence, coordination of economic policies and adherence to the relevant provisions of the Stability and Growth Pact. Meanwhile the Commission seems to have recognised the irrelevance of the Maastricht EMU convergence criteria for assessing the applicants' economic development. This is due to the fact that a policy of restricted government spending is incompatible with the need to foster high growth rates in the applicant countries for several years to come.

VII.3.2 Adoption of the Acquis

In Agenda 2000 the Commission confirms that its attitude towards the granting of derogations from the *acquis* to applicant States will be no different in this enlargement than it was in the previous one. There will, according to the Commission, be no place in the Community for countries only partially adopting the *acquis*. Nor will there be any diluting of the *acquis* through enlargement.

In reality both these principles will suffer from exceptions. The Union is likely to grant prolonged 'temporary' derogations to the next entrants on a scale never experienced before. Also the length of the negotiations, with two or even three waves of entrants over the next 10 to 15 years, means that the Union will be developing policies while negotiating the same policies with the applicants. It will do so in the knowledge that what may once have been possible for the 12 or 15 may no longer be possible for the 26 or 30. This in effect may imply some diluting of the *acquis*.

VII.3.3 Administrative and Judicial Capacity to apply the Acquis
The Commission pointed to the absence in several countries of the structures needed to apply regulations on environment and technical inspections, banking supervision, public accounts and statistics. It also pointed to the widespread problem of corruption in several applicant countries. In terms of the countries' ability to enforce the *acquis* once the appropriate legislation is passed the Commission speaks of the dire necessity for the retraining of legal practitioners and members of the judiciary. The Commission even goes as far as to recommend the 'replacement' of many judges.

Commission conclusion on other obligations of membership
In the light of the main trends observed in the candidate countries, the Commission concluded that, if current efforts are reinforced, Hungary, Poland and the Czech Republic should, in the medium term, be able to take on the major part of the *acquis* and to establish the administrative structure to apply it.

Slovakia, Estonia, Latvia, Lithuania and Slovenia would be able to do so only if there is a considerable and sustained increase in their efforts.

VIII. PRINCIPAL QUESTIONS ON THE WAY TO ENLARGEMENT (IMPACT STUDY)

The Commission's interim report on the effects of enlargement in the context of the Union's current policies and their future development, presented at the Madrid European Council, came to two main conclusions:

(a)   Enlargement should provide dividends in terms of peace and security as well as economic growth and development in Europe as a whole. An enlarged market of 475 million people will bring considerable economic and political advantages.

(b)   These advantages could be undermined by potential sectoral and regional adjustment problems and an increased difficulty in further developing the *acquis* unless adequate preparations are made.

The report pointed to the necessity that the pre-accession period is used to the full in order to ensure that the applicants make adequate preparations for membership. Too slow an adaptation to European standards, especially in the social and economic sphere, could undermine the unitary character of the *acquis*, warns the Commission. The financing of these improvements must come from private and public funding within the applicant countries, from the Union and from other providers of foreign capital.

According to the same document, areas which require particular attention include agriculture, cohesion policy, implementing the Single Market, implementing environmental standards, transport, nuclear safety, the area of freedom, security and justice, border disputes and the application of Community rules in advance of accession.

IX. A STRATEGY FOR ENLARGEMENT

According to Agenda 2000, accession negotiations will define the terms and conditions on which each of the applicant countries will accede to the Union. In order to allow for an accession process that is as smooth as possible the Commission proposed a two-pronged strategy for enlargement:

(a) The start of *negotiations* based on the principle that the *acquis* will be applicable on accession.

(b) A *reinforced pre-accession strategy*, for all applicant countries, designed to ensure that they take on as much as possible of the *acquis* in advance of membership.

IX.1 Accession Negotiations

The proposal is that these should be based on the following principles:

(a) Membership on the basis of the *acquis*.

(b) Application of the *acquis* on accession.

(c) Transition periods (limited in scope and duration) but no derogations or opt-outs.

(d) Commission reports on progress made by applicants.

IX.2 Reinforcing the Pre-accession Strategy

Agenda 2000 recognises that the original pre-accession strategy approved in March 1995, including the 'structured dialogue', was incapable of coping with the intensity of contacts to be expected in the future. It therefore suggested a new pre-accession strategy with two main components: accession partnerships and participation in Community programmes.

IX.2.1 Accession partnerships

Accession partnerships bring together all the different forms of support for applicant countries under one framework, including:

(a)   Precise commitments on the part of the applicant country, relating in particular to democracy, macroeconomic stabilisation and nuclear safety, as well as a national programme for the adoption of the Community *acquis* within a precise timetable, focusing on the priority areas identified in each position.

(b)   Mobilisation of all resources available to the Community for preparing the applicant countries for accession — in particular through PHARE, and through co-financing with the EIB, EBRD and the World Bank. The suggestion is for 70% of PHARE money to go to investment, primarily in transport and the environment.

In addition to PHARE (1.5 billion ECU per year), the pre-accession aid to be granted to the applicant CEECs from the year 2000 would consist of two elements:

(a)   aid for agricultural development amounting to 500 million ECU a year.

(b)   Structural aid amounting to 1 billion ECU primarily in the sphere of transport and environment (analogous with the EU's internal cohesion funds).

As mentioned above the accession partnerships for all 10 CEECs were approved on 30 March 1998.

IX.2.2 Participation in Community Programmes

Familiarisation of applicants with the Union's policies and procedures, through the possibility of their participation in Community programmes was already provided for in the Europe Agreements and should raise no problem of principle. As these programmes encompass most Community policies, covering education, training, research, culture, environment, SMEs and the Single Market, the Commission expects them to provide a useful preparation for accession by familiarising the applicant countries and their citizens with the Union's policies and working methods.

IX.3 Final Recommendations

The document finally goes on to recommend the opening of accession negotiations with individual countries according to the stage which each has reached in satisfying the basic conditions of membership.

It maintains that the decision on opening negotiations with particular countries should be based on the objective analysis of the Commission which finds that *none of the CEEC applicants fully satisfy the criteria at the present time. Nevertheless all applicants except Slovakia meet the political criteria of membership.* It also points out that several applicants have made sufficient progress in satisfying the economic criteria and those related to the other obligations for membership.

In the light of the above the Commission stated that *Hungary, Poland, Estonia, the Czech Republic and Slovenia* could be in a position to satisfy all conditions of membership in the medium term if they maintain and strongly sustain their efforts of preparation and should therefore be invited to commence accession negotiations in 1998. *The Commission also reiterated the decision of Corfu Summit to open negotiations with Cyprus six months after the end of the 1996/1997 IGC.* It also points out that although the invitations to commence negotiations are made simultaneously to these six countries, this does not imply that they will also be concluded simultaneously. In effect, the prospect of the group of 5 + 1 being split before the first accessions seems to be gaining support already at the early stages of negotiations.

Needless to say, there was more to the final conclusions than a simple decision based on the objective tests discussed above. Suffice it to say that up until very close to the publication date of Agenda 2000, the Commission President was still convinced of the wisdom of inviting only Poland, the Czech Republic and Hungary to the negotiating table. It was only after consistent pressure from within the Commission and from particular Member States for Slovenia and Estonia to be added to the list of invitees that the final conclusions were amended accordingly.

X. THE EUROPEAN CONFERENCE

The idea of a European Conference was put forward in Agenda 2000 as a way of bringing together all countries which aspire to membership of the EU together with the 15 Member States. The rationale was to give a sense of inclusion to those applicants who would not make the first round of enlargement and, above all, to try to deal with the ever-present problem of Turkey.

Questions of CFSP, relations with Russia and the Ukraine and matters of justice and home affairs were, according to Agenda 2000, to be the main areas of emphasis for the Conference. France was interested in giving the Conference real substance while Commissioner Van Den Broek proposed that First Pillar issues could also be discussed at the Conference. Meanwhile there was talk on whether or not countries such as Norway, Switzerland, Malta and Iceland, which are not actively pursuing membership, should also be invited.

When the concept of the Conference was approved at the Luxembourg Summit of December 1997, it became clear that it was to be primarily of symbolic importance. This fact led Turkey, the inclusion of which effectively gave a *raison d'être* to the whole idea, to reject the EU's invitation to the Conference. Ideas that Turkey would come round to attending the Conference when the disappointment of Luxembourg subsided were proved wrong when it snubbed the inaugural Conference.

The first European Conference was convened in London on 11 March 1998. Heads of State and Government of the 15 EU Member States, together with the 10 applicants from Central and Eastern Europe and Cyprus were accompanied by their Foreign Ministers, together with Commission President Santer and Commissioner Van Den Broek. The British Presidency sought to give some substance to the meeting by asking the attending dignitaries to concentrate on issues at the centre of citizens' concerns including drug trafficking, organised crime, the environment, regional economic cooperation issues and CFSP matters particularly the crisis in Kosovo which erupted precisely at this time. In reality apart from comforting words on all the above subjects the brief conclusions of the one-day summit produced only one concrete result: a resolution to set up a joint expert group charged with establishing a detailed inventory of the problems organised crime is creating for the countries present.

Although the decision to invite six countries to start accession negotiations was actually taken at the Luxembourg European Council of December 1997 and the start of negotiations was set for March 31 1998 it was decided that the European Conference was to mark the 'official' opening of accession negotiations.

The European Conference is expected to meet at least twice a year, once at the level of Heads of State and Government and once at the level of Foreign Ministers.

XI. CYPRUS

Cyprus's application for membership of 1990 was met with a positive Commission *avis* in 1993. The island was not invited to join the EFTA enlargement negotiations but the conclusions of the Corfu Summit of June 1994 stated that 'the next phase of enlargement of the Union will include Cyprus and Malta'. Until the freezing of Malta's membership bid in October 1996 the prospect of an EU enlargement just to the two Mediterranean islands was still on the cards. Since then it has become clear that Cyprus will only be able to join at the time of the first eastern enlargement. At the European Councils of Cannes, Madrid and Florence, Cyprus was told to wait till six months after the 1996–97 IGC before it could start negotiating accession. Once the negotiations get well under way Cyprus is likely to realise that it will again have to wait for the conclusion of the post-2000 IGC before it can actually accede.

But it is clear that Cyprus might be told to wait even longer, if the Union's commitment to allow accession even without some form of reunification of the island is overturned. At the London European Conference the French suggested that while it was the Union's vocation to take in Cyprus it was not the Union's vocation to take in a divided country. The Greeks, who have kept Cyprus's accession on course through persistent threats to derail the whole enlargement process, were not pleased with these comments. Finally the Conference reiterated the Union's commitment to take in Cyprus whether it remains divided or otherwise. France's suggestion that accession be allowed only for an as yet non-existent bi-zonal, bi-communal Cypriot Federation based on UN Security Council resolutions was rejected. France was placated with a simple decision that the Commission will monitor developments and report to the Council during negotiations in the same way as it does for the other applicants.

Agenda 2000 praised the vigour of the Cypriot economy, which performs better than several EU economies in terms of GNP per capita and employment. The Commission suggested that the adoption of the *acquis* should not pose any serious problems, even if renewed efforts will have to be made in the sphere of financial services and justice and home affairs.

Cyprus does not benefit from the PHARE programme but is the recipient of less generous EU funds under its fourth financial protocol with the Union. A particular pre-accession strategy for Cyprus was agreed to at the Luxembourg European Council and includes provision for participation by Cyprus in several EU programmes.

Meanwhile, efforts by both the Greek Cypriot government and the EU to include representatives of the Turkish Cypriot government in the accession negotiating team have not yet proved successful. At present the Union suggests that the effects of accession will cover all of the island of Cyprus. Nevertheless, the prospect of accession of only the Greek part of Cyprus continues to be mooted as a real possibility.

XII. TURKEY

In Agenda 2000 the Commission reiterates Turkey's eligibility for membership of the EU while at the same time setting out a daunting list of economic and political obstacles which make it amply clear that membership is not on the cards for the foreseeable future.

The Communication led to a furious reaction from the Turkish authorities, who broke off all political relations with the Union. Turkey refused to attend the European Conference and has since been focusing its foreign policy initiatives on its neighbours on its eastern borders. Turkey claims that the Union has been discriminatory towards it because the majority of its population is Muslim, citing the fact that it is economically much more advanced than several of the CEECs lined up for enlargement.

The chapter in Agenda 2000 on Turkey refers to the satisfactory implementation of the Customs Union Agreement (which gives the EU a trade surplus of 9 billion ECU). It also points out that 'political circumstances' have not allowed the financial cooperation and political dialogue aspects of the customs union to be brought into effect. In effect Greece continued to veto its implementation in the light of ongoing Turkish-Greek disputes in the region.

XIII. FUTURE PERSPECTIVES

XIII.1 A Crowded Agenda

The start of accession negotiations should be the cause of some satisfaction for the applicants. Although no one underestimates the dimensions of the task ahead, the Union is now firmly on the road to enlargement. The applicants' main concern should be to keep up the Member States' political will to proceed in spite of the distractions that will plague the Union throughout the years of negotiations.

The fact that negotiations will take place simultaneously with the launch of the single currency implies that the Union cannot give enlargement the undivided attention it deserves. A difficult or failed launch of the euro could potentially undermine the whole enlargement process. On the other hand a successful start for the new currency could help the Union through the daunting tasks before it. These include the ratification of the Amsterdam Treaty and institutional reform. The reform of CAP and of the structural and cohesion funds within new financial perspectives will also have to be completed in the medium term not least because of their implications for enlargement (see chapters 3, 7 and 13)

XIII.2 The 'Others'

The simultaneous accession of all the 11 applicants is clearly not in the interests of the Union and enlargement in waves is clearly more prudent and logical. However, in effectively splitting the group in two, the EU risks creating instability on its own borders. It is in the Union's interest to ensure that in denying these countries early accession it does not lose them altogether. The success of the new Accession Partnership in avoiding such a situation is perhaps their best test.

In the near future there is likely to be a membership bid by Moldova. Changes in the attitudes of the 'frozen' applicants of Switzerland and Malta also seem like a real possibility in the medium term. Meanwhile one can be relatively certain that relations with disappointed Turkey will continue to haunt the European Union.

XIII.3 Date of Enlargement

As the years since the Copenhagen Summit tick by the actual date for the next enlargement remains unsettled. Agenda 2000 suggests that 2003 would be the most likely date. Senior European politicians such as President Chirac and Chancellor Kohl have suggested that enlargement could take place as early as 2000 or 2001. Even though these dates are often only mentioned on official visits to candidate countries, the false hopes that these statements create are only likely to exacerbate the impatience of many Central and East Europeans (not to mention Cypriot) citizens.

Although the early enlargement rhetoric has not yet subsided, geopolitical developments seem to suggest that accession is likely to take place later rather than sooner. Positive developments in Russia, together with the confirmation of the imminent expansion of NATO mean that the need for the EU to project stability to the CEECs is substantially less accentuated than just two or three years ago.

These factors, together with the slowly dawning realisation in several CEECs of the sacrifices and dangers of an economically insufficiently prepared accession, make enlargement around 2004 or 2005 more likely.

This date also fits in more comfortably with the negotiation and ratification of another pre-enlargement IGC, whose necessity has now become generally accepted. An IGC starting in 2000 is unlikely to be concluded before 2002. Since its conclusions will have a direct bearing on the powers and obligations of the new entrants it is difficult to imagine that enlargement negotiations can be wound up before the IGC conclusions are ratified by the 15 Member States around 2003 or 2004.

XIV. FURTHER READING

The ideas and basic materials for this chapter came from several official publications of the Union together with the analysis and insight of the following recommended publications:

INOTAI, András: *What is Novel about Eastern Enlargement of the European Union? The Costs and Benefits of Eastern Enlargement of the European Union*, Working Papers, Budapest, Institute for World Economics, 1997.

MARESCEAU, Marc (ed.): *Enlarging the European Union, Relations between the EU and Central and Eastern Europe*, London, Longman, 1997.

MAYHEW, Alan, *Eastern Enlargement: a Win-win Enterprise*, Occasional Papers, Brussels, European Policy Centre, 1997.

NICHOLAIDES, Phedon and BOEN, Sylvia Raja: *A Guide to the Enlargement of the European Union: Determinants, Process, Timing, Negotiations*, Current European Issues, EIPA report, 97/P/01, Maastricht, 1997.

PRESTON, Christopher: *Enlargement & Integration in the European Union*, The Routledge/University Association for Contemporary European Studies Series, 1997.

SCHELLEKENS, Pierre: *The Role of the Commission in Accession Negotiations*, Bruges, College of Europe, 1996.

SOVEROSKI, Marie (ed.): *Agenda 2000: an Appraisal of the Commission's Blueprint for Enlargement*, Current European Issues/EIPA Report, 97/P/03, Maastricht, 1997.

SMITH, Karen Elizabeth and SENIOR NELLO, Susan: *The Consequences of Eastern Enlargement of the European Union in Stages*, European University Institute Working Papers, Robert Schuman Centre, 97/51, Florence, 1997.

Websites

Agenda 2000 online	http://europa.eu.int/comm/agenda2000/index.en.htm
DG 1A (External Relations: Europe and NIS, ...)	http://europa.eu.int/comm/eg1a/enlarte/index.htm
PHARE Home Page	http://europa.eu.int/comm/dg1a/phare/index.htm

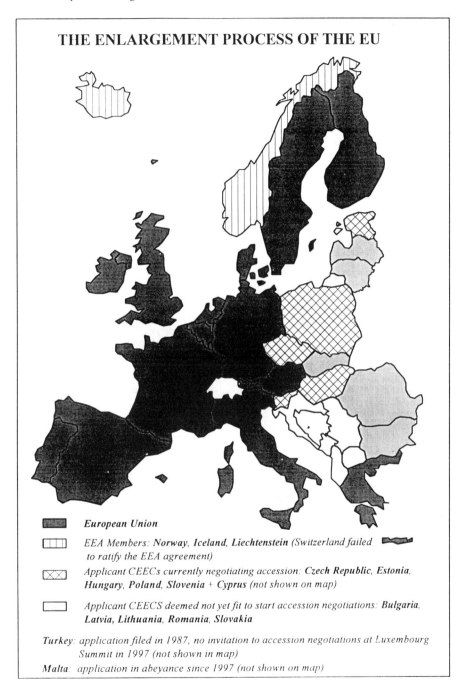

THE ENLARGEMENT PROCESS OF THE EU

European Union

EEA Members: **Norway, Iceland, Liechtenstein** *(Switzerland failed to ratify the EEA agreement)*

Applicant CEECs currently negotiating accession: **Czech Republic, Estonia, Hungary, Poland, Slovenia** + **Cyprus** *(not shown on map)*

Applicant CEECS deemed not yet fit to start accession negotiations: **Bulgaria, Latvia, Lithuania, Romania, Slovakia**

Turkey*: application filed in 1987, no invitation to accession negotiations at Luxembourg Summit in 1997 (not shown in map)*

Malta*: application in abeyance since 1997 (not shown on map)*

INDEX